BARS, BLUES, AND BOOZE

BARS, BLUES, AND BOOZE

STORIES FROM THE DRINK HOUSE

EMILY D. EDWARDS

UNIVERSITY PRESS OF MISSISSIPPI / JACKSON

www.upress.state.ms.us

The University Press of Mississippi is a member
of the Association of American University Presses.

Manufactured in the United States of America

First printing 2016
∞
Library of Congress Cataloging-in-Publication Data

Names: Edwards, Emily D.
Title: Bars, blues, and booze : stories from the drink house / Emily D. Edwards.
Description: Jackson : University Press of Mississippi, [2016] | Series: American made music series | Includes bibliographical references and index.
Identifiers: LCCN 2015034525| ISBN 9781496806390 (cloth : alk. paper) | ISBN 9781496806406 (ebook)
Subjects: LCSH: Blues (Music)—Social aspects—Southern States. | Musicians—Alcohol use—Southern States. | Drinking of alcoholic beverages—Social aspects—Southern States—History. | Music and race—Southern States. | Blues musicians—Southern States—Interviews.
Classification: LCC ML3918.B57 E39 2016 | DDC 781.6430975—dc23 LC record available at http://lccn.loc.gov/2015034525

British Library Cataloging-in-Publication Data available

CONTENTS

ACKNOWLEDGMENTS

I owe the deepest recognition to Doug Mokaren, who supported this project in a number of ways from encouraging me not to give up on it, for being an amazing photographer and having a camera handy at opportune moments, for his knowledgeable advice, and for being present during many of the discussions that supplied the stories here, so that they were always wonderful conversations rather than formal journalistic interviews. I also want to thank David Evans, the series editor at the University Press of Mississippi, for his careful review of this manuscript and wise suggestions, and Anne Rogers for her editorial advice. I need to acknowledge the "blues family" that I have encountered on this journey: music fans, friends, bar owners, drink house operators, and musicians and their families. Above all I want to thank the contributors, who were willing to share their adventures, photos, and insights. It was a privilege to hear every story. I want to thank my daughter, Marissa, for her indulgence. Finally, I want to express my gratitude to the members of the Piedmont Blues Preservation Society for their advice and support.

This book is dedicated to all those people who make our southern party possible and memorable and to those who enrich our lives with their musical talent.

For those stories that were not included here and others that I encountered after I had exceeded the word limit for this book, check out the website: drinkhousestories.org.

The conversation continues.

BARS, BLUES, AND BOOZE

INTRODUCTION

I was born in Florence, Alabama, four years before W. C. Handy (also a Florence native and the "Father of the Blues") died. Live music was a featured entertainment of the Florence and Muscle Shoals area, and still is. When I lived in the Shoals, my musical experiences largely consisted of front-porch music, lawn music, and house-party music. In the late 1950s, the area added "studio music," when Florence Alabama Music Enterprises (FAME) recording studios opened. When musicians Barry Beckett, Roger Hawkins, Jimmy Johnson, and David Hood of the Swampers created Muscle Shoals Sound Studio, the musical notoriety of the area continued to grow. There were no legal "juke joints," "drink houses," "pour houses," or "bars" in Florence during Handy's lifetime or while I lived there. As of this writing (2015), Lauderdale County still remains dry, although Florence became one of the two cities that turned "wet" in the 1980s, a few years after I moved away.

Even when Florence was dry, people still drank. And generally, wherever people were drinking, there was music.

Before Florence went wet, the drink houses were private homes and illegal bars. People willing to risk a drive over the state line to Tennessee to buy liquor and bring it back for resale or individuals willing to brew homemade liquor supplied the drink house or the house party. The more affluent country clubs found ways to skirt the law, serving liquor that belonged to the "private reserves of members." Although country clubs could be targeted for an occasional raid, law enforcement was more likely to target the less affluent drink houses or (more frequently) to wait at the Alabama state line to pull over anyone suspected of having a trunk full of bootleg or moonshine.

The musicians who provided entertainment were often the customers, performing in improvisational jams. Rarely were they paid professionals. Music, illegal liquor, and drugs were the backbone of these parties, which might travel from one house to another to avoid the law. Though not fully integrated, anecdotal stories suggest there was more racial mixing in these illegal bars than in most areas of southern social life in the 1960s and 1970s. The mother who objected to her young daughter swimming in the same public pool with "dirty black boys" would be shocked to learn that her daughter danced with black teens and young adults at an illegal house party, where the "crossroads" (some might say "cross-pollination"; others might say "corruption") of black and white music culture challenged the social stigmas of race mixing. In the mythologies of white, black, and blues culture, the crossroads is a place where journeys meet, where choices and opportunities wait. The crossroads is an important metaphor in blues music; it is an exciting but uneasy spot, imposing alternatives and the risks of choosing the flawed path.

In the late 1960s and 1970s, young white musicians, southern hippies who felt themselves proudly outside of mainstream American culture, appropriated the traditional African American blues sound. Rawboned blues music that portrayed the yearning, struggle, and personal loss of the black artists seemed to resonate with a white youth culture rebelling against the oppressive and segregated mores of their southern parents. "I know how to sing the blues," a young white musician told me after having been busted for drug possession in Florence in the early 1970s. "I may not be black, but the cops beat me, too." He added, "And they made fun of my hair." With odd, convoluted logic, this young musician felt his love for blues music and his waist-length hair connected him to exploited black men (but not oppressed women). He believed his hair was a signal to the cops that—like a black man—he was someone to be hassled. Sensitive to the proximity of black America and "its bitter, pissed-off readiness to mock beyond humiliation any white attempt to get truly down,"[1] white musicians, particularly southern ones, seemed eager to prove their "coolness" in the music scene. This was not only defiance of the liquor laws but also included all manner of risk taking: social, legal, and artistic.

I spent all of my young adult life in the South: Alabama, Tennessee, and North Carolina, where I finally settled and became a professor of media studies at the University of North Carolina–Greensboro (UNCG). In the summer of 1989, Dr. Rebecca Adams and I decided to follow the Grateful Dead on tour as part of a study of musical subculture. I produced a documentary (*Deadheads: An American Subculture,*

Films for the Humanities, 1990); Dr. Adams coedited a book (*Deadhead Social Science: "You Ain't Gonna Learn What You Don't Want to Know,"* Rutgers University Press, 2000). While videotaping Deadheads, I realized that the same music associated with the defiant drink house subculture in Florence and similar house parties in other communities was also in the core play list of the amateur musicians in "Tent City" (the nomadic community set up by Deadhead campers in the parking lots of the venues where the Grateful Dead performed). Unplugged parking-lot music included drink house staples such as "Frankie and Johnny," "Rising Sun Blues," and tunes covered by the Grateful Dead like "Iko, Iko" (a.k.a. "Jock-A-Mo"). Deadheads were largely a white subculture that championed the sound, soul, dreadlocks, and cool outsider status identified with black culture. Alternative and magical beliefs that flowed freely through Deadhead subculture were sympathetic to the hoodoo magic expressed in blues lyrics and the superstitions of the juke joint. Although the "tailgate bars" in Tent City were hardly drink houses, they shared a similar furtive quality and sometimes illegal entrepreneurship along with the drugs, alcohol, improvisational music, and outrageous stories about life on the road or at the concerts. I've always felt that the real key to this subculture—or any culture or subculture—can be found in its storytelling and the musical accompaniments to those stories.

I was a college student in the 1970s attending Florence State University (now the University of North Alabama). The university was a colorfully eccentric place to be in the '70s. Hippies played the newly invented game of Frisbee golf on the campus lawns and offered impromptu music concerts in the student center. One of the English professors was rumored to have wrestled a bear and another professor entertained students with banjo music. The university's mascot was Leo the Lion. In 1974, the university's president, Dr. Robert M. Guillot, brought a live lion cub to live in a den next to the president's home. It became natural for students who lived in apartments on Wood Avenue to hear Leo "barking" at night, just over the sounds of the music of whomever was throwing a party. Leaving campus at night, students found that most businesses were closed. The only place open to get anything to eat really late at night was the Pitt Grill, where you might enter just in time to see somebody famous, like Paul Simon, pay his bill at the register and leave without any public fuss. At the Pitt Grill you could sit down at two in the morning with some heavy philosophy over a cup of coffee brought to you by a waitress with the name of her current boyfriend tattooed on her arm above the crossed-out tattooed names of all her ex-boyfriends. It was a place frequented by students, musicians, hippies, and truck drivers alike. The Pitt Grill didn't serve alcohol, but it was the major destination for sobering up between partying and work—or partying and school. Because it was located in downtown Florence, the Pitt Grill was occasionally the destination of someone coming back from a run to the Tennessee state line, a "Pitt Grill" stop before the final destination.

I was one of those college students who hated the drive to the bars in Tennessee. These places just over the state line looked like the large warehouses that sold cheap furniture. Big dirt and gravel parking lots surrounded metal and concrete buildings with nasty dumpsters on one side and nastier bathrooms on the other. The clientele was white and the music tended to be country or southern rock. The reliable events of a trip to a bar over the line were that the law would bust somebody for drunk driving or transporting alcohol or somebody would get busted in the lip because tempers in those bars often seemed inflamed.

The better time, in my view, could be found in temporary illegal bars or house parties in the Shoals area, sometimes on the west side, sometimes in the low-rent east side, most often for me in the student "slums" nearer campus, but sometimes at other house parties across the river in Muscle Shoals, Tuscumbia, or Sheffield. Though white people made up the majority of the events I attended, these parties were apt to be racially mixed. There was a happy rebellion thumping in the heart upon entering some ancient house with a sagging foundation to hear the "one-four-five" of an unplugged blues melody coming from the back room. Here we could flout all social taboos with positive relish. It would be a lie of omission not to mention the drugs. It wasn't a far step from violating liquor laws to violating drug laws. Soldiers recently back from the Vietnam War brought legendary drugs to the party. The '60s counterculture that urged people to welcome change by defying existing conventions, hierarchies, and drug laws was late arriving in the Shoals but it had arrived, even if relegated to a minority. Among some artists and musicians there was an added belief that drugs and alcohol freed the creative spirit and encouraged it to greater achievement. If not to defy the established social conventions, musicians were known to experiment for the sake of their craft or because they knew their musical heroes experimented with drugs. Either older musicians with day jobs or younger musicians with unrealistically big dreams played without contract, just for the opportunity to play and maybe get a free drink. After all, there were major studios right down the street or across the river. Someone important might show up. You never knew. It was possible.

Those important "someones" never showed. At least, I was never at a house party where Paul Simon or the Rolling Stones or Cher showed up, even when we knew they were in town, but other curious strangers did show.

I remember once meeting a raging drunkard named Bucky at a house party filled with college students, the art and music types. Bucky's glamour was that he had served time in prison for killing a man. At least, that was what he said. He also claimed to have been a "super bad" guitar player until he broke his hand and the injury left him unable to play. Bucky was an older, scraggly man with brown teeth and a mean look in his eye. At some point in the evening, a bad cloud passed over Bucky and his mood turned ugly. He stood on a chair and announced to anyone listening that "the devil in me. Violence like a sickness in me. Sometime it make me so I just have to *do* something." At this point Bucky opened his knife to exhibit an unimpressive-looking blade, but Bucky's sincerity was scary. After yelling and threatening for a long, uncomfortable moment, nothing happened. Someone brought Bucky another beer, the bad moment passed, and the music played on. That incident combined with the invincibility of my youth and the rebellious optimism of the time created in me a belief that the right combination of a cold beer and good music could break down racial barriers, open the doors of artistic possibility, and calm any savage beast.

Well, sometimes it did and sometimes it didn't.

In more recent years I've become an ardent fan of the Piedmont music scene. The musicians that are the staple of this arena are talented men and women who usually fly under the national radar, often performing for free at bars that host jams, at street parties, or for fund-raisers when a fellow musician gets in trouble and needs a financial bailout. Though the blues music scene has aged considerably and several of the core musicians have died, the improvisational music and outrageous stories still circulate. With the deaths of vital Piedmont musicians like Guitar

Slim, Guitar Gabriel, Skeeter Brandon, and, most recently, Ray Burnett, along with ardent fans such as the flamboyant Naomi Alexander and Pat Freitag, I felt an urgency to document the stories before the old crossroads became a completely different kind of intersection. Many of these stories are not dignified or decent or filled with uplifting euphoria, but they are the real narratives of people who worked hard with their hands during the week just to celebrate the weekend with mood-altering music along with other mood-altering substances.

This book is a limited record of bar stories, particularly at the junction of black and white music cultures in the South. I wanted to preserve the stories of artists who may not be famous celebrities, but are men and women deeply occupied with their music, professional musicians with a day job. I also include stories from fans, bar owners, and family members, those people important to shaping a culture and helping to choose the direction it takes. My intention is not to rehash the history of blues as a genre or categorize the styles; other scholars have done this very thoroughly. My intention is to explore the "crossroads," that intoxicated intersection of spirituality, race, and music culture that helped to shape a rich southern vernacular. The stories from the drink house are personal narratives: tales of narrow escape (almost getting busted by the law while transporting moonshine), of despairing poverty (rat-infested kitchens and repossessed cars), of magic (hiring a root doctor to make a charm that will compel a deceitful spouse to become faithful again), and loss (death or incarceration). They are stories about race (remembrances of a black musician whose mother did laundry for the Ku Klux Klan, of defiant miscegenation, of forgetting race and going out to eat together after the jam and not being served). They are the assorted boasts of improbable hijinks that give the "blue-collar" musician a wild, gritty glamour and emphasize the riotous freedom of fans, ditching the genteel bourgeois for the culturally kaleidoscopic and tribal experience of drink house music. The stories reveal what it means to be drunk, dumped, broke, beaten, and yet to survive with humor or grim determination. They provide the inspiration for lyrics and the poignancy of musical performances. Included with stories from musicians like Chick Willis, Roy Roberts, Big Ron Hunter, Melva Houston, Abe Reid, Mark Harrison, and others are stories from fans and bar owners. If you are looking for historical accuracy and meticulous fact, this is not the book for you. Storytellers often forget names and dates. What storytellers forget as far as historical accuracy still contains important emotional truths. The stories candidly demonstrate what we search for in our good times and how these good times bring us together, or perhaps pull us apart. If frank statements and coarse language offend you, be prepared. Storytellers in this collection do not mince words. Some might question why such imprecise and salty stories deserve attention. I am convinced we know ourselves better when we explore the stories that are the foundation of our heterogeneity, especially those stories that happen at the junctions of our ever-evolving culture.

CHAPTER 1

Buckets of Blood to the Better Clubs: Defining the Drink House

There are different opinions about what constitutes a drink house. Ideas range from a very narrowly defined "blacks-only, illegal juke joint set in a private home" to "just any old place that sells alcohol" for consumption on the premises. Some storytellers distinguished between legal and illegal operations, labeling the illegal operation a drink house, liquor house, pour house, party house, or after-hours club. Others did not make this distinction. Both legal and illegal bars seemed to operate in all manner of buildings: houses, garages, warehouses, sheds, and barns. Almost any type of building could be repurposed as a bar. A surprise is that the ability to get a permit and legally sell alcohol did not discourage the illegal bars or make them less popular. Illegal drink houses continued to operate with gusto in the same cities that had legal bars. Storytellers suggest that working-class bars, both legal and illegal, were often the initiation for a musical career. As one storyteller declared, "These places were ground zero for local musicians."

North Carolina was the first southern state to vote for prohibition in 1908, helping to encourage federal prohibition following more than ten years later with the Eighteenth Amendment to the US Constitution (1919). After federal prohibition was repealed in 1933, North Carolina was among nineteen states to pass the Alcoholic Beverage Control bill (1937), allowing local communities to decide whether to permit liquor sales. The state of North Carolina maintained blue laws prohibiting legal sales of alcohol between two and seven in the morning, Monday through Saturday, and before noon on Sundays. Gradually, some communities across the state began to drop local prohibitions and authorize the sale of alcohol in retail establishments, but maintained statewide blue laws. As is true of most southern states, not all North Carolina communities ditched their bans on liquor sales.[1]

North Carolina is widely celebrated on Internet sites ridiculing "dumb laws" as the only state with a statewide law that prohibits off-key singing, suggesting that North Carolinians do take music seriously. I have not been able to find a statewide law against "off-key singing," but just as communities are allowed to set their own liquor laws, cities in North Carolina set noise ordinances. For example, Greensboro is a city that has ordinances on loitering as well as noise, but not specifically against off-key singing in bars or in any public location.[2] Rumored laws against off-key singing did not stop musicians from performing in North Carolina; neither did concerns for liquor laws stop bars (legal and illegal) from opening in the state.

From 1961 to 1980, Greensboro became an important gateway and safe stop for black musicians traveling the East Coast between Washington, DC, and Atlanta on the chitlin circuit.[3] In upscale, black-owned clubs that echoed the Harlem Renaissance of the 1920s, patrons could listen and dance to the music of James Brown, Jerry Butler, Otis Redding, Solomon Burke, Gladys Knight and the Pips, and Charlie and Inez Fox. These entertainers could stay the night at the local Magnolia Hotel before traveling to the next gig. The El Rocco and the Carlotta dinner clubs in Greensboro were recognized for good cocktails, good food, and nationally known rhythm and blues entertainment.[4] White-owned clubs like Green's Supper Club offered similar food and entertainment combos.

Greensboro had a vibrant and legal bar scene, where lesser-known acts could play for a cut of the door, a salary, or tips. Sometimes storytellers did not differentiate between the ordinary, legally operating bar and the illegal drink house. Storytellers did not always know whether a bar was legal or not. Both places might allow roving musicians to come in without special invitation or prior arrangement and play for tips or a "free" drink. Both could have a kind of gritty charm and both could become notorious. The biggest difference is that with the illegal bar, the "house man" had not bothered with a permit for his alcohol sales or any other business permit. This deficit meant law enforcement could raid the bar at any time and shut it down. Even so, stories suggest that a fair number of drink houses operated for decades without too much interference from police.

Tim Duffy: The Working-Class Drink House

Before Tim Duffy and his wife Denise established the Music Maker Relief Foundation in 1994 to preserve southern musical traditions and provide assistance to artists, Tim was a folklore student whose studies eventually led him to the discovery of Winston-Salem drink houses.

"In the poorer communities and little neighborhoods, every block there's a house where entrepreneurs open up their kitchen or their house to sell shots of liquor or beer. That's how they make a side income. There are other people I know, who have retired, and that's their full income. For twenty years, John Dee Holeman's wife did that for a living, just ran a full-on drink house selling fish sandwiches and stuff. They're like little restaurants that are under the radar. They're very much a fabric of the community. I'm here in a little town in Hillsboro and you could see them all over. You can usually spot one if you see a lot of people hanging around all day. It usually means that this place is a neighborhood drink house.

"The people I know who ran them, Sam and Ezelle, were working-class guys. A lot of the guys that were their customers were the guys who drove the garbage trucks. They were city workers or postal workers, or just people in the community. Like anybody else that lived in a culture where they have bars, they'd just go into the drink house and shoot the breeze with everybody and have a beer or something. That's the service the drink house provides. In the Deep South people know them as juke joints. A lot of people in the southeast call them liquor houses. There's a guy named Captain Luke that's a friend of mine, who just turned eighty-seven. He said he came up with the name 'drink house' in the '50s when he came up from South Carolina. It could be true. Something has to come from somewhere. . . . I think it's just a cool Americana term that people should know about. A juke joint in Mississippi is the same thing as what they would call a drink house or a liquor house here. Or even just a bar. . . .

"Sam and Ezelle were open twenty-four hours a day. They would sell shots of vodka, shots of beer . . . usually just vodka and beer. No drugs were involved. There would be always the cast of homeless characters that would be in and out, or their friends and family, like three or four guys that would always be there, and maybe the woman he was supporting, the old lady. Gabe [Guitar Gabriel] and I would go and play there. We would play the weekends or weeknights and Sam would actually pay us twenty dollars apiece and we'd make some tips. This still goes on and is very much a tradition. I met guys that made a living that way. For thirty years all they played professionally were drink houses. According to Sam and other people, there were some nicer places, more like real nightclubs, but they were all totally illegal. When I went—or still go—they were just in people's homes.

"Ezelle's and Sam's drink houses were genuine working-class places where working-class men and women went after the job. Others would sit there all day. If a farmer would pull up and needed hands, people would jump in the truck and go work. What Sam Red[5] was famous for was giving credit 'til the end of the month. Two weeks after the paycheck and you're out of money, he would give you credit on your drinks. Even sometimes he'd lend you money—cash—if you had a bill to pay off. They were a mixture of social welfare agency, bar, and clubhouse. In these sections of town there were no legal bars, but there's not a bar or tavern culture in North Carolina—period. In the northwest and other parts of the country, or in New England where alcohol is not a forbidden thing or looked down upon, they don't have dry counties per se. Every neighborhood has a neighborhood bar where you can walk to and get a drink. In the Bible Belt, for various reasons probably going back to the early days of this country, the liquor laws are arcane and complex. There's dry counties. . . . It doesn't mean people don't drink, both in white and black communities, poor to rich. Even the Baptist church after Sunday sermon . . . lawyers and judges are dealing moonshine in the back parking lot. This is just what happens.

"If you hang out with Captain Luke there's always another great drink house. There's always moonshine to sell. This is a moonshine state. Drink houses are the storefront for moonshine. They call moonshine 'chicken' in the Piedmont. That's a code word to keep it from 'the man.' In parts of Alabama they call it 'Joe Lewis,' because it has a knockout punch. At the heart of it, these places are for selling moonshine. I don't know the numbers, but there's no shortage of moonshine in the state of North Carolina.

"I fell in with these guys when I was a young man. That was twenty-five years ago. It was still going then, and twenty-five years later a lot of the guys have passed . . . but the drink houses are not gone. The one where I was just the other day, Miss Puddin's . . . you just go in and you'll go into the back kitchen. Miss Puddin' sells food and makes dishes. The ones that I go to now are really more like retirement senior centers. A bunch of old guys and old women that spend time together. Sam Red . . . he lives in one of the senior-citizen housing high-rises now. He has an apartment and he's still running a drink house to the old geezers."

Ralph R. Speas: The Bloody Drink House

Ralph R. Speas has been the archivist for the Piedmont Blues Preservation Society (PBPS) for more than twenty years and has been familiar with the music scene in the Piedmont of North Carolina since 1967, when he moved to Greensboro. Ralph described the diversity of bars, clubs, and drink houses that made up the Piedmont music scene, which included not only the illegal bars but also a "bucket of blood," which was a type of drink house known to be so dangerous that when the owner mopped the place the next morning, the dirty water in the bucket might also be bloody. The bucket of blood was the most violent of the drink houses, where patrons often released pent-up frustration with brutality. In the book Seems Like Murder Here: Southern Violence and the Blues Tradition, *Adam Gussow devotes a chapter to "Guns, Knives, and Buckets of Blood" (pp. 195–232), where both men and women could be jealous, possessive, and murderous. According to Ralph, there was one popularly known "bucket" in East Greensboro's past.*

"I've driven by the old Bucket in East Greensboro many times. Now it's long gone, of course. There's some people today who will still call any bar or drink house a 'bucket of blood' if something rough happened there. . . . The phrase 'bucket of blood' is old pirate slang that means a rowdy place where almost anything goes and you could get 'shanghaied,' drugged, kidnapped, and awakened the next morning not only hung over but literally 'lost at sea.' Seaboard houses of prostitution sometimes paid madams to deliver prospective unwary deckhands.[6] I believe 'bucket of blood' was also a term used in the old West for a saloon that

1.1. Ralph Speas, archivist and blues historian. Courtesy Emily Edwards.

had a reputation for being violent. The worst one in East Greensboro had an extremely bad reputation. Most weren't so bad.

"I came here to the Piedmont because I was recruited to teach at a black university because I'm white. A&T University[7] needed a white face on the faculty to meet federal guidelines. And in '67 that's what I did; I came here to teach. I eventually married a black woman, Betty Jean,[8] and got involved with the local music. Actually, there was mixed reaction to my going to listen to music as a white person in a black bar in the '60s. But it didn't take long—as the audience in the bar, 99 percent black—it didn't take them long to size me up, to figure out who I was, what I was doing there, and that I wouldn't cause any trouble. Then they went on about dancing and drinking and having a good time. I think the black drink houses were much more adaptive to me walking into their bar than white people would be to a black person walking into a white bar at that time. Once they got to know me, folks in the black drink houses were friendly. Sometimes there would be food, fried chicken or fish, and maybe there would be some gambling in the back. It's important to know that not every drink house was a bucket of blood. It depends on who the clientele is. If there is more than one violent episode, however, a place gets a reputation.

"Interestingly enough, women operated most of those drink houses. They were controlled by women and fronted by a man, but the woman made the rules. Like the old song says, 'Mama Don't Allow No Easy Riders 'round Here.' Well, 'But what I care what she don't allow, I'll bring my easy rider in anyhow. But Mama don't allow no easy riders in here.'[9] And that was a very interesting aspect of the drink houses, the women were in the back. There was almost always a male bartender because he had to be a big, tough guy to act as a bouncer if there was any trouble, but women controlled the money.

"I think what we mean by a music scene is the general ambiance, the overall feeling you get from a place. Audiences absolutely contribute to that. A lot of times we put our emphasis on the musicians, but audiences are a critical part. They are a motivator for musicians and they determine what kind of place it is. Can't have a drink house without the people who come there to buy the liquor and listen to the music. I try to put myself into the mind of someone starting up a new bar; they want a place where the audience feels at home. People want to let loose, so alcohol is important to everybody: musicians, bar owners, audiences, just everybody. The place where liquor is served minimizes inhibitions. It's for this reason that most musicians prefer to perform where alcohol is served . . . because it does loosen audience inhibitions. You'll hear a musician say to the crowd, 'the more you drink, the better I sound.' An audience will get up and dance and react more vocally, which the person who is booking and paying for that musician appreciates. Any substance that lessens inhibitions, the internal restriction not to do something because it's dangerous, naughty, or wrong, is very hard to fight against. You want to let loose and it's easier to do with alcohol. . . . Anytime the music is unrestrained and alcohol lets inhibitions loose, religious people are going to see the devil operating. However, the more restricted the thing that you desire becomes, the harder you try to get to it. A place that doesn't have its alcohol permit might even have an extra fascination for some people. Smelly, shoddy, rough, and dangerous—all that gives the drink house a certain charm . . . or maybe the stamp of authenticity.

"You can get a thrill just by being there.

"Tommy Johnson,[10] who preceded Robert Johnson, used to sing about drinking Sterno, which is not the kind of alcohol intended for drinking. Sterno is fuel you burn directly from the can, like for a camp stove. 'Canned Heat Blues' is about drinking Sterno, about doing what's bad and dangerous. Many musicians invite this 'bad boy' reputation. People are so repressed in their everyday lives; they need release, even if it's for just a few hours, even at the risk of flirting with the devil—or his stand-in, that bad boy musician. The musician, who is probably drinking himself, helps lead people in the audience to their own release."

Michael Bennett: The Campaign Liquor

Michael Bennett owns a guitar shop in Winston-Salem called the B String. He started playing guitar at fourteen, influenced by British rock and the Allman Brothers. Mike began doing guitar repairs as a kid and found his niche selling and repairing guitars as well as giving music lessons, but like many musicians, his earliest gigs were playing in the local bars. I interviewed Mike at his guitar shop in Winston-Salem in 2006.

"I played in drink houses or juke joints at an age where today it would be illegal for me to go in there—you were supposed to be eighteen to get in there.[11] The county I'm from, Burke County, was a licensed county. You could sell liquor but you had your blue laws, so you couldn't sell beer or wine on Sundays but some places didn't bother with a liquor license or observe the blue laws. We had a place in Burke County called Bear's Head. That one juke joint—the Bear's Head—would get raided all the time. Law would shut the place down and in a few weeks it'd be back open. It would open up or get really started at midnight and go on until the wee hours. There could be 150 people in there. The blue laws kept people going to those places, so they could party all night and all weekend. The place would get raided, the law would shut the place down, and

1.2. Michael Bennett. Courtesy Doug Mokaren.

in a few weeks it'd be open again with full bands, full bar, everything. If it was an election year, the place might get popped more often.

"There was a funny sort of bond between the law and the juke joints. I remember one time these bottles of moonshine liquor were dropped off in the back of the bar and the owner said the law was coming by to pick them up. This moonshine was campaign liquor, which means it was for a candidate throwing a party. Campaign liquor. There's a poetic irony there . . . moonshine as campaign liquor.

"The last time I played at the Bear's Head, I was warned ahead of time to get my guitars and amps out of the building—that it was going to get popped. I was grateful they told to me get my stuff out of the building because, when a place gets popped, the police are gonna padlock the joint and I wouldn't be able to get my stuff back until after the trial was over. That would put me out of business for a while.

"When I moved here [Winston-Salem] twenty years ago, I saw that there were some real good players and they were all in it together. When an opportunity to play at a bar or something came along, they'd get on the phone, call in a few people, write out a set list, and without any kind of rehearsal, they'd go play the gig. People would ask, 'How long have you boys been playing together as a band?' Somebody will look at his watch and say, 'About forty-five minutes now.' Folks are impressed, but a lot of that goes on around here. There's this continuity to the blues and country styles of music. You know where you're going musically and it gives you some freedom to improvise within the pattern. . . . Musicians around here will play for nothing just to play, to jam. Put out a hat and hope for tips, but sometimes it was for absolutely nothing . . . a good time. After I was married and the kids came along, I skinned it back some."

Big Ron Hunter: Getting Started in the Drink House

Big Ron Hunter is a vocalist and guitar player from Winston-Salem, North Carolina, who has played in Belgium and New York as well as at bars and festivals all across North Carolina. When I interviewed Big Ron in 2006 at an outdoor café on Fourth Street in Winston-Salem, he told me that as a younger man he played several drink houses for tips and experience.

"When I was just a knee-high kid, my cousins Netty and Bo Pete influenced me to play music. I first heard the guitar from them. Finally, my mom bought me a Mickey Mouse guitar and I started fooling around with that little thing. My dad played the blues. He wrote and played by ear. We used to sit out on the porch when I was a kid and play. I wrote a song called "My Father Said," which is about the things he told me about how to play the blues.[12] He told me, 'Son, I want you to learn how to make your guitar talk. When you learn to make your guitar talk, then after you become a man you can play with anybody.' So I worked out a sound to make my guitar seem full. After I was older, I started playing around in some of the drink houses. They weren't legal as far as the alcohol, but that was a good way for me to make some money. They would give tips.

1.3. Big Ron Hunter. Courtesy Doug Mokaren.

"Most of the drink houses in Winston-Salem were all black. Every once in a while, a white person would come in and he would be welcome, but mostly it was black people. . . . The hippie musicians didn't really come out to the drink houses around here, but I played with them some, too. We would hang out at a strip down on North West Boulevard in Winston, where all the hippies hung out. The hippies would come out and we'd play some. Then there was the Reynolda Gardens; all your hippie musicians, all your young people would go there on Friday afternoons. That wasn't a drink house. It was a garden, an open space and free to go inside. There was a big field usually full of people with all types of instruments—some folks would be studying and some folks would be playing Frisbee and some would be playing drums and guitar, you know, people from everywhere. All kinds of people. Every weekend. People would be all over the place out there and maybe you'd smell a little something in the air. Somebody might sneak in a bottle. Not now. Times change and they started locking the place up. Used to be the place was open all the time, all night long; then they started locking it up, keeping a closer eye on it.

"Well, the things people used to do they can't do anymore or they don't do anymore. People vanish. Times change. People got jobs. So the hippie scene faded out. Most of the real hippies moved on up to the mountains, up to Asheville or way off in the country somewhere. The others got jobs, got respectable.

"The black drink houses changed, too. And the music changed. Young black folks are not interested in blues music so much anymore. Actually, if you really listen to the music, it's still blues. They're still just singing about their surroundings, you know, the stuff they deal with. But the surroundings today are different for them now. Back when I was coming up, we lived in houses and out in the country. You know, our surroundings were different, and so our music was different. But the next generation—it's like when B. B. King sings about why does everybody sing the blues. When they came to the city, the people were living in projects. And that's what happened. The young people lived in the projects all on top of one another and it was a different atmosphere. They didn't venture out into the country. They didn't travel. It was just that one atmosphere they were in and rap comes up and they just rapped about that one environment they were trapped in and what happens to them there. So it's blues they sing, but it's a different type of blues. They don't play instruments. Maybe nobody showed them how. Maybe nobody got them any instruments, and so they just rapped. Made the beat with their voices. Music without instruments.[13]

"When I was growing up, we were all spread out. We traveled and we learned to play instruments. Young black kids today maybe don't have that same opportunity . . . the generation before me had to travel for work. My mother had to travel for her success in life. My uncle came to take her to New York. My mother couldn't raise me; she had to find work. She knew she had to make a better life, so my mom . . . gave me up [at six months old]. Some black folks back then were making hard choices for a better life. Kids today may not have those same choices; they may not have someone to get them a Mickey Mouse guitar. They may not have relatives or people that can teach them how to play.

"I decided I wanted to show my appreciation for the folks that came before me musically: Guitar Gabe, Howlin' Wolf, and all them. So I've been keeping the blues going in my own style. I quit playing drink houses for tips and started playing in the ministry. I've been playing in the ministry for eighteen years now. What I've learned is that music—all kinds of music—is healing. You can reach people with music when you can't reach them with anything else."

Lorenzo "Logie" Meachum: Neighborhood Drink Houses

Lorenzo "Logie" Meachum is a vocalist, guitar player, and storyteller turned scholar and educator. Logie is one of the founding members of the Piedmont Blues Preservation Society, the group responsible for organizing the Carolina Blues Festival in 1987, which continues at this writing (2015).[14] *I interviewed Logie on the front porch of his parents' house on Aloe Road in Greensboro, near the Old Oak Stump Garden, on June 2, 2014, after visiting his cousin Po' Ray's drink house or "social house" a few days earlier on Memorial Day. According to Logie, drink houses were sprinkled all across the black communities from the 1960s to the 1990s. He believes most of the old-fashioned drink houses have closed now. The ones that still operate, like Po' Ray's, are called "social houses." A social house is convenient, usually located in a residential neighborhood, and the only place to go when all the legal bars have closed their doors. Logie added that the contemporary social house never involves musicians sitting in the corner to jam. Another woman I met at Po' Ray's for the Memorial Day event also operated a social house nearby. The proximity of these establishments meant that the clientele could roam from house to house.*

Po' Ray's Memorial Day event in 2014 looked just like any neighborhood cookout, with children playing on the lawns of other nearby houses. Although Po' Ray's social house was open early in the evening when we visited and was also selling plates of fried fish, that was an unusual occurrence. Logie described the contemporary social house as a place that normally will not open until midnight or later, rarely serves food, and, unlike earlier drink houses, was not a place to jam.

"The old drink houses, they didn't have no license. There were several of them around here. The one off Cherry Street was nicer than others. It had nice new café tables. They sold food. The sisters were coming in setting things up and they had the traditional stuff in liquor houses. Jars of pickled pig feet, pickled eggs, Penrose sausages, and crackers. The liquor was some dark, some white, and some homemade, and that was it. You couldn't get any scotch or rum. Vodka, whiskey of any kind, cheapest you could get.

"You know. People would just come to the drink house to sit and talk. . . . I would take my older cousin; his name was George Reynolds,

1.4. Lorenzo "Logie" Meachum. Courtesy Doug Mokaren.

but everybody called him Booney Coon. Booney Coon liked to drink his whiskey . . . and he always enjoyed Georgia Skin parties. Georgia Skin is a card game, a gambling game. Literally, the rules for Skin are the same as the rules for dice, except you're using cards. The old-fashioned liquor houses had lots of gambling going on. Sometimes it wouldn't be in a liquor house; people would have the liquor-house dynamic come to their private homes. What they were doing is they'd throw a Skin party. You can make some money if you throw a Georgia Skin party because the house always gets a cut. People buy food from the house and the house gets a cut of the take. There's always a lot of money at a Skin party. People are sitting there with fists full of money. You bet against the dealer and against the other players. Because you've got twenty dollars bet with this guy and you've got five dollars bet with this guy and you've got two dollars bet over here. When the number comes up, everybody starts paying. Money is flying from every which a-way. It depends on who's betting and for what on the deal.[15]

"I would take Booney Coon to every liquor house he wanted to go to, like Ivory Reed's. In this neighborhood there was a liquor house on Carter's Grove called Ivory Reed's, a big-time liquor house. Then there was the Bucket of Blood, Frank's place. It was called the Bucket because on any given night, it could turn to a fight pretty quick. Yep, knife fights in the sixties. The Bucket was all fights and knife fights. Brothers didn't shoot each other. All the men in my generation, down until my generation, we all have false teeth and stitches because we're all alive. We fight; we survive. There was never anybody putting on guns and shooting nobody; that was uncivilized. That was cretin. Damn, that's low-life. You were not a man if you had to pull a gun. You were a hooligan. A gun is detached. You can't be a child of God and take a person's life and be detached like that. If you're going to send one of God's children home, you got to make it personal, up close. You make it a special delivery. You can't detach yourself; you've got to be special delivery Jones. You can't be twenty feet away and shoot some fucking body. Anyway, the Bucket could usually get a good fistfight; somebody might get cut and there's even been a few shootings there. Frank ran the Bucket out of a garage. . . . He'd move the cars out and he'd put the sawdust down. He'd set the pickled eggs and pickled pig feet out and turn the music on the jukebox. We called it a 'piccolo'—turn the piccolo on. He had recorded music.

"Two doors down, my cousins had a liquor house called the Hut. It was really a family liquor house for this community because this was an all-black community. My grandfather sold all the chaser that you needed. His little store was that little black building down the road. You could go upstairs and dance. You could come downstairs and buy drinks and cookies, cakes, pies, pickled eggs, pickled pig feet, and stuff like that, and shoot pool. But he only sold chasers. No liquor. You'd stop by my granddaddy's store and get your Nehi Grape or Nehi Orange or maybe a Pepsi. Then you would drive real slow around the corner to the Hut, pull up, and top it off. That's where James sold the liquor to go with your chaser. You could get a fish sandwich and your liquor there. Over in Hyde Park, Pop Presley had a little house. He also sold liquor, but the most famous house in this area—there were a lot of little liquor houses around, but Shirley's, up by the airport. Shirley got them when they got off the airplane. Unfortunately, Shirley's is gone now but that was the best chitlin sandwich, fried fish, potato salad, greens anywhere around. . . .

"I was out at the Bucket one time when a fellow got shot. I was still a kid. This man and his wife would come down there every weekend. Then for a long time the wife would meet up with her guy at the Bucket and that was kind of like 'their place.' The husband didn't come out there when the wife was meeting up with her guy. Except this one night the husband came . . . and here he comes with a shotgun. I saw him coming. Nobody had glass on the windows or screens back then. The window is open, so if you're a kid and you're not supposed to be there with all the drinking and dancing and gambling, you sit down in the open windowsill and watch. You enjoy watching the older men slow dance, slow grind with the women. You're watching how they hugging and squeezing the women. And then here comes this man with a shotgun. . . . Pow! He slammed in the door with that shotgun and, boy, I was out of that window and under a '64 Chevy as fast as I could go. Here he comes with his shotgun. . . . Pow! That wasn't special delivery Jones. . . .

"Now, the Carlotta was a whole different kind of place. This was a club. This was an upscale place. You paid a cover charge to get in there. I was too young to go in when it was still in business but you knew who was going to be at the Carlotta by the marquee at the Magnolia Hotel. The sign would say, 'Here tonight, the Blind Boys of Alabama, Sister Rosetta Tharpe, Mahalia Jackson, James Brown.'[16] Greensboro and the Magnolia Hotel were stops along the eastern seaboard for black performers and black travelers. There used to be a black book that showed you all of the places up and down the coast that black entertainers could stop in and get rooms or food. Back in those days, a black entertainer couldn't just stop and be welcome in any old place, but the Magnolia Hotel was the one to welcome them here."

Rob Slater: Driving a Cab

Rob Slater is a guitar player who has twice competed at the International Blues Challenge as a player in two different bands: Lawyers Guns & Money

1.5. Rob Slater. Courtesy Doug Mokaren.

in 2012 and Toot and the Long Shots in 2013. He is currently a member of the Luxuriant Sedans. However, Rob's early experience with North Carolina drink houses came not as a musician but as a cab driver.

"I came back to Winston in 1980. My friend Gary found out where they were hiring drivers for Bluebird cab and we got the gig. . . . We were told that because we were white boys and it's largely the black community in Winston, we had to watch ourselves and our fares. White folks in Winston-Salem have cars and live in the suburbs. The cab company primarily served the black community. We were told that it would not be a good idea for white boys to drive on the weekends or at night. Driving a cab was a real tough way to make money. . . .

"One Saturday morning, I decided to do a shift anyway. I went in early, got my cab, and my first haul was east of Patterson Avenue. This was back before the urban development in Winston, and there was a section near the Reynolds facilities downtown where there were these old row houses. They must have been built at turn of the [twentieth] century or just afterward. So I get this call. . . . I go to the neighborhood and there's a row house. It was up off the street on the hill. I'm sitting there in the cab waiting for the fare and the front door opens. Out on the porch comes this really nicely dressed young guy. Nice leather jacket. Got a polo shirt on and some nice slacks, really looking incongruous with the house he was leaving. He comes down the steps and gets in the front of the cab, in the front seat, which is always kind of suspicious. I was always leery of anybody who got into my cab and got in the passenger side of the front. We sat there. He's a handsome guy, well turned out.

"He looks at me and he says, 'I hope you got all day.' He says, 'Because I'm going to keep you.'

"I said, 'Well, I'm doing a shift. You're my first fare. Sure. Why not?' I thought, well, this is interesting.

"Anyway, he started chatting me up and he gave me an address. We drove to this address and he said, 'Just leave it running. I'll be out in a minute.' He gets out of the cab and disappears in this house for about five minutes. Comes out, gets back in the front seat of the cab, gives me another address. And he chats me up. He's talking about the weather and sports and real glib.

"He has me drive him to a series of these houses all over east Winston. It must have been five or six of them. It's the same M-O every time. He gets out, goes in the house for maybe five, maybe as many as ten minutes, but no longer than that. Then he comes back. Anyway, after like five or six of these, he comes back, jumps into the front seat of the cab, digging in his pocket, and he pulls out this wad of cash. It was literally—choke a horse—wad of cash. It was all tens and twenties and hundreds, rolled up in a roll that must have been three or four inches across. I mean, it was a pile of dough.

"Being the young lad I was, I wasn't really hip to what was going on . . . and it was kind of . . . well, none of my business. The meter is running the whole time, so I'm going to make some money today anyway. Another couple of places and the same thing happens. By now it's lunchtime and he comes out with this incredible bankroll.

"My curiosity gets the better of me and I inquire. It turns out that what we were doing was he—and I don't know exactly how the hierarchy works—but he was working for somebody who ran drink houses and card games. He actually referred to them as 'drink houses.' I think there was some girl and dope action going on in some of these places, too. Apparently, he was working as a runner for whoever it was that was getting a cut of the action at these places. He was basically collecting debts or dues or whatever you want to call it, at each one of these houses. We'd been to eight or ten of them all over east Winston on this beautiful morning. He had this really huge wad of dough. Huge.

"After it became clear what was going on, I looked at him and I asked, 'Aren't you kind of nervous, running around town with this mountain of cash that you've got in apparently every pocket on your person?'

"He looked at me and he smiled really big. As he smiles, he leans back in the front seat of the cab and he pulls his shirt up and he's got this cannon stuffed down his pants. It's a revolver. It's the biggest firearm I've ever seen. It was a pistol, but it looked like a rifle. It was huge. I don't know anything about firearms, but it was a revolver of some kind and it was gigantic. He's grinning at me and he says, 'No, man, I'm not worried about nothing.'

"I thought, okay. Good. I guess I'm okay, too."

John Dee Holeman: A Chapel Hill Drink House

The musician and National Heritage Fellowship recipient John Dee Holeman was so moved by the violence of one drink house that it inspired his song "Chapel Hill Boogie," which he cowrote with Kenny Wayne Shepherd. The song became a signature number for Holeman. He played a version of this song at the New River Blues Festival in 2012 with Andy Coats.[17] *Afterward I asked Mr. Holeman about his drink house experiences. We were sitting under the musician's tent; Mr. Holeman was looking out at the New River, mesmerized by the water flowing north in front of us. This is all he told me.*

1.6. John Dee Holeman. Courtesy Doug Mokaren.

"There was this place in Chapel Hill, in the old Chapel Hill, which was called Tin Top. . . . It was rough. It was really rough. That's why I wrote that song. 'Well I go to Chapel Hill, Chapel Hill is a ball. Go to Chapel Hill, get a drink of alcohol.' That place . . . someone might throw a bottle or something at you."

Max Drake: Juke Joints and Tobacco Barns

Max Drake plays guitar, mandolin, lap steel, and banjo and is known for a fifteen-year run with the band Arhooly.[18] *He has played with B. B. King, Lightnin' Hopkins, Skeeter Brandon, Bo Diddley, Mick Taylor, Nappy*

1.7. Max Drake. Courtesy Doug Mokaren.

Brown, Big Boy Henry, Lightnin' Wells, and Johnny Copeland, among many others. He currently plays with Mel Melton and the Wicked Mojos.

"I grew up hearing blues music all my life from the time I was two years old. I grew up in Stoneville right on the edge of the Blue Ridge Mountains. It was always around. My family is from Yanceyville. We had all these descendants of slaves and itinerant workers out here singing all the time in the fields. I was exposed to it from day one. I remember the drink houses out here on [Route] 158, coming out here to my grandmother's. On weekend nights, there was a place coming out of Reidsville right before you hit [Highway] 29. On the weekends, there would be so many people there that they would stop the traffic. It was a black joint. I remember seeing the really cool dapper guys, really gaunt skinny fellows with the black pompadour hair and the wraparound sunglasses and the skinny suits and the Cuban roach-killer shoes. I would sit in the backseat going, 'Man, that is for me. That is too cool for school.' They were partying down. There were just piles of people. It would be 150 people it seemed like to me. There was also this relative of mine by marriage, younger than me. He converted a tobacco barn into a little juke joint. Bars like that were all over the place. These country people had to party someplace."

Robin Stamps Doby Easter: They Wanted Me to Run a Drink House

Originally from Lynchburg, Virginia, Robin Stamps Doby Easter is a vocalist for the band Doby and has performed with various bands. Robin had never been inside a drink house or a social house, but knew what they were. In our conversations, Robin mentioned that for a very short time she was a bartender at a legal bar in Greensboro that is now closed, but while she was bartending, she was approached about opening a drink house.

"I knew they existed because I heard of all these places . . . my ex-husband would go and I have a girlfriend whose father would go. When she needed money, she would say, 'I got to go find my dad.'

"I said, 'Where is he?'

"She said, 'He at the liquor house.' She called them the 'liquor house.'

"I said, 'What are they doing in there?'

"She told me, 'They play cards there and get a good game of bid whist or spades.'

"So the liquor house is not just for drinking, it's for socializing, but it wasn't for me. Once when I was bartending, I was approached by a man who wanted me to have an after-hours liquor house. I was like, 'What do you mean? I don't want to work after—' [and] they said, 'No. What happens is you have the place; we supply everything else: the ice, the liquor, the people. You're just providing the place.'

"I said, 'Well, what happens at my place?'

"He says, 'After a certain hour, like when this bar shuts down, then people who want to drink all night come to your spot and they drink.

1.8. Robin Stamps Doby Easter. Courtesy Doug Mokaren.

We supply the liquor, the cash, everything. We pay you a certain amount to run it. We'll have the people there that'll take care of everything. If you want to wait on the people you can. If want to sleep you can, but what we're doing is we're using your place, but we're providing the people, the staff, everything, to come in there and run it. We're going to pay you just to use your place and we'll pay you handsomely.'

"Now, it was an enticing offer, but I just could not—I was more afraid of who would be showing up. Would there be fights? Would there be arguments where people actually stab or shoot each other? Anything could happen and I wouldn't know who these people were in my house. But, if you worked at a regular bar and people go in, then they have to show their ID and people know you at the bar, but to have just anybody come in your house? Boy, did I think about it, but I eventually said, 'No thanks.' Yeah. The other thing was they didn't harass me about it. It was like, 'Here's the offer.' I could take it or leave it. I left it."

Roy Roberts: The Nightclub Is Classier

Roy Roberts grew up in Kentucky in the '40s doing heavy farm labor in order to buy his first guitar, a Silvertone he says was popular with young musicians because it was considered well made but inexpensive. He mail-ordered his Silvertone from Sears and at eighteen, Roy left the farm to live with an uncle in Greensboro. Roy got his big break in the '60s when Solomon Burke let him sit in on a set, and then took him on tour. Roy began to cut records as a session player with artists like Stevie Wonder, William Bell, Solomon Burke, and Otis Redding. From the beginning of his career, Roy explains that music was always his business, never his pastime. For Roy, there was a clear distinction between the "drink house" and the nicer, legal bars and club scene.[19]

"The drink house is a place where everybody just gets together. They're cooking chicken in the back, you know, drinking liquor, gambling, and all that mess is going on. It's just an old big house where everybody gets together. They used to get together on the weekends and that's where they partied. It could just be somebody's house or a garage. Compare that to the nightclub, where you can go out and give a big performance and that type of thing. A nightclub has more space; it's classier. For one thing, when the musician was going to play the nightclub, he knew he was going to get paid. When he was over there in the liquor house, all a musician might get is a drink and some fried chicken or maybe a sandwich. He can put out his hat and maybe get a dollar or two, if he's lucky. I've never had any interest in a drink house. I came out starting in the business with musicians like Solomon Burke, Stevie Wonder, Eddie Floyd, Dee Clark, and Otis Redding—all these people are the ones I came up with. These guys are classier than some little dude sitting over there in a drink house, you know. I avoided that. In my career, I've always been looking for bigger things, greater things. The drink house was too

1.9. Roy Roberts. Courtesy Doug Mokaren.

small for me. That was on a level that I didn't want, because first of all, I don't drink, so I didn't care about getting paid with any liquor.

"The clubs are a whole different situation. With the nightclub, I can go in and do a show, and then go on about my business—and I'm getting *paid* for it. It's classy. With the drink house, it's more like something where musicians would get together: 'Hey, let's run down to Joe's house tonight and jam down there, man, and have a little party down there.' Well, that just wasn't my bag. The dude at the drink house, he's bootlegging. So you're going in there and getting yourself a little fifty-cent shot, back in the day—or twenty cents or two dollars—whatever it is at the time, shot of liquor and a fifty-cent chicken sandwich. This was not for me.

"There was an old guy here in Greensboro who had this old big house out in the woods and he just opened up this juke joint out there. Everybody would run out there in the woods, get drunk, shoot pool, and gamble. That was not my scene. The worst one was the Bucket. If you got killed out at that place at night, your cold, dead body could just lay there on the ground until the next day, because ambulance drivers would not risk coming out there at night to get you. That's how rough the place was."

T. L. "Poppa T" Lineberry: Introductions to a Juke Joint

T. L. Lineberry is retired from the retail music industry. He was a local promoter and founder of the Greensboro concert venue CafeJAM. At the time of this story, T. L. was a chaplain for the sheriff's department of Cumberland County and a sworn officer of the court who had been issued a uniform that he never wore. He explained that as a chaplain, his job was to do the "death notifications."

"They send a chaplain out, just like they send a military chaplain out, to tell a family that their son or daughter's been killed in service. I would go to the family with the uniformed officer, knock on the door, and say, 'I have some bad news. Your son's not coming home. He was killed in a car wreck—or, he died in a drowning accident.' I was the bearer of bad news. It's one of those jobs that nobody really wanted to do. It's mostly what I did as a volunteer for the sheriff's department, community service, basically."

The night of this story, T. L. was not performing a death notification but doing a ride-along with the deputy sheriff, who had become a friend. It was a warm summer night when the deputy drove out of his jurisdiction into Sampson County, North Carolina, and into an area unfamiliar to T. L., but the deputy knew exactly where he was going.

"I don't remember what we were talking about. We might have been talking about music. He knew I had been in Mississippi prior to living there and that I was a guitar player. He knew I liked music, all kinds, but especially blues. . . . Anyway, we crossed the county line and he said something like—best I can remember now, he said something like, 'Let's go have some fun,' or something like that. It was just something off the cuff. Shortly after that, he turned on to this little dirt lane.

"I might have said, 'Where're we going?' because we'd never been down that road.

"He said, 'I'm going to show you a juke joint.'

"And I said, 'A juke joint?' I do remember saying that.

"We pulled up in front of this little white house in the middle of—in the dark, it looked like pastureland, or part of a farm, or something like that, because that's about all that's down in that area . . . farms and hog farms, farmland. Best I remember, there was music playing, and the music stopped once the sheriff's car pulled up in front of the place. There were probably twenty or thirty cars, maybe, around the house. I don't remember exactly, but there were a lot of cars jammed in around in the yard and around the house. There were a lot of people standing around outside, too . . . some couples and some guys just standing around. Most every person had a drink or a cigarette. He looked over at me, we were sitting in the car, and he said, 'Let's go in.'

"I do remember looking at him because I wasn't really sure why we were there or what we were going to do, but he wanted to show me the juke joint. We got out. I followed him onto this little side porch, which was probably the main entrance to the little house, and we walked through a handful of people, not a whole lot of people, standing near the door, but I don't recall speaking to any of them, but maybe a head nod or something like that. Of course, they didn't know why we were there, and I didn't know either, but J. D. [the deputy] knew why he was there. We walked in, and on the right in the main room we went in, there was a pool table. I do recall that the room was packed. There was a larger room off to the left, which would have probably been something like the living room, maybe. We didn't go in there. The place was packed with African American men and women. Besides the ones playing pool, most of them either had a beer or some kind of drink. There was a cooler in the room back in the one corner. I don't know if it was an old Pepsi cooler or Coke cooler. It was a chest-type cooler . . . something of that nature.

"Anyway, he said, 'Who's in charge here?' This one guy spoke up and then he turned around and stepped into a smaller room in the back, and this older gentleman came out and said something like, 'Can I help you, sir?' or 'What can I help you with?'

"That's when J. D. makes up a story. He told the guy that we had a loud-music disturbance call. He said, 'You need to turn the music down.'

"The guy said, 'Yes, sir, yes, sir. We'll do that. We'll turn it right down.' He was real cordial.

"Then J. D. says, 'If we get a call again, we're going to have to get the ATF boys out here.' . . . I don't know what kind of alcohol, but they were selling beer, and probably liquor without a license; it was one of those off-the-radar, off-the-grid juke joints.

"The guy said, 'Oh, yeah, yeah. We'll turn it down.'

"Of course, I'm kind of uneasy about being there, but then when I was standing there listening to J. D. make up this yarn. . . . We didn't get any disturbance call. I'm thinking, 'I'm not believing this.' He turned around and I followed him. We got in the car. Before he even backed out, I looked over and said, 'Are you crazy?' I do remember saying that. I said, 'Are you crazy? What are you doing?'

"He just laughed. He had a laugh like Deputy Dawg. He wanted to show me the illegal juke joint that was operating out there. He probably had been there before because he knew exactly where it was. What he was going there for, or had been out there for, I don't know. There weren't any white people that I remember, but there might have been in the other room. We didn't go in there. He wouldn't have turned anyone in, I don't think. He told me, 'They're not hurting anybody,' but he had to have an excuse for being out there. You don't go unless you're called. There was no call from the county for a loud-music disturbance. He just wanted to show me a juke joint."

Moneek Allah: The Liquor House Rules

Moneek Allah is a factory worker who relocated to North Carolina from New York. He says that in the South, after-hours clubs are called "liquor houses," and still do a thriving business in 2014. However, live music in the contemporary liquor house is rare, reserved for a special occasion like a birthday or private party. Moneek explained that even though the liquor house has no license, the "house man" is less concerned with police than with a robbery or home invasion, so some liquor houses hire security or become very particular about their clients.

"A liquor house is just like a club. Bigger houses have different clientele and different atmospheres. You have the low-class ones. One time I was at one of those . . . usually a woman may approach you and ask you about buyin' 'em a drink, but this guy asked me if I could buy him a drink. I told him, 'No,' . . . but then the guy asked me for a cigarette. He says, 'Can you just save me a short?' It was really tacky, you know. I've been in some other ones where you thought you were in a nice club, you know. . . . I ate food, everything, drinks, but, of course, you're buying everything at a higher price than the usual liquor house. . . .

"I went to this liquor house . . . back in the late '80s and a young lady was sitting in this chair, and this guy was drunk and saying it was his chair. I went in the other room, came back, and then I heard a loud sound where he had shot this woman in her head. He killed this woman over a chair because he was drunk. I was right there. Everybody scattered because it was an illegal place, so nobody wanted to get caught there with the situation that happened, so everybody just pretty much just went separate ways. You know, quick exits.

"You learn about a place usually by word of mouth . . . and some people, they have followings, you know what I'm saying, like an entourage. They go, 'Let's go to this one, and this one,' and then it'll be a pack of people going from liquor houses like bar hopping, but liquor-house hopping. People out partying and stuff, after everything closed off, they don't want to go home, so they find someplace else. . . . Lot of 'em will be working people; you'd think you're at the club. People want to get out, they're just getting off work, and want to hang out before they go home and stuff like that. There'll be nice cars parked out there, nice music going on, nice decor, and everything.

"I know this one place, this one girl, I laugh 'cause hers is not upscale, but she has a pretty good clientele, but the thing made me think about hers, it's a place where all the strippers go after they leave the strip club. There'll be packs of 'em. Yeah. They be doing some business there, too. . . . Then you have the real crazy people, you know, the alcoholics that every time you see 'em, they're getting put out of the house because they don't know how to act. They curse people out; they're being malignant and stuff, you know? The illegal businesses don't want to draw attention. I'm sure the police pretty much know what's happening there 'cause every Sunday the whole block is packed. Then you'll get your

DWIs leaving there, so the police know what's happening. They lay and wait for 'em to leave. . . .

"Prices not as high as the bar, but they're high. Plus a lot of times, the alcohol they serve don't be top shelf either. There are people that do it different ways, but a lot of houses have a designated area like maybe the living room or kitchen, people just sitting around drinking in there. A lot of 'em have families, like they have little kids in the back and stuff like that, especially in the early mornings or late nights. There's no drinking in those parts of the house. You stay in the part of the house where the people are drinking. They start congregating; they go out in the backyard and stuff and keep the noise down.

"A lot of times the people that's running it, they be real particular. They like to make sure you know [the rules]. . . . 'Don't park in nobody's driveway.' They don't want no complaints. No use of drugs out in the open and stuff like that and don't bring no [outside] liquor into the liquor house. That's a cardinal sin. Hang 'em high. And they try to keep the noise to a level. All them people and the music and stuff, but then, a lot of times, people are outside arguing. They tell you you've got to move off the premises; take it someplace else. They ain't trying to draw too much attention, even though, in a lot of places, it's obvious there's a liquor house there."[20]

◆ ◆ ◆

With the exception of an upscale club, oral histories about the drink house may not always clearly differentiate between a legal and an illegal venture. *Drink house, liquor house, juke joint, bar,* and *club* are often interchangeable terms. *Honky-tonks* are considered the country music version of a juke joint with white patrons, which made them distinctive. Although the illegal drink house was the only operation in a dry county, both might operate in a wet county. The older drink house and juke joint might have once been "ground zero" for the local musician, but contemporary illegal bars (liquor houses, pour houses, social houses) tend to rely on recorded music. Sometimes patrons did not know or care if the "house man" had a legal permit for alcohol sales, and this was a principal feature that set the two apart. Other distinguishing features were that the illegal drink house was

- less likely to advertise,
- more difficult to locate, if it was in a rural area,
- more likely to have unusual hours (opening very late at night or operating only on weekends and during those times when blue laws would be in effect),
- less likely to card underage customers,
- more likely to have underage employees, and
- more likely to sell cheaper alcohol, generally corn liquor or bootleg.

As one storyteller suggested, "A drink house is just a bar. You people [meaning academics] seem to need to classify everything, even bars. But the most important thing to know about any bar or drink house is to go where you know you will be welcome, where someone won't beat you up because of your skin color, and where you know you can find your good times."[21]

CHAPTER 2

The Bar as a Music Venue

While a few drink houses may have offered a starting point for the musician looking for that genuine sound, some stories suggest that legal bars could be just as important or even more important as a training ground and music destination, especially those bars that held jams or made music part of their identity.

Mel Melton: The Goal Is Not to Lose Money

Mel Melton is a chef and harmonica player who was raised in North Carolina but became heavily influenced by the Cajun lifestyle when he moved to Lafayette, Louisiana, in 1969. In Lafayette he began playing in a band with Sonny Landreth, known as the "King of Slydeco" for his zydeco-inspired slide guitar playing. To help support his musician's lifestyle, Mel found work in Cajun restaurants in Lafayette. When he moved to Austin, Texas, three years later, he was still cooking and playing. Mel took his Cajun inspiration with him to Chicago in 1986, opening two restaurants, but by 1990 he was back in North Carolina as a restaurant consultant and executive chef until he opened his own Papa Mojo's Roadhouse in Durham in 2008. We had this conversation on August 22, 2014, a few days after he had made the decision to close Papa Mojo's Roadhouse.

"In North Carolina it's pretty easy to get a liquor license. When I was in Chicago, I had a real small quick-serve restaurant downtown, but to get a liquor license there . . . no way. As far as I can tell in Chicago, they don't give them out. It's nearly impossible. . . . There's none to be had. I've heard it's like that in Manhattan, too, and in Florida or Miami. If you want a liquor license, you've got to buy somebody out and if you don't have a couple hundred thousand dollars, you're not getting one, because

2.1. Mel Melton. Courtesy Doug Mokaren.

it's all locked up in those cities. There's kickbacks and all kinds of things going on, but in North Carolina, it's a pretty simple process. You just tell them what you want. There's three different ones to get. You can get malt beverage, unfortified wine, and spirituous liquor. We obviously want all three. They package them together. You get a yearly license and they're like under two thousand dollars.

"The reason so many North Carolina drink houses just don't bother with a liquor license—even though it's pretty easy to get one—is . . . because number one, they don't want to follow up on the hours of operation. They'll stay open all night if they can. Number two: they don't want any kind of age code, although those places are not usually kiddy shops.[1] But the most important thing, when you own a bar or a restaurant with those licenses, you pay several dollars more per bottle than you'd pay for liquor if you just go in and buy a bottle of booze at the ABC store. You're supposed to buy from a licensed wholesaler. I ran Papa Mojo's for seven years. I had the ALE [Alcohol Law Enforcement] come in there. I had the alcohol officers come in there and after a while they just never came back anymore because they knew we were running it by the book. If you start playing around with them, then they're never going to leave you alone, so we always did the right things and they never really bothered us. . . .

"My goal with the music was just not to lose any money and if I did lose money, try to not lose too much. I considered the music as part of the marketing, the branding of Papa Mojo's. It worked because we got this reputation. You brought a band in to perform and you paid for their food; you paid for some drinks. The hotels for the bands were barter; we got the rooms for gift cards and a small amount of catering. That made it doable but I don't know how a club that's dealing with national touring acts can do it if they're having to fork out hundreds of dollars for hotel rooms or whatever. The other thing in terms of Durham, I can't speak for other places, but the Durham music audience has a local indifference to national talent. They would prefer to go out and hear some part-time, weekend-warrior band that they know and they're all friends. You book a local band and the band brings its buddies prowling in here and they're all drinking heavy. But that's the other thing. A lot of times you got problems . . . because you get people going out to the parking lot and drinking in their cars. You find the little airline bottles in the bathroom, in the trash can, in the parking lot. . . . I'm telling you, the last two years there have been many Friday and Saturday nights where I was thinking, I could be relaxing at my house right now, instead I'm listening to this band. It's not even that good of a band. Plus, I'm surrounded by the same drunk people that come out to hear the same crap every weekend. But when you bring in somebody like Rick Estrin[2] or one of these big-time operators, you can't even get the house filled up. It's not worth trying. . . . If I can be Papa Mojo and I can come in here and be the front person and, you know, I don't mind getting a little gumbo on my shoes, but I'm not going to be the guy that's in here wrestling this whole beast. . . .

"I'll say this about Papa Mojo's: we never really had problems with audiences being overly rough or rowdy. We've had maybe three incidences with that kind of problem and that's in seven years of running the place. Wednesday nights we had one of the most popular open mics I've ever seen. It was probably 80 percent African American. The leader of the band that fronted the open mic was a black professor [Brett Chambers] from Central [North Carolina Central University].[3] They would come in and do a short fifteen-minute set. Then he had a sign-up sheet where everybody got two songs. Once he built the crowd up on Wednesday nights, if you didn't get in the door by 7:30, you couldn't get in the door at all. That was every Wednesday. He brought in some pretty astounding talent—a lot of jazz guys, a lot of touring guys who were coming through town. Mostly black musicians. It was more R&B and soul music than anything else. We had spoken word, too. It was a pretty eclectic lineup but it was popular. I met a lot of really nice people on Wednesday nights. Maybe we did finally integrate the southern party before we finally closed her down."

Burley Hayes: SomeWhere Else Super Jams

Burley Hayes is a drummer, but he is also the owner and operator of the SomeWhere Else Tavern (SWET or the Tavern) for more than thirty-five years in Greensboro. From its beginning, the Tavern had a reputation as a colorful, lively place for bands playing original music, generally blues and rock. The Tavern's emphasis continues to be original music, because, as Burley says, "You can go hear a cover band almost anywhere." I asked Burley what inspired the music emphasis of the Tavern.

"Well, when I was young I lived in the country and my mom gave us the choice to go live with my father and my father lived downtown. Right across the street from him there was a club called the Blue Max and Bill Kennedy owned it. He brought in a lot of acts, Nashville acts and stuff like that. He and my dad were friends, so they let me go in and clean the club during the day and hang back in the wings at night, because back then underage was not cool. I was probably twelve or thirteen. I would hang out in the back and I remember the first time hearing live music in my life there. . . . You remember Screamin' Jay Hawkins?[4] He was an old blues player they brought out in a coffin with all the eerie music, smoke and stuff. Then the coffin opens up and he climbs out. I'm going, 'Whoa! What *is* this?' It's been on ever since. I've never been the same after watching that. That was my first time with live music and it's made me do what I've done to this day. That's the power of music. . . .

"We opened the SomeWhere Else Tavern on July 3, 1979. My older brother is the one that really wanted to open a club. I was doing electrical work. I came off the road a week after we opened up. The music part actually started when these two fellas walked in—Dwayne Leonard and Aubrey Henley [Mother Magoo]. They asked to start doing a jam in the

2.2. Burley Hayes. Courtesy Doug Mokaren.

bar. We were doing music from the beginning but the main aspect of the club came in when they started the jams. We started the 'Sunday Night Super Jam' and we did 586 consecutive Sunday nights. The SomeWhere Else is basically a music venue. . . . A drink house is—well, back in the day it was where people could go to get their drink on and live music might be involved; a lot of it was just drinking and gambling. I don't usually think of a drink house as a music venue; these days they're mostly about the alcohol . . . no license, no music.

"It's not really hard to get a license to open a bar. I mean you just got to have a good record and abide with all the state laws. I've been doing it for so long that I couldn't even tell you what a license costs now. You have to reapply every year, but you know, I don't have a liquor license anymore. I used to have a liquor license and back then to get a liquor license it was like five hundred dollars and now it's something like three thousand. You're also separated as far as law. If you got a beer license, you're controlled by the ABC, the Alcohol Beverage Control. If you have a liquor license, you're controlled by Alcohol Law Enforcement, which is a state organization and stern, much sterner laws. They're on top of you all the time. . . .

"After we started doing the jams, we became more of a music venue. . . . It was always a music mecca. You never knew who was coming through the door. It just exploded and musicians that were touring knew about the jam and they would all pop in on a Sunday night. You never knew who was coming to play. It was incredible. One of my favorite players to come through was Elvin Bishop.[5] He just came through touring and he was eating at a Waffle House. One of our friends popped in and started talking to him and told him, 'You need to come down to this little jam.' So he came down to the Tavern and sat down at one of the little tables, listening to the jam. I introduced myself to him; he was just so nice. I said, 'Hey, Mr. Bishop, nice to meet you.' I asked him if he would like to jam.

"He said, 'I thought you'd never ask me.'

"Then he went up and played all night long. All morning long. . . . We finally got him out of the club like at seven in the morning. They played all night. We had a blast. He got so drunk we had to carry him out . . . his manager that was with him took him by his feet. I had him underneath his arms and we were carrying him out and the last thing he said when he was going out the door, he says, 'One more song. One more beer.' But, he had to go. They had a tour date. That was the way that place was; you would have seasoned players coming in all the time. We'd have as much as two bass players, two sets of drums set up. A hundred guitar players lined up and wanting to play. But it was one of those deals where the players . . . well, you had to earn the respect to get up with the big-dog talent. So we would let them play a little set with somebody. We'd pick them out to go up there and play and then, if they made the cut, I'd say, 'Would you like to go play with the big dogs?' There were always some big dogs playing in there. We don't do the jams like that now. . . . We're still a music venue with original music . . . bands doing their own stuff. There's no cover bands. . . . We depend on each band bringing in their twenty or so friends. The only support that we actually get is friends . . . the bands' fans, friends, and family come down and support them. Everybody gets a shot. Mainstream America don't understand it. They'll come in the door and go, 'What's going on here?' They'll come in and hear music that they're not used to hearing . . . music they don't hear on the radio, so they don't like it. . . .

"The original location of the Tavern was past that strip mall where they had that nightclub, the Cosmos. It was a black club at the time, but you go a quarter mile down the road and we were on the left. It was a wild neighborhood, but I mean we never had any problems, ever. But it was one of those deals like moms and dads didn't want their kids going down there because it was on the wrong side of the tracks. You don't never tell a kid they can't go somewhere, because they going to go right there to it, right to where you tell them they can't go. And they did. . . . Nowadays we got kids coming in here who tell us their parents used to come in here as kids. I'm thinking, 'Yeah. You were probably conceived right out there in that parking lot.'"

Max Drake: I Played with Lightnin' Hopkins

When Max Drake was touring with Arhooly, he got to play in some celebrated music venues, places like the Double Door in Charlotte, Ziggy's in Winston-Salem, Papa Mojo's in Durham, P. B. Scott's in Blowing Rock, Fast Company in Hickory, Sloppy Joe's in Key West, and Tobacco Road in Miami, among others. While all of these places served alcohol, they had the distinction of being known for bringing nationally recognized musical talent to their cities.

"I knew Stevie Ray Vaughan for a little bit. Well, he used to come play at the Double Door and we used to play at the Double Door. Shoot, at some point, we all crossed paths. We went to the same parties, tore up the same person's apartment or house. . . . But, the thing that I want to be remembered for as far as this kind of stuff goes was I played with Lightnin' fucking Hopkins. I don't care about the rest of it that much. A lot of it was really a great adventure, but I played with Lightnin' Hopkins[6] and that is the top of the heap. It was Arhooly that backed him up. I just keep telling people, I don't give a shit what you did or what you didn't do. I played with Lightnin' fucking Hopkins. . . .

"He was cool as shit. I first discovered Lightnin' from watching Johnny Carson. He used to go on *The Tonight Show*. . . . Lightnin' was from the great tradition of the older bluesmen who were natural orators. He was our hero, the biggest hero next to John Lee Hooker—not B. B.—but Albert King and John Lee Hooker and Lightnin' Hopkins. We liked those dangerous-sounding guys, the older guys. We met up with Lightnin' Hopkins at P. B. Scott's in Blowing Rock.[7] He comes walking in, and he's got those sunglasses, and he's got that cool-ass little hat

2.3. Max Drake. Courtesy Doug Mokaren.

and a long, wool, beautiful overcoat. He's really, really sharp looking. He comes in, and he sits down. We introduce ourselves. He said, 'I was just in a festival.' He said, 'I had mud up to my ankles. The weather was that bad.' All of a sudden, we just look at each other . . . we're sitting there going, 'Goddamn, he's talking about rain and mud up to his ankles, and I'm completely spellbound.' He had this way of talking . . . that just completely took you in. You were zoned in. You didn't see or hear anything else. Then we made the mistake of asking him about practicing. He laughed, and he said, 'I haven't practiced since I was ten years old.' That was when he started playing professionally, when he was ten. The guy's got like 300 albums, and he's the most successful solo artist ever, no need

2.4. Max Drake and Lightnin' Hopkins. Courtesy Max Drake.

to practice. We're all sitting there going, 'Sorry, sir.' Then he tells me to come by the room. The drummer and I go by his room before the gig. He opens up his guitar case, and he hands me an Old-Timer, single-blade folding knife, which I've got one in my hand right here exactly like that one he handed me. It's about a six-inch knife, close to seven inches. It's a big knife.

"He told me, 'Before I go on stage, you hand me that.'

"I'm carrying this knife around all afternoon. I'm a little white kid going, 'I've got Lightnin' Hopkins's *knife*, I'm going to steal it. He's going to forget about it. Dave'—I'm talking to Dave Clark, the drummer—'What do I do? Do I keep this thing?'

"Then, to add more to the misery, he gives me his guitar after I play this Dobro Bottleneck set that we had, and asked me to tune his guitar to my tuner. I had a Conn Strobe tuner at the time. I go and tune it up, and it's sitting up there. I gave him an amplifier. I used one of my amps that I long ago sold. We were back in the dressing room. He's standing at the door. He's got his guitar strapped on.

"All of a sudden, he turns and he goes, 'Where's my knife?'

"I look at Dave, we're going, 'Shit!'

"'Okay, Mr. Hopkins, we've got your knife.'

"We didn't want to, but we gave him back his knife; that was his personal protection while he was on stage. He endures us until the end of the set, and he goes off. We all go back and ogle at him and just torment the shit out of him, admiring him and everything. He politely goes back to the room. We all go home, and he goes home. . . . Well, ended up, he died. I believe it was in January [1982]. Our gig was three months before he died. He went back to wherever it was—Texas—I don't think he ever came back to the East Coast. Then Billy Gibbons of ZZ Top hit a popular magazine with the question: 'Who was the last man that played with Lightnin' Hopkins?' We think that I was the last guitar player ever to play with him on the East Coast. . . .

"A lot of people played P. B. Scott's. It's a dome structure. Bonnie Raitt played there. We played with B. B. there three or four times. We opened up for B. B. We opened up for James Cotton too. That was cool. That was the opposite end of the spectrum, the really hypermodern, fiery-modern Chicago blues. We got to see it firsthand. It was a really good training ground for us. Then we saw Muddy live in full force there. I talked to Albert King a couple of times there. He was a guy you didn't want to mess with. You didn't want to cross him. He was serious but he was an effective bandleader. Back in those days [1980s], the majority of the musicians that were out there were the biggest pack of fuckups you could ever imagine. That's one thing I did not enjoy about working in that time period. People honestly and stupidly thought that getting hammered was actually the thing that they needed to do to play better.

"I took Nappy Brown[8] out a couple times and there were nights where he was in no condition to even be on stage. He had just gotten so fucked up. . . . On the other hand . . . you put Pinetop Perkins, and you put Lightnin' Hopkins and those Chicago guys . . . those guys were professionals at it. They drank whiskey for breakfast. . . . They knew how to pace themselves.

"Some of the funniest stuff happened when I was playing with Skeeter Brandon [Calvin Thomas Brandon, 1948–2008] and Highway 61. Skeeter was this blind piano player and vocalist. He was completely blind from the time he was four years old. He was in the backseat of a car, driving somewhere with his uncle. They say it was a drunk driving thing, but there was an accident and shattered glass flew back into his eyes. They couldn't save 'em. He had no eyes, but he always wore those sunglasses. Anyway, we'd be playing somewhere and the girls would come up and be dancing in front of him, leaning over, shaking it, just putting on a show. Of course, he couldn't see any of it.

"Once when we were up in Boston playing at Harpers Ferry, Skeeter was being interviewed. He discovered there was a case of Budweiser in the room, longneck bottles. Skeeter would have a beer in his hand, take one drink, and completely suck all the beer out of the bottle in one swallow. We were setting up to play, but as the interview went along, we were checking in on him. Skeeter drank, if not the whole case, almost the whole case of beer. I'm gonna tell you what: he flat rocked that place that night. That night he was drunk and inspired and he tore that place up. It was probably one of my favorite shows that I ever played with him.

"Now Tobacco Road in Miami is this old bar that dates back to your prohibition times, the oldest bar in Miami. Arhooly was playing there when B. B. King was in town, so we called and left the message that we were playing at Tobacco Road, inviting him to come jam. We knew he wouldn't. So we were playing the late show, as luck would have it, doing the song 'Phone Booth' and in comes Robert Cray and his guys, saying, 'We heard somebody wanted to jam.' That was a night. B. B. had invited us to come back to his hotel room, but we ended up drunk, driving around Miami getting lost and telling Don Johnson jokes."

Michele Seidman: Misbehaving Women

Michele Seidman is an actress and musician from Wilmington, North Carolina, and the vocalist for Michele and the Midnight Blues, a band she says grew from the blues jams in Wilmington. Her band took first place in the Cape Fear Blues Challenge and went on to compete at the International Blues Challenge (IBC) in Memphis in 2006. When she was in Memphis, Michele noticed very few women in the bands. Afterward she formed the network National Women in Blues as a way to help level the playing field but also to find mentors. Her current ambition is to create a searchable database of female talent to help connect women to lucrative gigs in reputable venues.

In 2014 and 2015, Michele's group presented a showcase of female blues talent at the IBCs in the Center for Southern Folklore in Memphis. She admits that certain bars, especially those with really heavy drinking, can be a challenge for women to navigate, but the music is worth it.

"I've played bars . . . I don't know if you'd call them drink houses but I've played places that have the beers and a rib rotisserie going. Those usually weren't too bad . . . most of them. Most places where I play, I have a rapport with management; I have a feel for the place. There have been places and events I wouldn't have ever booked my band. But I've been around a long time so I know better what to look for now.

"For the most part I was always able to check out a place before we ever played it and I knew the clientele. There have been occasions where I played places that I wondered if this was a good idea. I think the biggest thing is it really depends on whether or not the artist is aware and self-aware and the band is aware if this is a decent music venue. It also matters whether or not you've got a drunk band or a sober band. Because it doesn't matter where you are, if you are a performer you're dealing with drunks in bars. . . . When alcohol is involved, people do stupid stuff. I've seen some really dumb stuff. . . . But if you're sober, these things are easier to manage.

"I had a woman one time grab my mic stand and start dry-humping it while I was in the middle of singing a song. Yeah, the door guys [bouncers] had to come and take her away, because she kept falling onto the floor. I had to take the mic off the stand because she kept yanking it away from me while I was trying to sing. And my guys, my bandmates, were just grossed out; it was that disgusting what this woman was doing. . . . She was dry-humping my mic stand. . . . This happened at a local bar that eventually got shut down for a lot of infractions. It originally had been a really nice bar but I guess the new management that had taken over at that point wasn't paying attention to their crowd. They weren't managing things and getting people out when they'd gone too far. . . . I hear more horror stories from my musician friends who also drink, because it's harder for them to keep a cool temperament and handle the situation more methodically and carefully when they are drinking heavy. . . .

"But I rarely hear about problems from my friends who stay sober when they're performing or at least manage their alcohol, like my bandmates. My bandmates always drank but if any of my bandmates drank

2.5. Michele Seidman. Courtesy Michele Seidman.

excessively, I stopped working with them. The bandmates I work with, they would have maybe three drinks, maybe four, maybe even more if we had a long night or if we had a long setup and they'd eaten a hearty meal. But they always stayed reasonably sober. . . . They could always play all their licks and they were never losing their temperaments and getting out of hand. So, if the band is calm, you usually don't have a lot of problems. . . .

"The blues crowd is not typically a volatile crowd. That's why everyone freaked out when that woman jumped on stage at the Russell City Blues Festival when one of the older black artists, Lester Chambers, made a dedication to Trayvon Martin. She punched him out on stage and the video went viral.[9] Everybody freaked because you don't see those things very often in the blues world. And not from a woman, usually. . . . The worst thing that happens at a blues thing is some girl or guy gets jealous. You might get one or two people who are just a little too drunk and a little too rowdy, maybe they throw a plastic chair or something. . . . I think the blues world is one of the most integrated worlds I've ever been part of. There's all that business about Caucasians hijacking the music, but I've seen a wonderful increase in young black artists getting back into the genre that is their heritage. And that to me is—that's a great sign. If it took some white folks to keep it alive for a while just to make sure it didn't die out, so be it."

Mike "Wezo" Wesolowski: Don't Spit in My Harp

Harmonica player and vocalist Mike "Wezo" Wesolowski has been playing and teaching blues harp for more than thirty years. Wezo was presented the Keeping the Blues Alive Award from the Piedmont Blues Preservation Society in 2006 and has been a Hohner harmonica endorsee but as of this writing is a Seydel Söhne harmonica endorsee. Wezo's career has taken him to a variety of bars and although some actually looked like houses or had originally been houses that were converted to bars, most of these places (he believes) had legal liquor licenses. When I interviewed him in June 2014, Wezo was playing with the band Blues World Order as well as conducting Blues in the Schools performances and lectures. Currently he plays in the band the Luxuriant Sedans.

"You know, I used to play as far back as the mid-'70s, late '70s, shit like that. I played around Winston with the various bands, and there was this place called the White Horse. It doesn't exist anymore. . . . Jay Stevens bought the White Horse for a dollar and moved it to a new location. That bar was the original Ziggy's.[10] It was just a small white house. Jay took the sign, big frigging sign with a white horse on it. It said 'White Horse Pub.' It was hanging in Ziggy's at the bar area where they served liquor, but originally it was just in this little house. . . .

"I don't think I've ever been to a run-down scary bar that I didn't like. I like them like that. I tell you what, man. The Checkerboard in Chicago was the coolest. I heard about that place my whole life, seeing all

2.6. Mike 'Wezo' Wesolowski. Courtesy Doug Mokaren.

these albums. Buddy Guy and Junior Wells recorded there. You know, it says, 'Live at the Checkerboard.' You go there, and you think it's going to be this fucking great, cool club. It's a hole-in-the-fucking-wall but that's what's so cool about it. I mean it was just this side of having a dirt floor. But, man, you start looking around . . . well, the Checkerboard's closed now [April 2003], but when it was open, you start looking at all the goddamn pictures on the wall of people who played there. Good God almighty. It's like a history lesson just being there and looking around.

"Chicago has some good bars. Back in '91, when I got married, April and I went to Chicago on our honeymoon. . . . We get there and the Chicago Blues Society was featuring a pub crawl. You could go in any of the bars, the Checkerboard, Rosa's, Buddy Guy's, and several others.

You paid like fifteen bucks. You get a little thing on your arm, and then every forty-five minutes, a bus will pull up, and a guy walks through the bar with a big sign saying which bar they're going to next. They don't say who's playing. The sign just says, 'We're going to this bar. Get on the bus.' Everybody gets on the bus. If you've got the armband, you get right in without another cover charge, because they're all on this list. We started out at Buddy Guy's . . . then we went to the Checkerboard. There was this harmonica player in there who just looked like he'd been living in the streets. He looked like he hadn't changed his clothes or took a bath in years. He was playing like a motherfucker. I looked at April, and I said, 'That's fucking Junior Wells, man. You've got to be kidding me.' So it's Junior Wells. After his set, he came up to the bar. He was going to order a drink, and I said to him, 'You're Junior Wells, aren't you?'

"He said, 'Yeah, I'm Junior Wells. Get me a Budweiser.'

"I got him a Budweiser, and then I exalted him as much as I could, told him what a big influence he was and everything. He was drunk as shit that night, but he sounded like God. The next day we look in the paper to see what is going on and there's this harmonica blow-off at Junior Wells's club. All these guys were playing: Junior Wells, Madcat Ruth, Sugar Blue.[11] Junior Wells's band was the house band, and they featured him that night. It was badass, man. . . . I had gone to a workshop by Howard Levy[12] two months before. I didn't know he lived in Chicago. We were sitting in the front row, eating our ribs and shit, and in the door walks Howard Levy. I said, 'April, that's Howard Levy.' I went over to his table, and said, 'Man, I just did a workshop with you two months ago in Winston-Salem,' and he remembered me. . . .

"I said, 'Man, I just got married. We're here on our honeymoon.'

"He asked, 'Well, where are you sitting?'

"He came over and talked to us for about an hour. I mean, just hung out and talked, and then he got up on stage and played.

"Junior Wells's band was the house band for all these harp players. It was time for Junior Wells to come out. The band was doing this vamp thing and here comes Junior Wells walking from the back, completely pimped out in a fucking yellow suit, gold chains, gold watch, gold rings, and, I mean, a big fucking fedora. He's strutting through audience, completely different from the night before when he looked like he hadn't taken a bath in years. It's cool to go in a place and meet people you know and even more cool meeting one of your heroes. . . .

"Here's one of my favorite stories about gigging in a legal bar. I don't even remember the name of the place we were playing. It was some grubby, pool-hall kind of place. I was playing with Ministers of Sinister [Calvin Johnson, Russ Wilson, and Max Drake]. We got there early but the place was already filled up with a bunch of drunk rednecks. They even had a drinking contest and shit like that going on. We're setting up and there's this railing—kind of like a small pony wall next to the stage to separate the stage from the dance floor. It's about waist high. I set all my harmonicas up there. I've got them in all the keys, A, B, C, D. I've got a bunch of harps lined up there, and my harmonica mic is sitting there, and my amp, and we're still setting up when this drunk redneck comes over. He's wearing one of these trucker hats that says 'Southern by Birth, White by the Grace of God.' I mean, it's got Rebel flags and shit on it.

"I'm thinking, 'Oh, no. He's one of those motherfuckers, and worse, he's drunk.'

"He says to me, 'Hey, man. How come you got all them harmonicas?'

"I was trying my best to be nice, so I tell him, 'Well, man, all these harmonicas are different keys. You know, there's A, B-flat, C, D.' I explain, 'Like when the guitar player changes keys from E to G or something, I do too, and it just makes it easier—' and the motherfucker cuts me off with, 'Hey, man. You play that "Train, Train," that Blackfoot song, "Train, Train," do you play that one?'

"I said, 'No, man, I don't play that one.'

"He says, 'Oh, come on, man.' I know you play "Train, Train." It's got harmonica in it.'

"I said, 'No, man, that's kind of southern rock. We play more blues tunes, like Chicago blues and stuff.'

"The guy is insistent, 'Come on, goddammit, I know you play "Train, Train." You got a harmonica; it's a harmonica song. I know you got to play "Train, Train." Come on, man, play it for me.'

"I said, 'No, man, I really don't play that one. I don't.'

"I was starting to get annoyed. This guy was . . . harshing my mellow. He was bringing me down, and I couldn't keep my eyes off of his hat. I kept looking up at that nasty hat, 'Southern by Birth, White by the Grace of God.' I'm thinking that I'm about two seconds away from taking my microphone and using it like a roll of quarters to just flatten him. But I kept patiently explaining to him that we don't play Blackfoot. He starts walking away like finally he understood. He took about eight steps going back toward his pool table, and then he stopped. You could just see a light come on above that trucker hat. Then he turned and walked back, and he says, 'Come on, man! Which of them harmonicas has got "Train, Train" in it?'

"I couldn't say anything.

"Finally I told him, 'None of them do, man.' I mean, what do you say? He wanted to hear 'Train, Train.' He was adamant about it. It might've been the first time he'd ever seen a harmonica player and he just knew that if I played harmonica, I must play 'Train, Train' because it's got a harmonica in it. . . .

"But here's the real aggravation about gigging at some of these old bars. People are always wanting to sit in. They want to be a singer. They want to play guitar. They want to play the harmonica. They want to use—and this really bugs me. Now, the harmonica's a pretty personal thing. It's like having a toothbrush. A lot of people come up and say, 'Hey, man. Let me play one of your harmonicas. Let me sit in.'

"I say, 'Sit in. Did you bring any harps?'

"And they'll say, 'No, I'll use one of yours.'

"No, you won't. Like hell! You've got to be fucking kidding me! You want me to spit into your mouth? I mean, how'd you like that? Yeah. I just ate some eggs; you want to play my harp now? Pickled! I mean, goddamn, man, I mean. . . . If you play harmonica, you know. . . . Well, if you don't know, you *should* know. Never play anybody else's harmonica. What if I got something, HIV or something? That's what I should tell these people. 'Well, if you don't mind HIV. Use this one right here. There's spit in that one.' Or maybe, 'My gums are kind of bleeding a little bit. I can't afford the dentist. If you don't mind a little blood, go right ahead.' The nerve of some people.

"The 'Train, Train' guy was a drunk motherfucker with a racist hat, but at least he didn't ask to spit in my harp."

◆ ◆ ◆

If a bar is a self-proclaimed music venue, that bar may be the best place to discover your musical heroes. If you are lucky enough to land it, musicians will say the self-proclaimed music venue is the most promising place to find that dream gig. That forgettable neighborhood bar may not be famous, but it could also be memorable because of the characters experienced there. Finally, the bar or drink house that hosted a jam might be the place for a young musician to launch a career.

CHAPTER 3

Blues, Booze, and "Occupying a Dive"

Chick Willis

Robert "Chick" Willis is a blues singer born in 1934 in Cabiness, Georgia. I met and interviewed Chick in 2008 when Roy Roberts brought him to Greensboro to play at the Zion Bar and Grill. He was also in Greensboro to perform at the annual Blues Festival held by the Piedmont Blues Preservation Society that same year. I also spoke with him briefly at the annual New River Blues Festival in Grassy Creek, North Carolina, in 2012, where he was playing but not singing due to cancer he had developed that made it difficult for him to sing. He still played with passion, walking out into the crowd to play the guitar with his tongue, which he said always impressed the ladies more than playing guitar with the teeth. Chick passed away in December 2013 in Forsyth, Georgia.

Roy Roberts and Chick Willis had had a long musical association, which includes a CD, From the Heart and Soul *(2001), recorded in Roy's studio in Greensboro, Rock House Records. The CD took the Best Blues Album Award from* Living Blues *magazine in 2003. Chick has recorded many other albums and CDs with Ichiban Records, among others. Chick is the cousin of the late rhythm and blues singer Chuck Willis (1928–58). After a short time in the military, Chick joined his cousin on tour as a driver, singer, and eventually a guitarist, even opening for him. Chick won a talent show in Atlanta, Georgia, which led to his first recording in 1956, the single "You're Mine." After cousin Chuck died in 1958, Chick continued with the live circuit. The year before he died, Chuck Willis's cover of the song "C. C. Rider" topped the R&B charts and also performed well in the pop charts.*

Chick's biggest disappointment came with his biggest hit, "Stoop Down, Baby," in 1972. This song was too raw for the radio but it became a major success as a jukebox staple in clubs across the South. The disappointment was that LaVal Records financially mismanaged his triumph. However,

3.1. Chick Willis. Courtesy Doug Mokaren.

the song's widespread impact was that Chick Willis had an enduring reputation as the "Stoop Down Man."

Chick began his story by explaining the secret to winning the constant financial struggle as a bluesman.

"I recorded my first record in 1956, but I haven't made a living with music. The reason I'm sitting here right now—ain't starved to death and homeless—is because of women. Women. Women. Women. I've always had somebody—a woman—in my life that had a good job or a good trade that could help take care of me while I'm doing my music. See. I couldn't have made a living in music. It's almost impossible to work on a construction job in the daytime and do blues at night. You know. Yeah.

Can't work night and day both. One of them is going to go lacking. . . . I got covered up in a ditch like that. Daydreaming and somebody got a hoe backed up in on me and three other guys . . . we almost didn't get out. Yeah. But in order to concentrate on music, you got to have somebody in your corner. You got to have somebody to say, 'Fine. You go ahead and play the blues, you know. I'll pay the bills, I'll pay the rent, I'll buy the groceries.' You know. But, here it is: if you don't hurry up and become a star right away, they'll be saying to you, 'Yeah, I don't know. I think you ought to go out and get you a *real* job.' So. Yeah. And then they better not come to the nightclub and see the girls comin' after you. Oh no, no, no. They see that and they'll be saying, 'You gotta quit this and you gotta get you a job.' I was the kind of guy to say, 'Well, this is what I want to do.' So then they'll be about through with me. I left. Headed for another city.

"This is what I do.

"The big break I thought I had was in 1972. I was living in New York after Chuck died. There was a song that everybody used to do, but it was a song that nobody had the nerve to record. See. So, I had a little ole three-piece group and I went downtown to New York, 1697 Broadway, and I got me some studio time and we went in and recorded this song. Okay. I had it on tapes and I made what they call an 'acetate.'[1] I took it to different places. Walked all up and down Fifth Avenue, Americas Avenue, everywhere. I was going into these record companies, playing it for these record companies, and they were, 'No, no, no. I can't do nothing with that. Oh no, no, no.'

"I got turned down, and turned down, and turned down.

"Then I was in a show with a guy called—well, two guys. One called Rudy Ray Moore and one called Jimmy Lynch. Jimmy Lynch was called "Funky Tramp" and Rudy Ray Moore was called "Dolemite."[2] Okay. Okay.

"They heard the song and they say, 'Man, that is a *great* song.'

"I say, 'Sure enough?'

"They say, 'Yeah, man. I know a man that will take that *right now*.'

"I said, 'No kidding.'

"So okay. They give me the guy's phone number. Name of Vic LaVal.[3] And I called him up and said, 'Man, I got this song and Jimmy Lynch and Rudy Ray Moore said you'd love this song.'

"He said, 'Man, play a little for me on the phone.'

"So I played a little bit for him over the phone.

"He said, 'Man, when can you get it up? When can you get it here?'

"I said, 'Any time.'

"He says, 'Bring it on. Bring it on.'"

"So we drove to Kalamazoo, Michigan, and they immediately put that song on and went wild over it. . . . 'Stoop Down, Baby. Let Your Daddy See.' Okay. They immediately went to the pressing plant with it. Right. While they were pressing it up, he gave me a thousand dollars to put in my pocket, you understand, took me down to his Dodge place and bought me a fifteen-passenger van with 'Chick Willis' on the side. 'Stoop Down, Baby' right under there. We had about three thousand 45s with 'Stoop Down, Baby'—and on the other side was 'It Ain't Right.' We put them 45s in that van and we didn't go to no radio stations, because we knew radio stations would not play it.[4] He [LaVal] had addresses to every jukebox company throughout the South. We stop at a jukebox company, they would play it, and 'Oh. Yeah. Oh, yeah. Give me about a hundred of those 45s. I got a hundred jukeboxes. Give me two hundred.' By the time we got to Memphis, Tennessee, had to turn around and go back to Kalamazoo to get more. It had been 300 and something thousand copies already ordered by the time we got to Memphis.

"In Chicago, 'Stoop Down, Baby' was a number-one hit over Aretha Franklin and everybody. But it's a jukebox hit. And the disc jockeys are saying, 'What? What? Why we don't have that?' But the distributors couldn't keep it—couldn't keep it. Walk down Beale Street in Memphis and every joint had 'Stoop Down, Baby' on the jukebox. So. One of the guys that was helping to promote it, he booked me in the Grand Ballroom on the South Parkway of Chicago on a Sunday afternoon on my birthday in 1972, September the 24th—and standing-room only. Grand Ballroom was jam-packed. And the band that was backing me up was Oliver Sain out of St. Louis, Missouri.[5] It was standing-room only. Now. We sit down and pick it out. Guy got hold of me about the first check. A hundred and ninety thousand dollars. . . . I went to his [LaVal's] office on that day. I was there, Rudy Ray Moore was there, Jimmy Lynch was there—everybody that was on his label was there.

"It was royalty time.

"While I was waitin' there, I saw these guys keep coming out the office with these long sour looks on their faces. Damn, you know, they ain't looking so good.

"Come my time she [the receptionist] say, 'Mr. Willis? Mr. LaVal would like to see you.'

"'Yes, ma'am.'

"I jump up and go in there, say to him, 'Hey. How you doing?' I was shaking hands. He goes and sits behind his desk.

"'I got bad news for you.'

"I say, 'Yeah, what is it?'

"He say, 'I ain't got no money.'

"I say, 'What do you mean you ain't got no money?'

"He say, 'I'm filing bankruptcy.'

"'*What*?'

"What happened to him was, he was a big numbers man. He loved the numbers. He had books. You know. He had number books but he wanted to be a big man. So, he was going into it in a big way. And they told him, don't do it. See. We got enough people in it, we don't need nobody else up in here. So. You keep your books. He went anyway. So many people in a time hit him and he didn't have enough money to pay them all. He had to liquidate everything he had to pay them off, to stay out of Lake Michigan and the concrete boots. That's where our money went. My money. Rudy Ray Moore's money. Jimmy Lynch's money. We all had hit records. Rudy Ray Moore had out a hit called 'Eat Out More Often.' . . . Jimmy Lynch had one called "Funky Tramp." I had one I called "Stoop Down, Baby." LaVal had to pawn and hock everything he had in order to pay off the bets. He got rid of all that money. He died on us."

With the financial failure of LaVal Records, Chick returned to touring and playing live performances, largely in the South and East. The popularity of "Stoop Down, Baby" made it fairly easy for him to get gigs at a variety of drink houses, bars, and festivals.

"I had to work. So I start booking. You know, back then you booked like the first three hundred dollars and then fifty-fifty after that. You know. That's the way you booked. See. Because back then you didn't have to worry about having a crowd. You knew you were going to have a crowd. You didn't need all that radio and TV advertisement back then. You just take a poster down to the beauty shop. Take one to the barbershop. That's all you need to do. Put one up at the club. See. That night you have a packed house. So you figure they would be charging four dollars or five dollars to get in and you got a couple hundred people in there, you doing all right. Everybody gets paid. You only had to have somebody working on the door. Club owners have somebody working on the door. And you have a roll of tickets. Tear a ticket in half. They get half; you get half. Then when you get through and you look at the numbers, deduct that number from this number . . . take your three hundred dollars off the top, then count the rest and you get 50 percent of that. You didn't get rich, but it kept you going. You couldn't buy no mansion, but you could eat."

Legal and Illegal Clubs

Chick worked all types of clubs when he toured, those that legally served alcohol and some that served bootleg liquor. He acknowledged that there were risks to booking in an illegal joint, but sometimes it was a financial necessity. He told me that the business end of things worked out pretty much the same way for the musicians, whether the bars were legal or illegal. Working a bar that sold bootleg was generally less risky for the band than for the bar owner.

"Both legal clubs and illegal clubs . . . they worked the same way. Illegal clubs had better profits because they were bootlegging. The only thing you had to worry about that was, being on the bandstand and all of a sudden the Man comes in to haul everybody off to jail.

"Let me tell you something.

"I was in Chicago, the big town of Chicago. I was in Chicago, playing in a club called Rosa's. Her son's named Tony. Tony was running the place and Rosa is behind the bar. Okay. I was on the bandstand playing and playing, you know. All of a sudden all these guys come in with these suits and stuff on, cops, and the cops say to us, 'Stop the music. Stop.'

"A guy was about to leave the bandstand and a cop says to him, 'Stay on the bandstand. Don't come off.'

"'Yes, sir.' We do just what he said.

"The guys went over to Rosa and ask, 'Where's Tony?'

"Tony was gone.

"I'm still sitting up on the bandstand, thinking, 'What the hell's going on?'

"And what happened was—Tony supposedly had the waitresses selling more than beer. See. And I guess the cops had got wind of it. And they come and raid the joint so they could search the joint. They wanted Tony, but they couldn't find Tony. Tony was gone. Oh, yeah. Tony was gone. But we had to stay on that bandstand while they were searching and everything. Everybody lined up on the wall. Yes.

"They say, 'Don't get off of the bandstand.'

"'Don't you worry, officer. I'll be right here. I'm going no place.'

"And that was supposed to be a *legitimate* joint.

"Now I have been raided in joints that were not legitimate and everybody was charged with 'occupying a dive.' Occupying a dive, that's what they charged everybody with. And it cost twenty-five dollars. Yep. The next morning it cost everybody twenty-five dollars and they keep you in jail just overnight. And if they lock you up at like three or four o'clock in the morning, you don't even go to jail. You just sit there in the paddy wagon and they just take you off to court. They take you to court and the judge smacks his gavel down and says—smack—'Twenty-five dollars.' Smack! 'Twenty-five dollars.' You can't say, 'Not guilty.' You can't say, 'All right, your honor, I'm not guilty,' 'cause that's where they got you at. They caught you. So the judge puts his gavel down and you pay up.

"Anytime we played these kind of clubs, we knew the man didn't have a license. We knew it. No liquor license. We knew it, but, you know, good money. They pay pretty good. . . . Monroe County [Georgia] usually—if there's a club—they just didn't have a liquor license maybe. But Monroe County had legitimate clubs, but they just didn't have a liquor license because it's a dry county. But they bootleg. So if cops came in and caught them bootleggers, they—the bootleggers—would be the only ones to go to jail. You see. But the club had a restaurant license, just didn't have a liquor license."

As discussed in chapter 1, some joints had a reputation as a "bucket of blood," meaning that these were rough places to work. Adam Gussow tells us that the violence of the "bucket" was intimate violence that black people inflicted on each other: "cuttings, shootings, razor slashings,

3.2. Chick Willis. Courtesy Doug Mokaren.

beating, and murders."[6] Chick didn't seem to think these bars were such a big deal and the violence described might be overemphasized.

"Now a 'bucket of blood' just means some old club that had a few fights and gambling and killings and stuff. 'Cause I'll tell you, back in the '60s through Louisiana, almost every club in Louisiana had gambling in the back. You know. They opened it just like Las Vegas until they changed governors and stuff. When I played through Louisiana it was just like Las Vegas, twenty-four hours a day, music in the room, and go through that back door and they were back there shooting craps and playing cards. Gambling in the back. The club business used to be wide open like that. Politicians changed all that. Everything is against the law now.

"Back in—oh, in the '50s—I played in a place in Hattiesburg, Mississippi. It was called the Hi-Hat.[7] I used to play there quite often. It was real funny. I would be in the club and it would be jam-packed with black folk. Jam-packed. You could go outside and look out at the road and all these cars would be lined up outside on the dirt road and all these white kids would be sitting on top of the cars, drinking beers and listening to blues coming outta there. That's how long back the white kids be liking the blues. Even though some newspapers was publishing ads that say, 'Do not let your white kids listen to blues music, because blues music teaches them voodoo.' Yeah. It was in the newspapers. 'Blues music teaches voodoo.'

"Later on down the line they started realizing that blues music had something that no other music had. It had this thing that grabs you. A vitality. They started experimenting with it. Guys like Elvis Presley. Even before Elvis Presley, though, there was a guy that—as far as I'm concerned—that was a better singer and everything. Had more soul than Elvis Presley. That was Carl Perkins. Now the first guy to really record blues with a twist was Bill Haley and the Comets. But they didn't want to call it blues. They don't want to call it 'rock 'n' roll'; they call it 'rockabilly.' But blues music has been an influence on everybody in the music business. I don't care what color you are or where you came from. Blues music has an influence."

Brainwashing: Blacks, Whites, and Blues

One of Chick Willis's first questions to me upon learning that I was originally from Alabama was, "How did George Wallace allow a girl like you to listen to blues music in some old Alabama drink house?" Of course, George Wallace didn't take any personal interest in me or my favorite music, and the liquor laws in Lauderdale County were not Wallace's responsibility. However, for a good portion of Wallace's long career as governor of Alabama, with four nonconsecutive terms, Wallace's goal was to put an end to desegregation. In the early 1970s, Wallace likely did believe that white children listening to black music risked cultural corruption, or worse. Chick didn't fully accept my argument that suffering is part of the human condition, which is why so many different kinds of people appreciate blues music. He countered that black music is so infectious that even slave owners in the pre–Civil War era loved the music without fully understanding what they heard.

Chick's opinions about race in America were complex. He told me that he looks forward to the day when miscegenation is so complete that racial makeup is impossible to decipher. When that happens and when all the bitter memories of injustice have passed away with the old folks, then he believes we will have solved our race problem. Yet he also told me that integration was the worst thing to happen to African Americans. He believes integration hindered black achievements in business and education. More affluent blacks moved away from the old neighborhoods and the once tight-knit, cohesive communities took a downward spiral. When black customers patronized white establishments, black businesses suffered. Chick explained that it was never "even-steven" for black kids in a white classroom or any African American in a white courtroom. Finally, he believed that white appropriation of black music prevented black artists from seeing the rewards of their achievements with the ultimate result that the music is losing its power and meaning for all audiences.

"With my fifty-something years of sleeping in my car after working hard in some club or dance hall or some fraternity party for an all-white college or white-only club because I couldn't get a room in the all-white hotel, I paid some dues to sing the blues. I worked in all-white clubs that I couldn't go to the bar and get a drink or sit down to the table and eat, so I had to eat in the kitchen. I have suffered way too much to see my music changed and twisted and renamed. Most of all, I refuse to be left out of my music.

"One thing—the blues has afforded me to go to places that people will save up an entire lifetime to go. I've been to Germany, Japan, England, and all over Europe. But what's happened now is they're ruining it, because the people over there are getting a lot of watered-down blues. What I'm saying now—if you write this, make sure you tell people that Chick Willis says: 'Demand the *real* blues.' The real blues is black. Black. Black. Black. Don't get me wrong. I also want people to know that I got a whole bunch of friends out there that play the blues—white, Chinese, Japanese, Mexican, you name it—lots of different people play the blues. What I'm saying when I say, 'Demand the *real* blues,' that don't mean to stop listening to the blues played by other people but make sure they got somebody involved that knows what the blues is all about. As long as you keep somebody involved that's the real thing, then the blues go further. It don't die. But if you cut out the people that invented it, then it's gonna die. Its soul is gonna die.

"The blues they're stuffing down people's throats now, it's not the blues, not the real drink house music. Now don't get me wrong. I'm not saying the kids can't play. Some of 'em are great players. But they are not playing the blues. See. You can play the same changes, you can sing the same words, but you're not singing the blues. You're not a blues person. See. You can go on and learn how to speak Chinese fluently. But that don't make you Chinese. You're just a Chinese-language speaker. Speaking the language doesn't make you Chinese."

Chick further explained why he thought so many young African Americans had abandoned blues music for hip-hop and rap.

"This is what I'm saying. If the blues is made inviting to the youngsters, they'll get into it. But as long as the blues is made to where kids think, 'They don't let me play. They don't let me rise to the top. They don't let me make a living at this, so no sense in me getting into it. That's the attitude of young blacks. Lots of young blacks want to play blues, but they think, 'Man, I can't make no money. I can't make no living at this. I want to rap.'

"You see. They can put out a rap song and they don't have to hire no musicians or nothing. They just sample other folks' music and put out a rap song and make a million dollars. Also, when you mention the blues—oh, lawd have mercy—it brings up George Wallace and all those people. It brings up Martin Luther King being killed. It brings up Medgar Evers. It brings up the bad time in life. The blues doesn't bring up anything good to them. My kids wouldn't have made it in my day. They wouldn't have made it because they wouldn't have took what I took. They'd of kilt my kids. They'd of ended up like the Indians. They'd all have been dead because kids today wouldn't have took what I took. But see, I had to take it for them. Because if I didn't take it, they wouldn't be here. You just have to hope and pray that one day somebody's gonna come along that's gonna straighten this stuff out.

"Now my pet peeve is my music, which is the blues. Don't get me wrong—I want everybody to play the blues. I want everybody to love the blues. You see. And I don't hate anybody. It's not in me to hate anybody. But if you want to do a festival over here and you got twenty slots, why can't ten of those slots be somebody black playing the blues? Why do you got to have seventeen or eighteen of those slots be white girls and boys playing blues and only three slots of the oldest, blackest, broken-down bluesmen you ever seen in your life? This is what's happening. Now, if you throw a blues festival, but you don't have no blues players on it, that's not a blues festival. See. They're using the word 'blues' now because the government declared the year 2003 the 'year of the blues' and all this kind of stuff. And there's so many grants you can get by just saying you keeping the blues alive. That's why they give so many awards. So-and-so win the award of the year for keeping the blues alive. Club won for keeping the blues alive. The blues organization won for keeping the blues alive. Everybody is keeping the blues alive and killing all the black blues players.

"Like I say, the blues was not invented as a music, per se. Keep that in mind. The blues was and is a language. Everybody don't understand the language. Only the older guys and the older ladies understand it. The blues was a way of communicating among your own, you see. The blues was not only a communication device, it was a soothing device. It was a soul-searching device. Blues was something that . . . your mother could die; you could use the blues to lighten the burden on you. Your wife or your husband could leave you—and you could use the blues to light the load on your heart. Know what I'm saying? You could be mad, pissed off at somebody. You could use the blues to keep you from going out and killing up somebody. And if you was a slave in the day and your master was treating you bad, you couldn't walk up to the master and say, 'You gotta leave me alone,' you know, but you could sing about it. And the other slaves could relate to it and say, 'Man sure is treating Chick bad over there. You heard what he just sang?'

"But the master is saying, as he is clapping and clapping, 'Hey, that's a nice song. Sing that again. Sing that song again.'

"We had to survive. We didn't even know which way to go to get back to Africa. We're here in a place where we got to survive. We don't want to disappear. Blues helped us survive. That was back there then. Now I wish with all my might that the races would just intermix so much that nobody knows which race we belong to, we just belong to each other.

"Nobody understands it but there was a brainwashing going on—all down through when I was a child, when my father was a child, when my grandfather was a child. Now this brainwashing do not leave you. This brainwashing stays with you. Anytime you can walk somewhere and know that you're being disliked, you can feel it. You can feel it. Like somebody saying, 'Hey, hey, hey, you're not supposed to be in here.' You can feel it right now. Right in these days. You can walk into a place of business right now and if I'm not wanted in there, I can feel it.

"This is something I've never been able to figure out. If I didn't like you, you couldn't cook my food. You couldn't see after my children. But they must trust us. When I was a little boy, our bed used to be full of little white children that my momma was keeping and stuff. Taking care of. They'd spend the night there, eat with us, and everything. And those kids and myself, we were crazy about one another. Until you start growing up and you get bigger and they start pulling away from you. Okay, now all of a sudden, we're the same age but now I got to start saying, 'Yes, ma'am.' I didn't have to do that when you and I were little children playing together. If they would just leave it like that. Don't put anything bad in your kid's mind and it'd be a great world.

"Brainwashing.

"Our folks—our American people—have a lot of blood on their hands. A lot of blood on their hands. We've been killing folks and maiming people. And taking from this person and taking from that person. We can't get to heaven like that. Whatever you want to call it. Heaven or whatever you want to call it. I don't know your religion and it's immaterial. But I would rather do what I think is right, do what I think that would get me to that place called heaven or whatever, and find out that it ain't there, than to *not* do those things that would get me in to heaven and find out it *is* there."

Home and Heartsickness

Chick talked quite a bit about growing up in Monroe County in Georgia. Although he spent his teenage years in Chicago, his early years in Georgia taught him some of his toughest lessons about racism in America. It was a special lesson after having served in the air force, to return to his hometown only to be slapped and insulted.

"Monroe County is one of those places with good ole boys running it. When I was a little boy, the only way you could go to college was to work for a well-to-do white family that would pay for you to go to college. See. If you didn't have the money yourself, somebody had to pay it for you. So, if nobody didn't pay for you to go to college, you couldn't go. The people we were working for mostly would say, 'What do you need with college? You don't need college to milk the cows . . . or plow the fields. You don't need no college for that. Your granddaddy can teach you all that.' So we didn't go to college. I always felt that if I had went to college, I'd be a genius. So okay, the only thing you got to do to make a living in Monroe County is plow the fields, milk the cow, plant the cotton, work at the sawmill, pick the cotton, cut wood. All manual labor. All hard work. Sunup to sundown. Then come home to our own chores—cutting the wood, feeding the cows, milking thirty-seven cows, feeding the pigs. More hard work. It wasn't the life I wanted.

"I had an auntie who lived in Chicago. I asked her, 'Can I go back with you?' I was thirteen years old. I had already got out of elementary. I didn't go to high school, never been to high school a day in my life, but I passed flying colors to get my GED. So I went with her to Chicago. I lived with her in Chicago and got a job downtown in the Harrison Hotel. When I became sixteen, I became a member of the Illinois National Guard. While I was in the National Guard, they mobilized the unit I was in. Korea was heating up. They gave us thirty days to choose whatever branch we wanted. I chose the air force. When I went into the air force entertainment, I was singing, playing drums. Played a little bass. I wasn't playing any guitar at all. I stayed in that until they stopped doing it. Then I went into the Bomb Wing. I was supposed to be a tail gunner for the B-29. I went to school for that. When I got out of school for that, they 'obsoleted' the B-29 and the 47 took its place. B-29 had eleven guys to operate it but the 47 only took three. So I was out of a job. So I went back into special services, going around to play at the Admiral's Club, NCO club, and even clubs in town. At that time I was based in Shreveport, Louisiana. I started going to the clubs downtown. I went to a place called the Cotton Club. I hung out at that club. Every weekend . . . I would hang out at the club, every weekend. I started singing and waiting tables for them. I hung out at that club until I got out of the service. They

3.3. Chick with the son of Zion bar owners Max and Lara Clarke. Courtesy Doug Mokaren.

said, 'Anybody with eighteen months or over can get out.' 'Cause the war was over.

"End of Korea.

"So, I got out of the service. They give you your transportation home. They give you the money. I put it in my pocket. Hitchhiked home, saving my money. I caught a ride with a guy and I drove for a while . . . out of Shreveport coming to Atlanta. And then I stopped driving and he started driving. I went to sleep. We got to Monroe County. Cops pulled him over. We both got out. So. They was asking me where I'm coming from. So I showed him my papers. I said I just got out of the service and was on my way home. Blah, blah, blah. So the cop was asking me questions and asking me questions and I was answering. So he [the cop] slaps me. Pow!

"'Nigger, don't you know how to say, "Yes, sir"?'

"This is my county. Monroe County, 1954. This is where I live. I couldn't do nothing about it. Now I *wanted* to do something about it, 'cause I had been in the service now. I mean, *hey*. I was a soldier. You know. But the other cop put a gun in my ear, pulled the hammer back. So they took me in."

Chick explained that part of the humiliation was that the cop who slapped him was about the same age as Chick, yet demanded to be called 'sir.' Chick was arrested but had the good luck to get a judge who had been in the service and had some sympathy for servicemen. When the judge learned that the arresting officer had slapped Chick for not saying 'sir,' the judge chastised the cop for not respecting a serviceman.

"Of course, the judge didn't do anything to him, but he talked to him real bad. That was about it. That was my first encounter with Monroe County since I left when I was young. First time back. So I left Monroe County and went back to Chicago for—oh, I guess, four or five months. Hung out in that area, then I started traveling with my cousin, Chuck Willis. I was driving for him and valeting for him. And then after I was out there for a while, I started opening the show for him. He died—of course—in 1958. I went back to Chicago after that.

"My mother was glad I went to Chicago with my auntie as a boy. I was very aggressive and she was just sure that I would end up dead if I stayed in Monroe County. I was rebellious.

"'Kiss my so-and-so.' That was me.

"She was glad I left. Going to Chicago probably saved my life. So she was glad I left. When I was a boy, there have been a couple of times people came to our house to get me, and my mother stood them off with a shotgun. My mother'd tell them all, 'See those four little black young 'uns? Those are mine. Don't ya'll put your hand on 'em. If they do anything against you, do anything you don't like, come tell me. Understand. Don't put your hand on 'em.'

"They all would say my mother was crazy. But they never did mess with her. She was working for Cary Bittick, the sheriff. That's who she worked for.

"My mother was in the kitchen one day ironing clothes that she had washed. And she had ironed these robes—and me and my brother was playing with them like kids do. Put the hood on and . . . and she was mad when she caught us. 'Put that hood down. I'm gonna beat on you. Leave them robes alone!' Because she was ironing 'em and folding them up and stuff and they were Ku Klux Klan robes. The hoods and everything. Listen. See. That's why I know what was going on in Monroe County. See.

"My mother I can say had some clout. My mother actually worked for two sheriffs. She worked for Sheriff Cary Bittick in Forsyth and she sold liquor for Sheriff Budd Pope of Bucks County. This is why I tell you that liquor was illegal because they wouldn't let them vote it in. They controlling the liquor. That county is still dry and all the counties around them went wet. They controlling the liquor. Same in Arkansas and Texas. The line might be right in the center of town. Walk on the other side and buy you some liquor and then walk back.

"You see what we did was we made it for the sheriff. So, we couldn't get caught. We were never in jail because we made it for the sheriff. Whenever the revenuers—you know, the big boys came in from Atlanta, we just rack his up and wait. He'd get with the revenuers and go around and bust everybody else's still. The sheriff of every county was usually the crookedest person in whole county. The Freedom Riders wouldn't be dead but for the sheriff. The sheriff set 'em up.[8]

"The sheriff of my county, Monroe County, back when I was a little boy, the sheriff was the grand wizard. Sheriff Cary Bittick. And guess who is the sheriff now? Sheriff Cary Bittick Jr.

"That's why we have the blues."

CHAPTER 4

White Kids on the Chitlin Circuit

Rob Baskerville and Penny Zamagni

Rob Baskerville and his wife, Penny Zamagni, formed the band the King Bees, meeting, touring, and recording with dozens of traditional blues musicians, artists like Jerry "Boogie" McCain, Charlie Bristol, Neal Pattman, Thomas "Guitar" Gable, "Chicago" Bob Nelson, Bo Diddley, Beverly "Guitar" Watkins, Roy Roberts, Doctor Dixon, Ironing Board Sam, Tinsley Ellis, and Chick Willis. "Hound Dog" Rob Baskerville is the guitarist and organist; Penny is the vocalist and bassist. In the 1980s, the couple sought out traditional blues artists and began touring with them on the chitlin circuit. Many venues on the circuit were drink houses or juke joints but also included any southern venue considered safe for African American entertainers. By the 1980s, some of these venues were still in operation and new venues and festivals had been added.

By 1991, Rob and Penny were married and continued on the road, backing up some of the legendary blues artists and playing in some colorful venues. In the mid-1990s, the King Bees were signed to Amsterdam's Tramp Records and released three CDs. In 2002, the band became regionally known as the host for the annual New River Blues Festival in Grassy Creek, North Carolina, which featured traditional blues musicians in the lineup. Grassy Creek is in a remote mountain area of North Carolina that tends to approve of bluegrass more than blues. I talked with Penny and Rob on September 21, 2013, asking about their fascination for blues music.

Rob: I grew up in an extremely racist household—really, really, badly racist. But the one thing that was okay—the one black person and the one black thing that was okay was music and Count Basie. My dad would somehow or another get over his racism enough to take me to see Count Basie, not only to listen to the music but to take me backstage to meet Count Basie

4.2 Rob "Hound Dog" Baskerville. Courtesy Doug Mokaren.

and to see the whole band. This happened numerous times. So my quest to answer that question—about the power music had to overcome my dad's racism—brought me to this interest in blues music. That and also going to see a chitlin circuit show here in Greensboro of Z. Z. Hill, Bobby Bland, and B. B. King when I was about sixteen. That actually just got me hooked on real blues—not rock blues, but the more traditional stuff.

I was always playing some kind of instrument as a kid. I was in a garage band in high school playing bass and playing keyboard, tuba in the band. Yeah. And my grandmother was an organ and piano teacher, so I grew up around music. But those two things right there—my father's adoration of Count Basie and seeing that chitlin circuit show—are the reason for my quest to figure out what all this is about: this music, this social exchange, the cultural journey. I haven't figured it out yet, but I've had some truly great experiences.

Penny: My experience is similar but reversed. My dad was the son of Italian immigrants and learned firsthand that prejudice can be a very painful and—of course—unfair thing. He was extremely open to black music. He had a fabulous collection of 78s starting from the 1920s. His collection included a lot of Louie Armstrong, King Oliver, Sidney Bechet, all of those guys—so I constantly heard that music growing up.

4.1 Penny Zamagni. Courtesy Doug Mokaren.

Music was always part of our house. My older brothers were in bands. The first music I heard my brothers playing was Jerry Lee Lewis and Fats Domino. I just said to myself, "This is the music; this is the music for me." I started playing drums in about fifth grade, chorus and band all the way through grammar school and high school. I did some acting and singing in musical kinds of stuff. Strummed a little guitar, then got away from it completely and went into clinical psychology. That'll really mess you up. Then I realized I wanted that music back again. And about that time I ran into this guy [pointing to Rob].

Rob: I was playing in some bands at that point.

Penny: We met in 1985. Bob is ten years younger than I am and I thought well, this is an interesting fellow; this is a nice friendship. But then we just fell completely in love and the music was our bond. We came from very different backgrounds. Rob would always say, "You look like someone from the Grateful Dead," you know, the hippie thing. Maybe it's the long hair. I really wasn't exactly a Deadhead, but blues was an important part of my music. I remember seeing Hendrix when I was a teenager and I remember thinking. "Wow, there is so much blues in that." My mom took me to see the Beatles at Shea Stadium when I was about ten. I guess they really made a big mistake exposing me to so much music as a child, because the clinical psychology went to the wayside and the music took over. After Rob and I met, we started traveling to the Delta to see traditional blues artists.

Rob: Yeah. When I was growing up, my sister Ann would be playing Hendrix and my dad would be playing Basie and they would be at loggerheads over their different musical choices. And I thought, what's the big deal? They're both playing blues music. They're both playing blues but just in a very different way. That was the thing. I don't believe music is meant to separate people; it's meant to bring people together. It did that for Penny and me. We had records by our blues idols and we thought—what happens if we just called them up? We were crazy like that. What would happen if we just showed up at Big Jack Johnson's[1] home in Clarksdale and chased him around when he was driving in his oil truck? What if we just found him and introduced ourselves? So we just drove to Clarksdale one weekend and followed Big Jack Johnson's truck around and ambushed him. And that's how we started out a friendship with him.

Penny: This was about 1986. We went to Jack Johnson's job at the oil company to meet him. Went to his house. We got to become friends. And so one day Jack said, "Let's do a gig." So we go and pick up Sam Carr[2] and we go to Frank Frost's[3] house, which is right downtown. It's like a storefront downtown.

Rob: It's an apartment with a storefront.

Penny: So we're all riding down the road together having a great time, driving over the bridge to Helena to this neat little juke joint over there.

Rob: This juke joint doesn't have a name. It's not a tourist place at all. This is a storefront where people are selling liquor, and dancing, and hanging out in the street. And there's this huge industrial fan. This is the main thing I remember. There's the huge, huge industrial fan—

Penny: —in the middle of the dance floor—

Rob: —with no guard on it. So you have drunk people dancing all around it. I'm ready for like, you know, people to just be chopped up—

Penny: —pulverized—

Rob: —for people to have serious accidents, but they didn't. Not one drunk dancer boogied into the blades of that industrial fan. They nearly did. It seemed like they were going to, but no one got hurt. It was amazing.

Penny: We did several gigs there. We hung out at Wade Walton's Barber Shop and went on KFFA in Helena, on the "King Biscuit Time" with Sonny Payne [KFFA AM 1360]. We played there with the Jelly Roll Kings, Frank Frost, and Sam Carr. We ended up playing several gigs together with Jack Johnson.

Rob: Jack was a monstrous guitar player.

Penny: They called him the "Oil Man" because of his job. He drove the truck for the oil company in town, in Clarksdale. He filled people's fuel-oil tanks. We went to his job; we went to his house and met his family. He had a big bunch of kids. Oh yeah. And he had, I don't know, six or seven kids. I don't know exactly how many. What I saw at the house was a whole bunch of kids.

Rob: He lived on Indiana Avenue, that much I remember. We played several shows—

Penny: —at this all-black juke joint in Helena where people were very welcoming.

Rob: The funny thing was that we never had any problem. Well, the most kind of unfriendly stuff we experienced was basically a dare, "All right, what you got?" You know. There was never any real fuss. Well, one time when we worked with Jerry McCain,[4] we were doing this all-black chitlin circuit festival, all through Alabama and Mississippi. Tyrone Davis[5] was the headliner. Black people did come up to Jerry and say accusingly, "Man, you got a white band." And Jerry told them, "I have a band of musicians."

Penny: And people would be standing with their arms crossed, challenging you, just waiting to see "what you got." No, people are not always welcoming to begin with.

Rob: They're not unfriendly, but they're not real sociable—

Penny: —and then when they see that what you got is workable, then it's like, "Oh, man, they're cool." You can play. You're all right. You're cool.

Rob: We played at the National Black Arts Festival on Auburn Avenue in Atlanta—
Penny: The first one they ever did was in 1988 on Auburn Avenue with Chicago Bob.[6] It was primarily all black acts, but there was one other white band that lived in Atlanta that played the festival; other than that, all black acts. James Cotton[7] was headlining and there was a lot of African art and dance things, and then . . . there was us.
Rob: We showed them what we had, and it was "all cool."
Penny: So we do this festival and we're about the only white faces at this very Afrocentric festival with really interesting African dance and James Cotton and afterwards Bob comes up and says, "I've got to show you something."
Rob: He took us to the Royal Peacock on Atlantic Avenue, which is the most famous of the most famous of the most famous of the R&B clubs in the Southeast, short of the Dew Drop in New Orleans. It's the club where Little Richard started out. It the club where Billy Wright[8] influenced Little Richard.[9] We actually got to meet and hang out with Billy Wright, which is a whole other story there. So we went down to the Royal Peacock, which is this seminal R&B club in Atlanta. White people don't go there, basically. And Bob took us in there and showed us the history.
Penny: The generosity with which these great musicians took us under their wings still amazes me.

Penny and Rob also played juke joints and drink houses with harmonica player Neal Pattman [1926–2005] from Madison County, Georgia. Sometimes called "Big Daddy Pattman," Neal Pattman lost his right arm in an accident as a child, but learned to make moonshine and play harmonica just fine without it.

Penny: Neal Pattman was a one-armed, Athens, Georgia, Piedmont-style harmonica player, whose style was a lot like Sonny Terry[10] but even predated that. He had a lot of this archaic late 1800s stuff that his grandfather had taught him. Neal took us to the dark side of Athens where he worked at a pool hall—
Rob: Now that was a juke joint, a pool hall, drink house all together, where Pattman was the one-armed bouncer. He would say, "I throw people out all the time." He was fun. You could have a conversation

with Pattman and his harmonica at the same time and your conversation would be punctuated musically. We played on Neal Pattman's first album, which came out on Global Village. We produced Pattman's second record, called *Lightnin' Twist*, which we put out on High John Records. We played a lot of gigs together. I remember when he came to our home after we played some festival and he was extremely nervous. He said, "I can't go in there."

Penny: He'd never stayed at a white person's house. And—Athens, Georgia, to Boone, North Carolina, was a whole other universe for him.

Rob: We had to coax him. He had never spent the night at a white person's house and he was afraid to come inside ours. This comes back to the whole thing about why I started this journey—the racism and the fear, the music and our cultural conversation. This was the 1990s. Neal Pattman was born in 1924 or '26, depending on when you asked him. The things that he had seen in rural Georgia as a black man were things I couldn't imagine, the scary things that today some people don't bother to think about. Now in the 1990s, this cat is afraid to come inside a white person's house.

Penny: Jerry McCain tells a story about Trumpet Records run by Lillian McMurry [1921–99] in the early 1950s.

Rob: Lillian McMurry was a white woman.

Penny: She was the proprietor of Trumpet Records. It was in a furniture store. She had a studio in the back of the store; this was in Jackson, Mississippi. So Jerry is going to do this recording and he is just shaking, because he's so afraid to go inside that store. He said there were these columns in front of the store and he just stood there shivering with the fear. But, of course Lillian McMurry recorded Elmore James, Little Milton, and Sonny Boy Williamson. She was a genius. She is one of my biggest heroes. She was white, living in the South, and she found all this talent, and she wasn't afraid to record it if the artist would walk through the front door. Lillian McMurry was the most seminal record label in traditional blues. So, Jerry finally went in the studio and got his career started that way. There was another time when Jerry was talking about a gig going up to Excello.

Rob: Yes. He was recording for Excello, which is a subsidiary of Nashboro Records. That was later in his career.

Penny: He did recordings in the mid-1950s for Excello.

Rob: Jerry was pulled over by a white cop once on his way to Excello. He left Gadsden, Alabama, and was crossing the Tennessee state line when the cop pulled him over. This time it would have been in the mid-1960s, around the time of all the civil rights turmoil and head smashing that went on then. I don't know too much about what happened, but Jerry told me a white cop pulled him over and beat him up. Jerry was a proud man, so he may have said something to rile the cop. I don't know. He may have said something about the cop being jealous because he was driving a Cadillac.[11] Jerry did get on up to Excello to make his recording but he had a busted lip, which could have made recording a challenge for a harmonica player.

Rob added later that part of Jerry's difficulty (in addition to driving while black) might have been that he was always armed and was not enthusiastic about the philosophy of nonviolence. Jerry also told Rob that after beating him up, the cop took a ten-dollar bill Jerry's wife had given him for the trip. The cop pocketed Jerry's money as a "souvenir" of the encounter.

Rob: Jerry McCain is my idol. He is also my biggest mentor and someone I've had hundreds of hours of phone conversations with, been by his house numerous times, eaten dinner there, played there, rehearsed there, hung out there, been insulted there with him saying, "You play like a hillbilly. You got to play *blacker*. I've got to show you how to play *blacker*." So we got our egos bruised but we persevered and basically gained some respect from people whose respect is nearly impossible to get.
Penny: Great musicians out of Atlanta will ask us, "Man, how did you get to know Jerry McCain? He hates everybody. How come he likes you guys?"
Rob: The quote was, "You are the only guys we know that he gets along with. How did you do it?" and I said, "We respect the guy."
Penny: Maybe that was it. We knew all about Jerry McCain's recording history. We didn't go in with just a spotty idea and outline. We knew everything he had recorded, with whom, and when.
Rob: I remember one of my first conversations with him. I told him, "I play the blues." He says, "Ha. You do?" He grilled me and I told him I played with Chicago Bob. He said, "He's pretty good, but he ain't no Jerry

McCain." In the course of our conversation, he found out that I knew his work. Finally he said, "I've got this little gig next week and I've got two bands. My white band is prejudiced and my black band is drunk."

Penny: That's a straight Jerry McCain quote right there.

Rob: He called it like he saw it. It didn't matter. And so he said, "Why don't you come down and do this little show with me?" And so we met him at Noccalula Falls outside of Gadsden, Alabama. And so we went down there. We said, sure we'd drive 350 miles down to Gadsden to do a "little show." Actually, we drove more than that because we left from Roanoke. We did a gig in Roanoke the night before going to Gadsden. We drove all night, got there, went and did this "little gig," which turned out to be Birmingham City Stages. This is like the biggest festival next to the Jazz Fest in the South.

Penny: They had James Brown. He was one of the headliners. We did that festival several years. We started playing with Jerry in about '91 or '92, so it was along in there. One year it was James Brown, one year it was T-Birds, one year it was B. B. The festival was right in downtown Birmingham.

Rob: Near the Tutwiler Hotel.[12]

Penny: Somehow they would fence off most of downtown and there were stages everywhere. We were on the Alabama stage because of Jerry. It was great fun.

Rob: Jerry McCain was my biggest influence. He was a master. He recorded on Trumpet. He recorded on Excello. He recorded on all the real seminal southern blues labels. Jerry would tell me stories like, "They kicked my black ass off the Martin Luther King peace march because I was carrying a gun." He was an extremely violent guy. I can't imagine what being black in Alabama might have been like when you have a talent and an ego like he had . . . and an arsenal like he had.

Penny: And a refusal to leave, because this was his home, damn it. He built his house, which was an interesting, fascinating home to walk into. It was like a monument to himself. Nothing but pictures of Jerry all over and he was always listening to his music constantly, always it was *his* music.

Rob: And he would play along with his own CDs. He'd stop, look at me, and say, "Ain't that great?" He had a huge ego but he backed it up by being a genius on his instrument.

Penny: So many white harp players like James Harman—all these people have paid homage to Jerry by covering his songs like "Steady" or "She's Tough."[13] He was one of the greatest talents and he was basically unknown outside of blues circles. We got to be friends with his wife Doris Jean, who was much younger than Jerry was. She died of cancer. I wrote a poem for him for her funeral and he read it.

Penny talked about the deterioration of the neighborhood where Jerry lived. In *A Change Is Gonna Come: Music, Race and the Soul of America,* Craig Werner explains that in the 1970s and '80s, several things contributed to the decline of black neighborhoods. White suburbanization redistributed the tax base away from cities, draining resources from areas that needed the funds for an aging infrastructure. But more problematic was the relocation of successful black families to neighborhoods with newer housing, better schools, and more attractive environments. Black flight diminished the rich cross section of economic conditions and social attitudes of black neighborhoods before desegregation. Poor black children were deprived of successful black mentors and the living conditions were increasingly ghettoized.[14]

Penny: Anyway. So Jerry's living in Gadsden and his neighborhood had decayed through the decades. He built his house in 1952 in an all-black community. We knew that segregation in some communities was a healthy thing because there would be black businesses; the schools would be black; the black church would be there; there would be black lawyers, funeral homes. You know, the community was self-sufficient. But then, decay started coming in and it seemed to come at about the same time—unfortunately—as integration did. Black businesses would get taken over by white people with more money. Neighborhoods began to decline. When we knew Jerry, his neighborhood was already in decline. There was a playground and a school yard right at the end of Henry Street where Jerry lived. And there would be kids playing basketball down there. But he knew they weren't playing basketball; he knew they were selling crack. *I* don't know if they were selling crack, but *he* was sure of it.
Rob: He wrote "Burn the Crack House Down."[15]
Penny: —which is based on older songs. We knew other artists who would sing about burning the drink house down. So this was an

extension of burning something down where all the bad shit was going on. Jerry McCain didn't just write a song about it. He actually went up to the playground with a chain saw and cut the basketball hoops down.

Rob: He said—oh, I'm not even going to tell you exactly what he said, but it was something along the lines of—there were so many crack dealers up there at the playground, they had to wear badges to keep from selling crack to each other. So he cut the basketball hoops down with his chain saw to discourage kids from going there to buy and sell crack.

Penny: One time when we got to his place—and this was slightly later—he said, "Come in. Let me show you what I got. Let me show you what I got." And he pulled out this huge case, like a steel case, and opens it, and inside is an assault weapon, but more than one. He had several of them. Assault weapons!

Rob: Oh, he had an arsenal.

Penny: I'd never even seen an assault weapon before. And he had all this ammo—

Rob: —green boxes of ammo. You have to picture this older black man with green vinyl shoes up on his stair-stepping machine, waving guns in the air like Yosemite Sam, saying, "Those crack dealers better not come around here." That was scary.

Penny: He trusted us enough to take us in his back room and show us this stuff. And he was raising his grandson, Joe.

Rob: Yeah. Because Joe's mom got murdered.

Penny: Jerry's daughter. Joe was her son. This was not unusual. This was rough shit. An ex-husband got out of prison and—

Rob: —he killed her. The whole violence around this scene is something no one really ever deals with because . . . well, it's like the blues festivals with the blues agencies sending out the acts. Everything is cleaned up. Everything is pretty. This isn't what the blues was about for Jerry.

Penny: White bands come along and learn the songs but never bother to really learn or understand the black history and culture behind them. White people sing the songs, put on the records, and dance—but this was real experience and it was really painful.

Rob: Jerry bought his harmonicas from a pawnshop in Gadsden, from Paul, [a] white guy who ran the pawnshop. Paul ends up murdering his wife for running around.

Penny: Paul was a friend of ours. Paul comes to film our shows, hangs out with us, drives us around, and the next thing we know, Jerry's saying, "Paul's in jail." "What happened?" "He murdered his old lady for running around with a black man."

Rob: Jerry was telling us, "Paul is trying to get me to get rid of his gun." That was Pawnshop Paul.

Penny: Paul played football for Alabama, Tuscaloosa. He got a scholarship. He said he hurt his knees. He would have been there in the late 1960s. He was a football hero but now he runs a pawnshop. . . . Paul and his wife had come up to see us all the time when we were playing in Gadsden. She has the long dresses and long hair . . . doing the hippie dance and they're just so happy and in love. And the next thing we know, Paul is killing her. He goes to the crack house, finds her with a black guy, and just blows her away. So, now he's in jail. Oh yeah, and another person we knew from Gadsden—the very guy who recommended us to Jerry—ends up killing somebody, or is *accused* of killing somebody. The rich guy.

Rob: Oh, Carl. Carl Weaver.

Penny: He wasn't a musician. He was an entrepreneur who eventually had a blues club and wanted us to be the house band. It's good that we didn't become the house band, because Carl Weaver ended up charged with double murder.[16] He wanted to call his club Boogie McCain's. He wanted to, but Jerry wouldn't let him.

Rob: It ended up being called the Second Street Music Hall or something like that—

Penny: —which we ended up doing a show there with Jimmy Hall[17] that got recorded by Johnny Sandlin.[18] If you remember Johnny Sandlin, the Allman Brothers' producer.

Penny: But Carl Weaver owned the blues club. His family had a lot of money. He had a house out on the lake. On the Coosa River somewhere. We played out there, too.

Rob: He opened this club that was going to feature Boogie McCain. Jerry and Carl had a relationship that went back for years. They loved each other and then they hated each other. Then they loved each other and then they hated each other. But anyway, Carl hired Johnny Sandlin to run sound and produce things at that club. That's how he recorded us. In the meanwhile, Carl is accused of eliminating his drug competition at a fishing lodge.

Penny: He was supposedly in the pot trade, growing and selling marijuana. This was around 1995. Some people were burned—killed in a cabin near where they were growing the marijuana—something like that. So, Carl was allegedly involved in two homicides.
Rob: On the chitlin circuit we got to see the seamy underbelly sometimes.
Penny: So we're hanging out with Jerry in about 1994 or '95 when Alabama Public Television decided they wanted to do a show on this great historic bluesman, Jerry McCain. Jerry called us to come down and be part of this show.[19]
Rob: He said, "I want the white people to be tellin' my story."
Penny: So this white woman from Colorado comes to interview Jerry and she's just jaw-dropping scared to death of him. So she takes us aside and says, "We went to the local radio station, because this is where Jerry did early shows decades ago and he wanted me to see this radio station. So we went there and this poor old drunk guy came up in the parking lot and was kind of trying to talk to Jerry. And Jerry pulled a pistol on him!" And we're like, "And? Is there an end to this story?" This was nothing new to us but she couldn't believe Jerry pulled a pistol on a guy. This was just how it was. Jerry McCain didn't think twice about pulling out a pistol. So another time we were on stage with Jerry. This was one of the street festivals—
Rob: —it was in Tuscaloosa. The Johnny Shines Festival.
Penny: Microwave Dave. He's from Alabama. Microwave Dave and the Nukes. So Dave really wants to get on stage with us so bad. Jerry doesn't need Dave on stage. It's just not going to work that way as far as Jerry's concerned. So Dave sees that there's a guitar, there's a bass, and there's a harp. Dave thinks, "I know what I'll do. I'll come on with my trumpet." And so Dave starts to come on stage with a trumpet and Jerry goes for his gun. That was the end of that.
Rob: And we're not gun people. We're not violence people. Sure . . . I grew up around guns. We hunt in North Carolina—
Penny: I didn't grow up in a gun culture at all. My parents were liberal progressive people. I never even saw guns. I never understood the attraction for guns. So I had to get used to all this stuff. And it took some getting used to. . . .

One of the more interesting chitlin circuit places where we worked was in Tallahassee [Florida] called Dave's CC Club. It was originally a clubhouse space for the Negro League baseball field. It was up a bumpy, bumpy old dirt road and the baseball field was still there. It was a clubhouse managed by a black couple, Dave Claytor and his wife Elizabeth. It had always been part of the black community in Tallahassee. Dave wanted the real-deal blues at his clubhouse, so we would bring Neal Pattman there, because he played the real old-style stuff. The audience was black people and white people. It was a fascinating mix. You had to come pretty far out into the country to get to Dave's clubhouse. And he'd always run out of booze and run out of food.

Rob: They'd have to go to the "city store and get more beer."

Penny: Yeah. Even though you're not supposed to buy it from a store. You're supposed to buy beer through your distributor.[20] . . . There would be hippies and conservative types and a large black audience all mixed together. We brought Chicago Bob there; we brought Sandra Hall[21] there. . . . It was a great experience but it's gone now. They lost money and it went out of business. . . .

Rob: Part of the reason was Dave had no head for business. We'd show up and Dave would be, "Rob, I've got an opening act for you." Oh, shit. Who is it? And it would be Magic Slim and the Teardrops.[22]

Penny: *Opening* for *us*? Uh, yeah. Wow. Dave, come here for a second. Let's reverse this, Dave. Let's open for *them*. And he'd say, "Whatever you guys want."

Rob: Yeah. It might be like, "Rob, I know you're comin' in with Nappy Brown[23] but I invited Eddie Kirkland[24] to come. Oh, and Bobby Rush[25] is in the neighborhood, he's gonna drop by. I hope you don't mind." Yeah. And so it'd be like a King Bee gig and here we are with Bobby Rush and Eddie Kirkland. Yeah. Eddie's in his station wagon in a parking lot over in Dothan, Alabama, wanting to know if he can come over here and play with us.

Penny: And it was an old, old station wagon. This would have been in the late '90s or early 2000s.

Rob: That was the kind of vibe the club had. And Dave would be like very casual about booking. He'd tell us, "Rob, I don't have any money but you can stay at my house." Okay. Sure, why not? Or he'd say, "Just come back through on Sunday." No advertising. "Just come on back, we'll do brunch. We'll get some people out here." Of course, this club was a beautiful, brilliant, heartfelt, soulful idea that was sure to fail as a business.

Penny: He was such a visionary. He would get on stage with us and start talking about his vision of the blues, the beauty of it, and what it meant to him. He would talk about our relationship. He would talk at length. It was very poetic and stream of consciousness. . . . That was the strength this guy had. He knew what acts to bring in, what people to put together. He understood the energy and the chemistry, but he didn't understand the money part.
Rob: He wasn't a musician but he had this vision of like, "Well, I bet Hound Dog would sound good behind Bobby Rush. And we're going to get Bobby Rush to lead the dancers home. . . . " Dave knew how to organize a good time for everybody.

Rob and Penny's travels inevitably led them to Chicago, which was and still is a major gig destination for a number of southern blues artists. Penny felt that even though they had played their way all over the country, touring with Carey Bell[26] from about 2004 to about 2008, they were still being "tested." Penny in particular felt that she was being "tested" in Chicago, when they played at Buddy Guy's Legends.

Penny: We had this long, frozen tour in about 2006 and we ended up in Chicago, where Carey is from and where a lot of his family lives. I'm getting ready to get on stage to play at Buddy Guy's. The all-black opening band is standing at the side of the stage, snickering behind their hands. Looking at me like this. [At this point, Penny rears back in her chair, eyes squinted and arms folded over her chest.] Very menacing, very hostile, and challenging, like, "What do you got?" I'm fairly confident by this point. Carey Bell wants me to be his bass player, asked us to be his band. So I get up there and they gave me a bass rig that was blown.
Rob: This is what you got—a blown bass rig.
Penny: —and so it's just sounding horrible on stage. It has no projection. But I'm playing and I'm playing everything I know to play, my best I know to play—that's appropriate for the music. The next thing I know, they're taking the bass amp off and bringing mine on and giving me my good bass. In other words, "Oh—she can play. She can play. Let's give her the good stuff. They knew that bass rig was blown; they were just waiting, hoping to see me freak out.
Rob: I think you passed the test on that one.

Penny: White *and* a woman. That was the thing. Buddy Guy's Legends. So then we had Needleneck sit in with us on drums. Needleneck was Carey Bell's son. Appropriately named, because he had a real skinny neck. He's playing and at the end of the gig he says, "Dad. Dad. I need a ride home, Dad." This was after he stood on the sidewalk and waited a half hour for a taxi that never came. Maybe he did that for show, because he knows a taxi is not going to pick up a black guy at two o'clock in the morning in downtown Chicago. Wasn't going to happen. Just doesn't. So he says, "Dad, I need a ride home." Okay, so we say [Penny adopts a cheerful voice], "We'll take you home. That's fine." [Penny groans.] Oh, it took us hours through the darkest, worst . . . most difficult—

Rob: —crime tape here, roadwork there. Detour here and get lost there.

Penny: People were just turning us around, telling us, "Oh, you don't want to go down that way." And Carey would say, "No, no, no. Don't go there, because they're gonna hijack your van; it's full of equipment." Oh my God.

Rob: Of course, Carey was in the habit of having a little nip all along and finally he's like, "Rob, Robbie, Robbie. Turn here. Don't turn here. Turn here."

Penny: He was getting lost. Needleneck was getting lost.

Rob: Everyone is getting lost.

Penny: We're so tired at this point.

Rob: Yeah. We spent two hours driving around downtown Chicago, through the crime scenes, going the wrong way on the roadwork, and we ended up back at Buddy Guy's. We didn't find our motel after two hours of driving. . . . Penny and Carey got to be really, really tight. . . .

Penny: I can tell you that he doesn't like rice. When were on tour and at Chan's in Rhode Island, a Chinese restaurant . . . a great venue.[27] I was going through the buffet line of Chinese food, and I'm always doing Carey's plates for him. . . . I'm asking, "Carey, would you like this?" And he was like, "No, no, no rice." He told me, "I ate rice every day of my entire life from the first day I can remember until I was thirteen. I got out of there and left Mississippi with Lovie Lee[28] and left the rice behind." Carey's mom died when he was three, so he was raised by a number of different relatives and his grandparents. And all they fed him was rice. He didn't want any more rice. So, he was learning how to play harmonica and Lovie Lee heard him play. Carey said that Lovie was like his dad, though he didn't know who his real dad was. He's actually Carey Bell Harrington, but his cousin was Big Chief Eddie Clearwater.[29] He said, "I got outta there." Carey never looked back, never went back, and he never ate rice again. Drinking was his downfall, sad to say. There were many places we couldn't go with him because he was no longer welcome. There was the Slippery Noodle.[30]

Rob: Indiana.

Penny: Indianapolis—a big club. And Canada. We don't know what he did but he did something. He was not invited back. He would get drunk and he could get grumpy with us. He could get ornery. He would get testy. But there was something about our relationship; he was always cool with us. We heard he got in trouble in other clubs quite a bit but he never got into trouble when he was with us. Never. We were never thrown out of a bar with Carey Bell.

Rob: I don't drink. I just simply drive. I'm the road manager; I take care of business—

Penny: —when you go into this business and you're working with the older black blues people, you have to be nurturing. They want it; they expect it. They want that respect. They want to be looked after, to be helped along. Get their luggage for them for Pete's sake. Get their keys for their motel room. It doesn't take anything away from you and it makes them feel appreciated.

Rob: And it's not a patronizing, paternalistic thing. It just makes everything go smoother and makes their life easier. It's not like the whitey plantation owner, "I know what's best for you." It's not like that. It's a generational thing, too. These are generally older players and you want to show them the respect they are due.

Penny: I'm thinking about when we were in Charleston one time and you and Carey did a show together. It was early. We'd played all night the night before and they had to be there early to set up at the library, the Charleston Public Library. Rob and Carey were supposed to do a duo at noon. I didn't go. I just stayed in bed. So Carey was drinking heavy the night before and we brought him into his bedroom. Literally, we put him on the bed in his suit, in his shoes, and threw a blanket over him. The next morning, Rob knocks on his door. Carey is still in his suit; he's still in his shoes; he's still on the bed. But he and Rob have this noon gig to do at the Charleston Public Library.

Rob: The whole time he's telling me, "Robbie, I don't feel too good. I don't feel too good." We walk up to the library past the line waiting to get in with him saying, "I don't want to be here." He did not want to be there at all. We get on stage, he says, "You know what I need? I need a bologna sandwich." This is like the first words he says to the audience. But once he gets past the bologna sandwich part, he proceeds to just blow them all away. And oh, he's sick. He's hungover. He's still drunk.

Penny: Wearing clothes from the day before.

Rob: And he's just magic. I don't know how. I don't know why, but he was magic.

Penny: The harmonica. That instrument. That was the instrument that took him out of Mississippi and took him to Chicago. Took him around the world. It brought him adulation and love. Before that he had been a car mechanic. His brothers and his kids ran a car shop in Chicago, but Carey became an artist.

Rob: On that day Carey goes from a burned-out, alcoholic, hungover, "give me a bologna sandwich" curmudgeon to a world-class musician right there in the Charleston Public Library.

Penny: He would be world class in spite of himself. Regardless of being pissed off and a big grump. Give him the music and he was beyond inspiration.

Penny: In 1994, we started going to Europe. We got signed to Tramp Records out of Holland. A great record label. For some reason they took us under their wing and we made three CDs. We started touring then. We toured Holland, France, and Italy and Belgium, Germany, Switzerland. We toured Paris with Neal Pattman and Johnny Mars.[31] We weren't expecting such blues music knowledge in Europe. But the average Dutch guy knows more than the average American southerner does about this music. We're playing in Holland one time and this Indonesian guy comes up to us and says, "I like it when you play Arthur Smith's 'Guitar Boogie.'" This guy knew who Arthur Smith[32] was. He knew the song "Guitar Boogie."

Rob: Arthur Smith. A guitar player, a country guy from Charlotte, North Carolina. And here is this Indonesian man from Holland who knows all about this about American roots music. What's wrong with this picture?

Penny: So the first gig we ever did, we're setting up on stage in a room that looks really, really empty. We're looking out about thirty feet and there's no one there. This is so depressing. And then we see that the back wall is actually sliding doors. The doors slide open and about 400 people come charging in, racing in like we're the Beatles or something. They're kissing Rob's shoes.
Rob: Kissing my red shoes! I had a huge ego after that. Then I come home, loading my gear into a sports bar to play for thirty people who don't want to hear me. It just like you go from people who are really knowledgeable and really value the music to those who don't. Some of it's a lack of education, but some of it's racism—probably the same reason that Champion Jack Dupree[33] moved to France.

Penny began talking about music traditions in the North Carolina mountains, Junaluska Mountain in particular, where there was a small African America community that became known for string bands or string music.

Rob: At the foot of the mountain you have Caldwell County, which is where I was born, surrounded by Burke and Wilkes Counties. Wilkes County is famous—of course—for moonshine and Tom Dooley.[34] . . . You've got Etta Baker[35] from there. Howard Colbert[36] from there, from Lenoir. He was a fascinating guy. He could play George Benson or he could play banjo. He could play serious funk on electric, then he could turn around and play traditional tunes on acoustic guitar, like on that *Real Folks Blues* CD. He could do folk tunes like "John Henry" or "Step It Up and Go," which is one of those songs you might hear Doc Watson play . . . oh, everyone has their adaptation of it. "Bottle Up and Go."
Penny: Neal Pattman had his version of it. Instead of "Bottle Up and Go," Neal called it "Bottom Up and Go."
Rob: It's a collection of traditional verses that float around in true blues tradition. Howard Colbert might have grown up in a community that has its own particular version of that song. As we were talking about Jerry McCain singing "Burn the Crack House Down," Howard Colbert is singing "Burn the Drink House Down." Come to find out the drink house is right next door. It's in his community.

Penny: Whatever the cancer is in your community that you want to get rid of—in Jerry McCain's case it was the crack house. In Howard's case, reaching back to an earlier time, it was the drink house.

Rob: There was another guy that we did some field recording with, a guitar player named Charlie Bristol.[37] Born in 1921. From Burke County. Chesterfield. Right on the Caldwell County line.

Penny: Charlie Bristol saw Blind Boy Fuller[38] play in the 1930s and had a lot of that material in his repertoire. Charlie had a drinking problem that made him kind of unworkable, but we brought him to Charleston—dragged him all around. But in the 1930s Charlie was in a drink house in Caldwell County and somebody sassed him back or talked shit to him and he cut the guy's head off. Charlie murdered the man.

Rob: "The guy deserved it," is what Charlie told us. So Charlie did time for murder.

Penny: So Charlie Bristol went to prison for murder. . . . After his prison experiences, Charlie said, "If you ever get in prison, don't ever let a prison guard tell you to go ahead and make a run for it, maybe you'll get out." I asked him, "What do you mean?" He said, "They'll encourage you to make a run for it. Go ahead and make a run for it. But, man, they got their gun on your back. They just tell you that so they can get in some target practice. I've seen that happen too many times. They'll shoot you. They just do it for target practice."

Rob: He'd seen people shot trying to escape.

Penny: The poor dumb guy that says to the guard, "Okay, maybe I will make a run for it." With the guard telling him, "Go. You can make it, man. Go for it."

Rob: Words of wisdom. Anyway, there's a lot of swapping of musical styles in this area. That's the beauty of the music for me. Scholars will label it "Piedmont blues." Musicians don't put a label on it. Musicians don't give a shit. . . . There's a lot of musicians from Appalachia I've worked with and picked informally with, like Ora Watson,[39] people like that, who would be playing blues. No one cared to label the music—

Penny: —Ora Watson. . . . She's passed now, but she was a very rural Appalachian musician. So, she was on tour with Johnny Shines.[40] Back in the '60s.

Rob: One of those folk heritage kinds of things. . . . Here is someone from the deepest part of Watauga County but her music knows no boundaries.

Penny: You learn music from people.

Rob: Records and CDs are great tools, but you really learn the music from the people who play it. This is why we set out to look for the players and I think we found some of the best.

CHAPTER 5

Muscle Shoals, Dry Counties, and the Hooch Run

Florence is the principal city in the northwest corner of Alabama known as the "Shoals" or the "Quad Cities," which also includes the cities of Sheffield, Muscle Shoals, and Tuscumbia. Even though the Shoals area was completely dry until the 1980s, the liquor flowed, making Lauderdale County the "wettest dry county in Alabama." The Shoals is additionally the site of some of the most nationally well-known music and musicians. The area has a history and folklore acutely connected to its music and its liquor.

The bit of the Tennessee River that runs through the Shoals area is called the "Singing River." The legend goes that long before the area was settled, an Indian girl came to the river to bathe and while she bathed, she sang. Her magnetic voice mingled with the sounds of water cascading over the rocks and echoed along the river. The people downstream, who couldn't see the girl, thought it was the river that was singing. The legend maintains that even to this day, if you listen carefully, you might hear the girl's voice in the water, especially after a big rain when Shoals Creek swells and babbles as it rushes into the Tennessee. On those days when the river flows rapidly—and especially if you've been drinking—you can hear the faint melody of the singing Indian girl that blessed the Tennessee River with music. You might even be able to see the flash of her white teeth in the sunlight reflected off the water or see her dark hair in the murky depths below. The legend further suggests that people born along the banks of the river are naturally inclined to music. That is her legacy to the Shoals.[1]

The area does seem to have an extraordinarily rich musical history.

William McDonald: Shoals Folklore and W. C. Handy

The "Father of the Blues," William Christopher Handy (W. C. Handy), was born in Florence, Alabama, on November 16, 1873. The Shoals historian William McDonald recounts the familiar local story: "Handy hankered after a guitar that he had seen in a shop window. On the sly he saved some money he made doing odd jobs like picking berries and making soap. When he had saved enough money, he bought the guitar, but when he brought it home, his family didn't approve of him playing a guitar. Handy's father made him take the guitar back to the store and spend his money on books instead. Handy was supposed to grow up to become a respectable teacher, not a musician."[2]

McDonald believes the attitude Handy's parents had about music still lingers in the Shoals area in spite of the legend of the singing river. He described Florence as a college town since 1872, but a town that never really identified itself as progressive or liberal. "The area has an active arts community, but the general feeling was that the arts are not a serious pursuit and musicians weren't generally considered to be respectable but more often thought of as drunkards and idlers." However, Handy was as serious about his music as his family was serious about him doing something more reputable. When he was a teenager, Handy joined a blues band in Florence, but he hid this activity from his parents, who did not support any idea of a musical career. Handy was highly educated and one of the few blues musicians who actually learned how to read musical notation, but reading music for some families is not a prized skill.

"Plenty of folks around here think that music is not a respectable or reliable way to earn a living. Music is something you do to pass the time and entertain yourself and your friends. Music is not the dependable aspiration on which to pin your dreams. And certain kinds of music are not highly regarded at all. Especially music associated with drinking and dancing. Given that attitude, it's remarkable that so many folks from the Shoals made a living and a name for themselves through music."

Handy wasn't the only influential musician from the Shoals. Sam Phillips, the man who founded Sun Studios and Sun Records in Memphis, Tennessee, and discovered Elvis Presley and Johnny Cash, was also born in Florence in 1923. Another Florence native was singer/songwriter Arthur Alexander.[3] Donna Jean Godchaux, a singer with the Grateful Dead from 1971 to 1979, was born in Florence and still lives and sings there as of this writing. Bass player William Doyce "Buddy" Killen was born in Florence and played music there until he moved to Nashville to become a record producer. James Joiner was also a Florence native whose

5.1. FAME recording studios. Courtesy Emily Edwards.

family owned a bus company, Joiner Transit. Joiner recorded demos in the back room of the bus station in the 1950s before recording his own popular single, "A Fallen Star," in 1957.[4] The Mississippi guitarist Travis Wammack settled in Florence in the 1960s and became Little Richard's bandleader from 1984 until 1995. There are many musicians that have called the area home. The region does not lack for musical talent.

In addition to the musicians, the Shoals was also home to several recording studios, among them Muscle Shoals Sound Studios, FAME (Florence Alabama Music Enterprises), Wishbone Recording Studios, Cactus Recording, Widget Studios, Broadway Sound, and East Avalon, among others. Rick Hall started FAME recording studios in 1959. Aretha Franklin's "Respect" and Wilson Pickett's "Mustang Sally" were both recorded at FAME studios. Norala Studios in Sheffield recorded Percy Sledge's "When a Man Loves a Woman" in 1966. Nationally known musicians such as Eric Clapton, Rod Stewart, the Allman Brothers, the Staple Singers, and Paul Simon have all recorded in the Shoals. In 1969, the session musicians for FAME, the Swampers, formed Muscle Shoals Sound. Not long afterward, Cher released the album *3614 Jackson Highway,* which was the original address of Muscle Shoals Sound Studios before it moved to a location closer to the river in the old Naval Reserve Building

5.2. Muscle Shoals Sound Studios. Courtesy Emily Edwards.

in 1978. The documentary *Muscle Shoals* (2013) helped to spread the legacy of FAME and Muscle Shoals Sound with featured interviews from a long list of popular entertainers who recorded there.[5]

Even though the Shoals area is rich with a relatively well-known music history, the musical influence of singing sharecroppers and back-porch musicians who never reached national stardom is fast disappearing even among friends and relatives. The population of traditional southern blues artists, both black and white, is aging and the character of the venues where they played has changed dramatically in fifty years. In the late 1970s, Lauderdale County churches campaigned hand in hand with local bootleggers to try to keep Lauderdale Country dry. Bootleggers had financial incentives to keep the liquor illegal; church leaders had religious dogma. In spite of their combined efforts, voters would ultimately make Florence a legally "wet" city in 1981 inside the borders of a "dry" Lauderdale County. In the same year, just across the river, Colbert County went wet. Afterward, the legal bars that appeared in the area were more sanitary and less dicey but perhaps not as colorful. By the mid-1980s, legal bars had essentially eliminated the necessity of the house party, bootlegger, and hooch run.

The city also restored the home where W. C. Handy was born and turned it into a museum to honor his life and music. In 1982, the Music Preservation Society in Florence began hosting an annual music festival in Handy's honor, which features blues music among other wide-ranging musical styles. Because it labels blues music as a colorful piece of the "new blues tourism" that encourages community leaders to "sanitize" and "repackage" a community in order to attract tourists to the area, a historic music festival, like the Handy Festival, may be an obvious indication that drink house music is part of a vanishing lifestyle.[6]

In Florence at least, the music culture of the illegal drink house has been cleaned up, contained, and legalized.[7] Singing, dancing, and even drinking are no longer a secret, Saturday-night taboo. Celebrated as part of a quaint historical past, music and liquor laws mark a cultural crossroads of racial interaction that left stories in its wake if not a sincerely integrated party. The stories typically involve the constant search for the good times, a hooch run to the wet counties just over the Tennessee state line, and a return to the party house, where both the bootleg and the musical instruments would be brought out and celebrated. One of the elements that make Shoals-area stories unique is the addition of the studio influence, which by the early 1970s had become a recognized part of the area folklore.

Max D. Russell: House-Party Blues

Max Russell plays bottleneck blues in the old Delta style on his National metal-body guitar. He has two CDs of original music: The Boys Got Rhythm *and* Alabama Moon. *In 2006, Max entered and won the solo division of the Magic City Blues Society competition and went on to perform in the Blues Foundation's International Blues Challenge in Memphis. This is the contemporary direction of music in the area. Musicians play in competitions, at festivals, and in legal bars where the liquor sold to patrons is also legal. However, Russell still remembers what it was like to play music in the Shoals in a time when liquor was forbidden and a white boy jamming with black boys was frowned upon. I interviewed Max at a music store in Florence on July 7, 2007.*

5.3. Max Russell. Courtesy Emily Edwards.

"I've been playing music longer than Florence has been wet. I played at some of those house parties myself over on the west side in the drink houses. I was usually the only white guy in the band—we used to have fish fries and stuff and have a big time in the garage of a house—a guy's house—we'd be in there jamming and there'd be maybe a hundred people dancing around on the street by that garage. Bunch of people. We'd have some cool parties over there. Those places are dangerous now. I wouldn't go over there nowadays. It's a bunch of crackheads and stuff and there's a lot less tolerance for white guys. That goes for musicians, too. I don't think they even play live music over there anymore. I don't know. But back in the day, if you knew somebody, it didn't matter if you were white. You were welcome if you played the music. You could get in and have a good time. Musicians just played at those for free—you didn't get paid. You played just to be playing. There weren't tips. I played in Memphis on the streets for tips. But there usually weren't any tips at the house parties. It was just fun. Lots of really good musicians just played to be playing.

"That area right over there—now it's an antique mall—it was a juke joint back in the 1940s and big entertainers like Duke Ellington played there. I don't know how many places there were around here, but I've heard there were a fair few that would get busted by the law for liquor because it was all illegal. The whole area was dry—Lauderdale County is still dry but the city of Florence went wet. . . . Franklin County and the Russellville area are still dry. But some of the other cities went wet and Colbert County is wet now. When that happened, the bars popped up all over but these were mostly top forty and country music bars. The old juke joints and drink houses just disappeared. There's never been a legal bar that catered strictly to blues or jazz music in this area, but that's what was playing in the drink houses . . . all those bars where they played blues were the illegal ones. There's another place right up the street that my old next-door neighbor used to tell me about that was a honky-tonk, which was mainly country music, I guess. But even at the old drink houses we played all kinds of music: blues, country, and rock. Whatever was popular. Whatever people wanted to hear."

There were places around the Shoals area where African American talent came to perform in the '40s and '50s. Max explains that one of these places was the stockyards. But after the studios developed, African American talent also came here to record.

"Florence, Alabama, is a studio city. Back in the day everybody was recording here. You had FAME, Muscle Shoals Sound, Widget, Wishbone—but the main recording studios were FAME and Muscle Shoals Sound. Everybody came here to record because it was private—like the Stones could hang out at the pool by the hotel and nobody would bother them, because nobody knew who they were. Maybe the ones who did know didn't care. So, there was the privacy thing. But the main reason why those famous musicians came here was because of the local musicians, the house band for Muscle Shoals Sound—the Swampers. There were artists who came in—black artists—who came in thinking they were going to have a black band backing them up and when the Swampers came out and they were a bunch of white boys, the black musicians didn't know what to think. But the Swampers were putting the music down the way they wanted to hear it. That's what got a lot of artists here: Pete Carr [lead guitar], David Hood [bass], Jimmy Johnson [guitar], Roger Hawkins [drums], Barry Beckett [keyboard], and the horn sections. Bob Dylan, the Stones, Allman Brothers—lot of big sounds came from the Muscle Shoals area.

"Over in Florence by the stockyard they used to bring in music. Mostly black musicians played there. George "Wild Child" Butler[8] played there. Mr. Graham, who owned a piano store in Florence, talked about going over there to hear the music. He talked about going over to the stockyard to hear Muddy Waters and B. B. King play. There was a lot of music around here in different places before '81, but no legal bars. If you wanted to drink legal, you had to drive to Tennessee. If you didn't care about being legal, you could help yourself at a bootlegger's or at a party house. . . .

"I am one of the few Shoals-area bluesmen still around—born and raised in Colbert County—just down the road apiece. I live here now. I play the blues. . . . When I was a kid my dad used to sing parts of songs he knew as a boy. I remembered hearing dad singing bits of songs his mom and dad sang to him. His mom and dad were sharecroppers from Tupelo—they sharecropped right along with black people—in the different farms where they were living. Then my grandparents moved to Alabama in a wagon with all fourteen kids. My dad's mom sang him songs that she learned from black people they sharecropped with. He kept saying to me after I was playing guitar—'learn that song I've always liked—learn to play that D-fellom blues.' I couldn't understand what he was talking about. D-fellom? What was that? Finally, I learned that he meant 'Deep Ellum Blues.'[9] My dad wasn't remembering the name right. So I learned the song and played it for him. I guess I turned my dad on to the blues after he turned me on to it. But he turned me on to this music without even knowing it was the blues. It was just music he liked. . . .

"I met Johnny Shines[10] one time and played him a couple licks on the guitar. Johnny played the slide guitar. He'd played a show out here at the "Hall of Fame" during the Handy Festival back in 1990 or '91. He's from over in Tuscaloosa but toured everywhere—all over the world. Johnny made the comment after hearing me play once, he told me, 'I used to play like that before the stroke fucked me up.' Johnny Shines had a stroke and he barely could play anymore. . . . But getting to meet him before he passed lit a fire under my butt. I was still pretty young then. The real bluesmen are all but gone. To be a real bluesman, you had to have lived the life, paid the dues, and then be able to sing about it with firsthand knowledge—be able to tell the stories. . . . I'm proud to be a bluesman from around here, because whether it's blues or country or rock, it's all good music. It was good music in the joints. It was good music in the studios. And liquored up or sobered up, it's still good music."

David Johnson: Eight Studios in a Dry County

When I interviewed David Johnson by telephone in 2007, he was the executive director of the Alabama Music Hall of Fame, a position he had to leave in 2010. The state had steadily cut funding to the museum, which was unable to operate on admission fees alone. In addition to being a museum curator for twenty years, Johnson had a long history in the studio-music scene in the Shoals. His experience was that music became a cultural crossroads, where southern musicians were color-blind.

"In the '60s there were eight music studios working in a dry county. We had a strong work ethic. There were no union people sitting in on a session. We wanted to work. But musicians did like to unwind afterwards with a drink. You don't want to tell a hard-working musician that he can't have a beer when the session's over. We could get liquor brought to the studio cheaper than trying to go somewhere. Of course, there weren't any legal bars around at that time. Sometimes we did go out to eat after a session. But it was the 1960s and it was Alabama. Music people never thought about racial difference that much. We had a great session, we wanted to celebrate, and we went on out to eat. I remember one time when we went out together and wouldn't get served. Forty-five minutes go by and nobody was waiting on our table. It took a black musician to finally explain why the tension was there. There was just a whole different mind-set among the musicians. We were way beyond thinking about race. We were thinking about the music.

"After Martin Luther King was killed and disco came along, it just killed the mood of the country. We suffered a serious setback after that."

George Lair: Muscle Shoals Sound and the Line

George Lair is a graduate of Florence State University. Now retired, he was formerly the manager of Southern Sound Records in Muscle Shoals and a former assistant to Jimmy Johnson at Muscle Shoals Sound Studios in Sheffield. He also spent nearly ten years doing research, conducting tours, and managing exhibits as a curator at the Alabama Music Hall of Fame. He remembers very clearly how wet a dry southern county could be in the 1970s.

"You were able to buy liquor at any time, any hour of the day or night, and regardless of age, because there were numerous bootleggers who stocked liquor and beer and things like that. Gosh, they were just everywhere. I can think of probably ten places just right off the top of my head that you could go at that time. Of course they're all gone now. Back then though, some of them were quite creative in that they even had drive-up windows, much like the drive-up windows now that you have at pharmacies and whatever, with a little drawer that would come out and you'd put your money in there and they'd pull it back. Then they would put in what you were getting and then push it back out to you. The prices were pretty high, but of course they were taking a risk, and it was very convenient to not have to drive out of town. Although, there was a steady stream of people who would travel the twenty miles or so up to the state line, and while there were no towns at the state line in Tennessee, there were numerous places to buy beer as well as drink houses and dance halls. I think there's maybe only one that still has music up there. It all just dried up once Florence went wet. After that happened, there was no need to drive up to Tennessee anymore.

"Those old dance halls and drink houses were just concrete block buildings, real simple and cavernous inside. You had a dance floor and tables and everything. They'd usually have a number of pool tables and maybe a shuffleboard table and an area for a band to set up.

"I didn't drink alcohol for a long time back in college unless it was wine and we drank that horrible Boone's Farm and Chianti and stuff like that. There was almost this association of beer and liquor with rednecks. During that early hippie period in the 1970s, I think several of us fell into that attitude that beer was for rednecks and we didn't care to be associated with rednecks, with that kind of bigotry and hostility. Plus there was a danger element involved up at the state line, because there were so many rednecks up there and—at least for the guys with long hair—you ran the risk of being beaten up pretty severely. One guy I knew was taken out back of this bar and rednecks cut his hair off. He was beaten and his hair was cut off. That happened at the Black Cat Lounge. Those places at the line had names like: the Dog House, the Black Cat Lounge, and Johnny's Place—names like that.

"In addition to those places at the state line, Natchez Trace Parkway is nearby. It's like another mile from where you could go up Cloverdale Road and buy your liquor. Then you go on up to a little roadside park there on the Natchez Trace, and a lot of us would gather up there and build a bonfire and sit around and drink, talk, sometimes play music. In fact, I even remember there was a fellow who was nicknamed "Trace" because he was always up there. That was more of what the hippies would do to stay clear of rednecks. Generally, it would just be that you would go and buy your beer or whatever and then ride around, go to someone's house or a park and avoid all those old bars at the state line.

"I know that there were some shot houses along what is now called Dr. Hicks Boulevard in Florence, but I never went to those. There were also several black bootleggers that I went to as well as white bootleggers in Florence. I remember there was one that was over near the hospital, [Helen] Keller Hospital, and you'd pull up there. It was just a real shack of a place. You'd go knock on the door. She'd invite you to come in. I remember, I went in this one time and there was a couple having sex right there on the couch in the living room. On the wooden floor there was a baby with a butcher knife. That baby was just in diapers and it was just stabbing away at the floor with this butcher knife. Then you walked on past all of that and go back to the old kitchen where she had her beer. She had a big freezer back there that she would keep the beer in and you'd pay her and she'd give you the beer. There might be some foodstuff on the beer cans. When you'd pay her, she kept her money in her bosom. She was a big-bosomed woman, and she'd reach down in there and bring out change or just put her money in there if you gave her correct change. That was always a colorful place to go to.

"For a long time people around the Shoals area had to entertain themselves and music is a great way to do that. I know that my grandfather played the banjo. He lived out in Freedom Hills, and they would have house parties out there. There'd be a fiddler and a guitar player, my granddaddy on banjo, and stuff like that. We'd just gather at somebody's house and move out all the furniture and dance. Even before that, it just seems like that kind of music party has always gone on around here. People congregated more with one another back then. In fact, I think it was almost a good thing that the county was dry for a period of time, because it forced people to socialize in one another's homes as opposed to going to some bar, where you don't get as close to people. I've always thought that that was a good thing, for me anyway, to interact with people in that way rather than in a bar. When you go into someone's home and see all of the trappings of his life, it's more personal. When I went out west, just about everybody would always go to a bar if you were going out to party. I kind of missed the house parties. Usually, at a house party, you're going to have people that you know in there. You're not going to invite a bunch of rednecks to a place with hippies and black kids, you know. The hippies and black kids were always okay together, but mix in the redneck element and you're going to have trouble.

"When I graduated from school, I hitchhiked out west and I stayed out there until 1979 and then I decided to come back home. When I came back to Florence, Diane Butler [director of publishing at Muscle Shoals Sound Studios] helped me get the job as Jimmy Johnson's personal assistant. I also knew Dick Cooper, who was working out there as Barry Beckett's assistant. That's how I got involved in the music business, working at Muscle Shoals Sound. I would work sometimes a hundred hours a week. It was very exciting to be around all those creative people. I got to meet all kinds of people: Levon Helm and the Amazing Rhythm Aces and Oakridge Boys, Lionel Richie. . . .

"When Jimmy Buffett came to town, he brought a lot of his band with him. He took all the plants that were in the front lobby of the studio there and brought them back into the recording area and set up a bar and made it like a little tropical club back there, an in-house bar. This was before Florence went wet.

George said that generally employees of the studio made the "hooch run" for musicians, but sometimes musicians requested to ride along, curious to witness firsthand this throwback to prohibition and seeing it as a kind of weird escapade.

"Having to haul your liquor was not the sort of thing people did in the rest of the world, so they saw it as an adventure.... Some musicians would be real businesslike when they were recording but others needed—well, I remember Chris Hillman and Roger McGuinn from the Byrds, when they came in to do an album, they brought their roller skates, and they would roller-skate inside the building. This was the building that was the old Naval Reserve down by the river. At that time, by the time I started working with them, they had moved the studio from Jackson Highway to down there by the river. Roller-skating was just something the musicians did to break the monotony of being in the studio, because frequently—well, different people would operate differently. Some people wouldn't come in the studio until late in the day, and then they would end up staying late into the night. Others would come in earlier and go home earlier, you know how different people have different hours when they feel more creative.

"Most of the people that came through the studio there were super-nice folks. They kept some video games in there and pool tables and there was a kitchen and I frequently would make food. Jimmy Johnson would just keep me around if there was a session going on. He might have me go out and get hamburger meat and fix burgers at midnight or something like that. I never knew what was going to go on there. I would go and pick people up at the airport. Once I picked up George Martin,[11] the fellow who produced the Beatles, at the Muscle Shoals airport. On the way back to the studio I was telling him all about the history of the area. That's usually what I would do for small talk. I would drive folks to the studio and tell them about TVA [the Tennessee Valley Authority] and the cotton fields and stuff like that. So when I get George Martin back to the studio, everybody is coming up to me asking, 'What's he like? What did y'all talk about?' Well, I didn't know who the guy was, so it was just easy for me to be real casual with him. Knowing who he was and his importance to the music industry might have changed what I said to him a little bit. But one thing you had to get over real quick working at the studio was any kind of hero worship. You just had to be yourself with folks.

"There are a lot of little stories from Muscle Shoals Sound when I was working there, like when Levon Helm was in town at the same time that Jimmy Buffett was. It was one of my duties to take Levon out to eat every day, and so we'd go to various places. The studio had a guesthouse overlooking the Tennessee River where the bands would stay. It was a huge sprawling place with lots of bedrooms. Jimmy Buffett was all set up to stay there at the guesthouse with all of his band. Levon and I went over there one evening after dinner and we walked into the den or living room, whatever it was, and everybody was laying around on the floor watching *Coal Miner's Daughter*[12] and they are watching a scene with Levon [who played the role of Loretta Lynn's father] and there is Levon Helm standing right next to me!

"One story I've got to tell you is about when Colbert County finally went wet in 1981. The very first store that opened up was over on the corner of Fifth Street and Waters Street in Tuscumbia, and the girl that I was dating at the time, Kim Belew, was maybe seventeen or eighteen years old. Kim had stayed out partying all night with this punk-rock band, but she got over there and got in line to buy her liquor. There was a huge line of people waiting to get in there and buy liquor on that first day once it went wet, but Kim had contacted the person working behind the counter and got him to go get a bottle of George Dickel whiskey and have it waiting at the counter for her, right up there at the register, so that when she went in, she went directly to the register and paid for it. That was how Kim bought the first bottle of legal liquor in Colbert County—and she was underage. Eighteen years old.[13] The television news crews were there. They didn't interview her, but you could clearly see her up front buying her liquor. Word got around that she had bought the very first bottle. I always thought it was funny that the first legal bottle of liquor sold in Colbert County was sold illegally because she was underage. She said that her grandmother couldn't go to the hairdresser for weeks after that because of the stir that it created and the embarrassment of it all."

R. Wayne Good: Hot Pursuit

R. Wayne Good, now a resident of Huntsville, Alabama, was a graduate of Florence State University (now the University of North Alabama). A retired photographer in 2007, he recalled what it was like growing up in the Shoals area and watching people on a hooch run drive to the "beer garden" destination in Tennessee.

"I attended elementary school at Wilson on the Chisholm Road in the early sixties. I recall that Chisholm Road is the way to Zip City and even further north, the state line and the beer joints and beer sales. Just over the Tennessee state line there were several bars that sometimes had live music but some of the bars just played country songs over a sound system. People would drive up there, drink a few, dance a little, and pick up some beer at a package store before heading home. People had to drive straight, slow, and careful on the way home because the Alabama Highway Patrol kept that stretch of road hot, chasing suspected beer haulers. No need for reasonable cause to stop someone back in those days. As kids we still looked up to 'the man' [police] . . . sometimes they would stop and talk to us at the school, which was maybe a hundred yards off the road. The troopers were there, watching the passing cars go by. Any car with a low rear end was suspect of carrying illicit loads and that would result in hot pursuit. There was more than one hot pursuit on Chisholm Road. One of my dad's good friends got his head severed on a late-night return trip on Highway 43 coming from St. Joe and the beer gardens. The crash took his head right off his body. That occurred over by Brush Creek.

"Living in the county there were still moonshiners out around Goose Shoals. They would always ask unknown adults if they were the law. If you were the law you would probably be killed. But if you weren't the law, the moonshiners would offer up a swig of white lightning, and then chase it with water. That was a rowdy bunch. My family and cousins did not drink, so I was never exposed to it much until I went to college down in Florence [in the 1970s]. It was all still dry. Hopped-up college kids looking for a wild night might find some liquor in Tennessee, unless they knew where to look for the house party in Alabama. You had to have a friend who knew somebody who was throwing the house party or you had to know which bait shop sold bootleg down by the river."

Steve Kelly: The Garage Band

Steve Kelly is the director of an independent production company called K2 Productions in Golden, Colorado, and is a graduate of the University of North Alabama. Steve ran a singing-telegram company for years, delivering more than 6,000 singing telegrams, even interrupting state senate proceedings in two different states. In the 1970s, Steve held several small jobs to pay his way through college. Although he was drafted and the GI

5.4. Steve Kelly. Courtesy Kate Kelly.

bill paid for classes when he returned from the army, Steve continued to take small part-time jobs, one of which opened an interesting garage door.

"I always had three, four, sometimes five small jobs. One of the jobs I had when I came back from the army was in the university cafeteria. I got a meal, either lunch or dinner, from the cafeteria for standing behind that window where you always put your trays. Grabbing those trays and sliding them into the sink, rinsing them off, and sticking them in the dishwasher that was an automatic dishwasher, I got a meal just for doing that. When I was doing the cafeteria job, I met a young black guy, a guitar player, who also worked in the cafeteria. I want to say his name was Jimmy, but I cannot think of his name right now at all. We talked and did all kinds of stuff to pass the time. We talked about a lot of stuff. When it finally came up, that yeah, I played guitar, he says to me, 'We have a garage band. You should come over and play with us some night.' He played bass guitar.

"I said, 'Yeah, heck yeah. When are you all playing? I'll come over and jam with you.' That was kind of the regular thing people did in Florence—jam. So we set it up for me to go over and play with them. When

I got over there, he introduced me around to all the guys that were playing. I was going to be jamming with my friend and several other guys, all black, and they had a garage door that opened right up onto the sidewalk. When you opened the garage door, you were standing on the sidewalk. It was a true garage band because that's where everything was set up.

"One of the guys who played keyboards was an old guy. He was already an old man at that time and his name was Pop Wright.[14] He wrote the song "When a Man Loves a Woman," and had made some money off of it. I played with those guys for hours just following these guys the best I could and doing some backup vocals and stuff like that. One of the other guys that was playing and doing backup vocals said that he was a member of the Pips. You know the group Gladys Knight and the Pips? They could have been razzing the white guy for all I know, but I didn't get that feeling. I thought everything they told me was true. Pop Wright was clearly who he said he was. This happened on the same block that W. C. Handy's house was on, which is interesting. That was a big deal for me because I played guitar. I wasn't a super guitar player. I played okay, I guess, well enough to keep up with them. I always sang and they liked my voice. I could harmonize with what they did."

Steve said everyone in Florence knew they were living in a studio town, but sometimes it was hard to believe the level of national and international musicians you might run into just doing normal things. When people told you Cher, Paul Simon, or another international star was in town, the tendency was to react with skepticism, even though you knew it was a possibility. Steve said he missed his chance to meet the Rolling Stones in 1970 because it was hard to believe that it would be as simple as going over to the local Holiday Inn to see them.

"I'm in the dorm, living in the dorm, and it's my first semester as a freshman. . . . Jeff Brennan was another student living in the dorm, too. He was really into photography at the time. He had a nice Nikon camera. One time when some of us had a card game going on, Jeff Brennan comes by the door, leans in, and he says, 'Hey, you guys want to go with me? I just heard the Rolling Stones are down at the Holiday Inn.'

"And we say to him, real sarcastically, 'Sure, they are. Sure. Why don't you go and bring them back to visit? We'll deal them in.'

"We just thought that was the most ridiculous thing we ever heard of, the Stones in Florence. He came back a couple hours later and he says, 'See these rolls right here?' And he holds up a fist full of film rolls. 'This is six rolls of the Rolling Stones. Yeah, they were really there and—yup—they had been doing . . .'—well, he tells us all these things that the Rolling Stones were doing and how he had gotten a bunch of shots of them. Sure enough, when he got the film developed, he had six rolls of the Rolling Stones at the Holiday Inn."

"There was another time when I went to the Corner Fruit to get a sandwich at maybe about two o'clock in the morning. I walked in and there was Rod Stewart,[15] also at the Corner Fruit buying stuff. It was just one of those things; I went down to get a bologna sandwich and there he was. The Corner Fruit was about the only place open all night where you could buy something to eat."

Steve described the house parties of liberal white college students as a combination of dry town, free thinking, a surplus of musicians ready to jam, and a drug culture experimenting with the "doors of perception." These parties were rarely about raising the rent money in the manner of some black house parties, so there was seldom a cover charge. People arrived on the doorstep and chipped in with beer, drugs, liquor, or music. A part of southern culture that the hippies had not turned their backs on was southern hospitality, even though this put a strain on the host whose house had become the designated "party house." The next day might be a full afternoon of really messy chores if the party had been an especially good one.

"In Florence at that time there were several different houses and these were the places that were the gathering spots. People knew which houses they were. We had one on Hawthorne Avenue where people dropped by to party and then there was another one on Wood Avenue. There was also the Tippers' house there, right close to us on Hawthorne. It wasn't too far. . . . That house became a party spot. The apartment had a little balcony, and they put a couch out on it. We used to go there and just sit, talk, and watch traffic go by all the time. There were a bunch of houses that were well known as the social gathering spots. The people who came here were the people that were into—and of course this is a much-dated term here—these people belonged to the hippie community. At the time, 'hippie' was not a phrase or a term that we denied and, in fact, maybe we even gloried in it a little bit. We were definitely the longhairs on campus. We also felt like we were the intelligentsia on campus. We were the smart guys and we were the freedom guys, the civil rights guys, the art and music guys, and the guys that thought about more than football and drinking beer. Of course, there was a big drug scene going on during that time, too. It wasn't just alcohol. A lot of the hippie crowd was doing mescaline and acid. I did not smoke at the time but everybody else, or it *seemed* like everybody else, was smoking pot. No prejudice stuff was going on, that's for sure. There was a black guy that regularly hung around there with us who was also in school and some other black guys that came around to party. As for music, I played the guitar a lot at the time. I played the guitar and I played the harmonica and drums. I remember jamming. Just about any time that there was a couple of guitars around, they got busted out and played and a lot of different people made music together."

Blane Edwards: The Hooch Run

Blane Edwards was still a college student at the University of North Alabama in 1979 when he got a job running the stage lights at Mr. C's Dinner Theater on Woodward Avenue in Muscle Shoals. The idea for the dinner theater was to provide an extra gig for musicians who were in the area to record at one of the studios. Blane tells this story about going on a hooch run to keep musicians happy backstage.

"The dinner theater was built by a local guy named Curtis Cameron, and a lot of famous musicians played there. It was Mr. C's Dinner Theater. People like George Jones[16] and Jerry Lee Lewis[17] performed there. Bands like Alabama and groups like the Tams[18] played there. One of my friends was working at Mr. C's and so Mr. Cameron hired me to run the stage lights. They had regular theater lights—Fresnels, scoops, and spotlights—so you could put on a real show. The idea for the dinner theater was that you would come in and pay your twenty-five dollars—or whatever it was—and line up for a buffet. You would get your plate, get your food, and then go sit at one of the tables in front of the stage, where you would eat your dinner and a famous musical act like Percy Sledge or George Jones would entertain you. A lot of these headliners that were in town because of the studios would be hired to come down to the dinner theater to perform.

"This one time they gave me the additional job of driving up to the state line to buy beer for the Drifters,[19] because they had requested that there be some beer backstage for them. Muscle Shoals was still dry at that time. So I drove the Pinto up to the line to get beer. I didn't get any hazard pay for doing this and I didn't have any trouble with the law. I just drove up there, bought the beer, and came on back. Actually, as a college student, I felt honored to be doing the hooch run for famous recording artists. The show must go on and if beer made the show better, then I was glad to go get the beer. I was happy to do it.

"The only problem I ever had wasn't because of bootlegging beer for musicians but because of running the lights. When George Jones came to Mr. C's to put on a show, his manager fussed at me afterward because I had used a follow spot, which I thought made George Jones look really good but apparently he didn't like it.

"The dinner theater didn't last very long. Local people came out there to eat when there were the nationally known big names performing, but a lot of times there weren't many people in the audience, especially for lesser-known acts. Maybe it wasn't advertised enough. The dinner theater was going down. I was laid off after a few months and it wasn't long after that when the dinner theater closed for good. I guess they just couldn't get a big enough audience to make it profitable."

◆ ◆ ◆

When national ideological changes were finally noticed in Florence, they had already shifted enough for Colbert County to vote wet (1981) and for the city of Florence to vote wet (1981), even though Lauderdale County remained dry. Florence also established a music preservation society along with the W. C. Handy Festival in 1982. Even though these changes seemed to usher in new times, the area perhaps still adhered to respectful and nostalgic images of race relations. People talking about the 1960s in the Muscle Shoals area recall the shock of seeing race riots televised from Birmingham, Alabama, just a couple of hours drive south and east. The bombing of the Sixteenth Street Baptist Church in Birmingham in 1963 would have been unthinkable at the same time period in Florence, where Rick Hall was already recording black artists like Jimmy Hughes singing "I'm Qualified." This isn't to say that Florence was immune to racism, but overt racism was impolite and bombing a church was un-Christian. (This was a disgrace I can remember hearing whispered about in Sunday school. It would be beyond hypocrisy to lead Sunday school class in a rendition of "Jesus Loves the Little Children" but pardon the murder of little girls.)

Like much of the South, the Shoals area had its passionate religious activists campaigning for prohibition. The crusade against alcohol could be particularly paternalistic toward black citizens, for the fear was that alcohol could make a black man especially crazy and violent. Still, it was no secret that much of the black and white populations took periodic hooch runs, whether it was to restock private stores, supply the party house, provide for the country club, or resell to the public at large. In Florence, however, liquor problems, civil rights issues, and the drugs of a defiant youth culture were just not part of polite conversation. As the '80s progressed, there was less reason for white citizens to go to the black bootlegger or to the black garage band to jam. The hippie culture, where courageous black students had come to party with the white kids, had faded. The infamous party house on Wood Avenue was demolished and other notorious "party houses" were reclaimed for different tenants once the students had graduated and scattered. Music that once seemed so innovative and dangerous during the 1970s had become safely celebrated and controlled.

In the Muscle Shoals area, there was politeness about racial issues, uneasy pride in the music, and an "under-the-rug" attitude about alcohol that did not like to see grandmothers embarrassed at the hairdressers.

CHAPTER 6

Juke Joints, Bootleg, and Moonshine

Whether they were in Alabama, Florida, Texas, Georgia, South Carolina, Louisiana, Mississippi, or Tennessee, many of the stories had consistent themes: liquor, live music, sometimes drugs, and sometimes violence. Some storytellers included motel lounge stories because *certain* motel lounges and *certain* drink houses have a similar vibe. Mississippi was the last of the southern states to repeal prohibition in 1966; however, many of the cities and counties in the state remained dry. As of 2015, a good part of the state is still dry, but juke joints have become destinations for people seeking the authentic drink house experience.

Bill Moore: A Mississippi Juke Joint

A few years after he had seen R. L. Burnside[1] play at the Fifth Annual Carolina Blues Festival in 1991 and had been "taken" by Burnside's performance, schoolteacher and bass player Bill Moore had an opportunity to go with his wife on a blues odyssey to northeastern Mississippi to try to find some of the artists from Fat Possum Records. A relative was looking after their two small daughters, so Bill and his wife at the time, Liz Seymour, began their journey, which would lead them to Junior's Place in Chulahoma, Mississippi, the juke joint of David "Junior" Kimbrough.[2] Junior's drink house burned down in April 2000, two years after Junior Kimbrough passed away and about nine years after Bill made his journey.[3] Bill told this story on June 4, 2014.

"We had a Toyota van in those days. So, I talked to somebody who was in the Blues Society and said I wanted to go see R. L. Burnside in

6.1. Bill Moore. Courtesy Doug Mokaren.

Mississippi. They said he's in Holly Springs in northeast Mississippi, and the way you catch up with musicians in Holly Springs is you go see the African American pharmacist on the black side of town, because the pharmacist, John Freeman, knew all about the blues in the area. . . . It wasn't until Sunday that we made it to Holly Springs. We went to the African American side of town and found the pharmacy that had been described to us without too much hope that anybody would be there at midday on a Sunday. I knocked on the back door of Freeman's, next to the Kentucky Fried Chicken on the east edge of town. No answer.

"We were about to leave when a car pulled up. It was Freeman, a tall black man in a pharmacist's V-neck tunic and suit pants. We told him our mission and he said, 'Sure, that's not hard. Let me do a few things here and I'll carry you over to see Junior Kimbrough.' We waited in the pharmacy while he finished up some business he needed to do on a Sunday. Then he conducted us over to meet Junior Kimbrough at a housing complex that looked a little run down. It was an apartment complex with lots and lots of small units. It was all African American and there were a lot of kids playing. This was in Holly Springs just a little outside of downtown. So he led us there; we followed his car. Sure enough, Junior Kimbrough was hanging out, sitting on the back of a car with some of his buddies, smoking cigarettes. He looked at me like, 'Who's this white guy and his white wife?'

"But the pharmacist introduced us: 'This is Bill Moore and his wife, Liz. They've come to visit with you and hear some blues if possible. Does that sound okay?'

"Kimbrough looked me over and said, 'I guess that's okay.' So we hung out for a little while. He said, 'Do you want to come to my juke joint tonight?' I said yes, indeed, I sure did want to see his juke joint. He told me where to go and I wrote it down. It was out in the country, outside of Holly Springs. . . .

"Before we went to the juke joint, Mr. Freeman showed us out to R. L. Burnside's house. We didn't call ahead or anything. I don't even know if there was a phone there. We drove down some country roads . . . went past the general store, took another right, and came up a side street. Then we pulled into a little dirt track and there was a really decrepit white house with a couple of big trees hovering over it. I think there were windows smashed. I don't mean to put down the guy's living arrangements but he was very poor even though he was a great bluesman. . . . They didn't want me inside the house, which was crowded and decrepit, but there was an oak plank set up outside under some trees. So 'Rule,' as his friends called him, came out to visit with us there. I had heard that the custom was that when you visit with a bluesman and you want to talk with them and maybe ask them about their music or hear their music, the custom was to offer to go for groceries. So I remembered that and said, 'R. L., can we get anything at the grocery store?'

"He said, 'Sure, that would be great. Let's go get some beer.'

"So he jumped in the car with me and we went back to the general store, picked up beer and snacks. We bought some very cheap beer that they drink a lot of in Mississippi. The preferred beer was the cheapest beer. We brought it back, cracked open a couple of cans, and sat on the plank. We got to talking and I asked him how he developed his style and how much he used slide. He had a guitar out there and he pulled a penknife out of his pocket, a jackknife. He played slide guitar with the back side of a jackknife. He was plucking with his hand and moving that knife up and down to make the chords and notes while he sang. Here is this guy so full of energy. And witty. And deep. Some of his blues were very deep but other songs were funny. . . .

"We proceeded in the late afternoon, sun still blazing hot, out to Junior Kimbrough's juke joint. There weren't too many people. It wasn't dark yet, but Junior Kimbrough was already there. The juke joint was really a very interesting place. I don't remember much about the outside of it except it was pretty much a big shack that sat back from the road. Maybe a dozen cars had pulled up on the grass and gravel. Men and women stood by the cars or under the jutting front roof of the juke joint, trying to ignore the heat. Once I went inside, it was hot as hell. It was a Mississippi July day . . . and there was no air conditioning. None. I don't remember if there were any fans. I don't think so. So everybody was sweating and starting to drink cold beer. Three-quarters of the way to the back of the place there was a jukebox and a cooler. Somebody stood by it and you could give the guy a couple of bucks and get a beer or something. . . . But what was really cool was that there were booths on the sides around the dance floor. And in each booth area against the wall there were folk art pieces of African American heroes with glitter added to the paints. Martin Luther King was there in one of the booths and a Jimi Hendrix portrait, I think, was there with glitter on it. They were all fabulous, so ornate and so gorgeous . . . but the outside of the juke joint was pretty dilapidated, as I recall.

"Anyway, I sat there and it was getting later. It was more like six o'clock by then. The drummer had showed up and Junior was there. I can't remember if there was another musician but they were waiting on a bass player. So I asked him, 'When do you think your band might be playing?" I told him we wanted to get to Clarksdale later on that night. And he said, 'I don't know when we'll play. The bass player is missing.'

"I paused for a minute, and then I said, 'I play a little bit of bass.'

"He said, 'Do you know my songs?'

"I told him that I didn't know them directly but I could try to follow him. He pondered over that. He had a way of looking . . . and he fixed me with his eyes again like he did in the parking lot before when I first came up to meet him.

"Finally, he said, 'Okay, let's try this.'

"So I got to sit in with his band. I got in a position where I could watch his hands. He did not make changes like white boys do, regular changes like rock and rollers do. He might stretch out some of his singing and keep on the same chord for seven bars, not four, not eight. So you just had to stay alert and see how he was moving. It was terrific fun. He had a bass amp and a bass guitar there and I hung with him for about an hour. It was just a real transcendental experience. One of R. L. Burnside's sons was the drummer. So I played and enjoyed the hell out of it. And then the bass player did finally show up. Liz and I drank some beer and danced when they started up the next set. . . . We excused ourselves at maybe eight or nine o'clock at night because we had to get on to Clarksdale. It was pretty dark by that point. The front and back doors were open and it had gotten a little bit cooler inside the place, but not too much. It was still plenty hot.

"So we drove across to Clarksdale in the middle of the night with the bugs slapping against the front windshield of the car. They have some big bugs in Mississippi. We're driving along in the dark and we turn off the lights so we can see the stars. It gets really dark at night in rural Mississippi. We're driving across the state northeast to northwest and eventually we found a motel. . . .

"I saw R. L. Burnside again sometime later when I went back to Mississippi on my own. He was living in a different place by then and this time he invited me to come inside. The living room was in the front. There were still lots and lots of people around but they were in the back or somewhere else. So there weren't too many people in the room with us. . . . I noticed he was holding onto a Kaopectate[4] bottle. I said, 'R. L. are you okay? What are you doing with that bottle?'

"He held it out to me and said, 'Have some.'

"I said, 'What do you mean? I feel okay. I don't need any Kaopectate.' He said, 'Smell that.'

"Ooh! Liquor! In the Kaopectate bottle was white lightning. And he was sipping on that. He drank a lot. Every time I've seen him, he was probably drunk. He was probably drunk when he was performing at the blues festival in Greensboro. He was one of those semi-functioning, high-functioning at times, alcoholics. I guess life is pretty tough down in Mississippi. I don't know how people get started drinking so much but he seemed to be a pretty heavy drinker. I don't think Junior Kimbrough drank nearly as much as R. L. Burnside did."

Joe Bill Loudermilk: Guns in a Motel Lounge

Joe Bill Loudermilk is a guitar player from Florida who says he cut his teeth playing with musicians in black drink houses but later played gigs in all types of bars, topless clubs, and lounges in Tampa. He spent most of his musical career in the South until he moved to New York City, where he became a songwriter for Leeds Publishing. He was also a studio musician and a singer-guitarist for the Ray Bloch Orchestra and the Peter Duchin Orchestra, but he also had his own band, Joe Bill and Grits. He said some more quirky bars were associated with motels or even bowling alleys. I talked with Joe Bill on June 23, 2014.

"There was this one time I was playing with my band in a motel lounge. I won't tell you the name of that motel. The lounge area had a little stage, a bar, and tables. It was near the area where the motel's front-desk clerk checks people in and out. Anyway, while we were doing our set, somebody comes in and shoots the desk clerk in the face. Kills him. Our music was loud enough that we didn't even know about it until afterward. We never even heard the shots.

"Another time we were playing in a very nice club in Sarasota, Florida. It sounds funny now, but it was in a bowling lanes. That was pretty big in those days because you had a ready-made audience. After the crowd finished bowling, they'd stay to drink and listen to you play. This particular club in the bowling lanes was *very* small and I had a four-piece band: me on guitar and vocals, a bass player and vocals, a drummer with a full set, and an electric keyboard and vocals. Add to that three amplifiers and three microphone stands and the fact that I was five foot eight and 165 pounds. My drummer was six feet and 185 pounds. The bass player was six foot two and 310 pounds. I'm not kidding; we are some big guys. To make it even worse, the keyboard player was six foot six and 200 pounds. You can't make this stuff up! We were with all our gear on a stage that was ten feet wide and six feet deep, with a small utility closet on each side of the stage door, facing inside the stage. It was tight.

"So, the dance floor was packed that night and there was a man and a woman dancing right in front of us, right next to the stage. Evidently, it was a wife skipping around, because a short time after we notice them,

6.2. Joe Bill Loudermilk. Courtesy Doug Mokaren.

Hubby comes into the club looking for her. Hubby sees her and comes right down to the front of the bandstand, turns his back to us, and rips her out of the other guy's arms. I can see from the bandstand that Hubby has a .38 Colt revolver in his back pocket. About then our *brilliant* drummer yells at the top of his lungs, 'He's got a gun!'

"So now everybody in the room is trying to get out of that place. When Hubby hears our drummer yelling about his gun, Hubby grabs the gun, spins around, and points it at us. Here we are, four grown men climbing over instruments and each other, trying to fit into those little closets on each side of the stage. . . . Thank God the guy didn't fire the gun at us but took off running instead. It looked like a Keystone Cops movie. The cops caught him a couple of hours later. It sounds funny now, but believe me, it was total panic when it happened. That was in 1966. I remember because I had a brand new '66 Ford Mustang."

Mel Melton: Chicken Wire and Cockfighting in Louisiana

Mel Melton also mentioned experiences in colorful bars in Louisiana and Texas when he was a young player, years before he opened Papa Mojo's Roadhouse.

"I played behind a chicken-wire stage a couple of times in Louisiana. They got it all wrong in the *Blues Brothers*.[5] They don't throw bottles and stuff at you. They flick *lit* cigarettes through the cage and try to hit you with them. That's their deal . . . some kind of bullshit there. Some places were really rough. I had threats and stuff. Finally I hired a bouncer to travel with me and stop any bullshit from happening on the road. He was a scholarship wrestler at the University of Southwestern Louisiana. His name was Big Steve and if I started to feel like there was any trouble, I said, 'Why don't you go over and talk to Big Steve? He's the man you want to beat up tonight. Not me.'

"On any given night, Austin was pretty rough. They didn't put up with a lot of bullshit. I've seen some pretty bad bar fights over there. These were cowboys . . . white cowboys in that crowd. The worst bar fights I ever saw happened because something took place with a girl and then—boom—here we go. But when girls started fighting with each other, then it's all hands on deck. Everybody. Their boyfriends get to hitting the other guys or somebody hits a girl and the fight is on. When girls start fighting with each other in a bar, my advice is this: go out the back door and go quick. Sonny [Landreth] would make a comment about me going out the back door. He said, 'I learned this the hard way. Never get between Mel Melton and the back door to a club if there's a bar fight.'

"So what happened was these two girls started a fight. One of them hit the other one on the head with a high-heeled shoe. Soon there was fighting everywhere. Everyone was fighting. The club owner gets on the microphone, trying to get everything calmed down. He tells us, 'Go ahead; start playing. You've got to keep the music going.' Well, we didn't even make it all the way through one song and here we go at it again; it

6.3. Mel Melton. Courtesy Doug Mokaren.

was fists flying everywhere. This big Breaux Bridge cowboy comes soaring up to the stage and hits me right at the kneecaps. This was in Breaux Bridge, Louisiana. I don't even know if he meant to. I don't know if he knew what he was doing, but I wasn't staying to find out. . . . Anyway, Sonny, unfortunately, yeah, Sonny is a little guy and he got between me and the back door. So I just tossed him out of my way.

"One truly memorable bar I played in was Jay's Lounge and Cockpit in Cankton, Louisiana.[6] They had the club and then they had this canopy kind of a tunnel to go into a cockpit arena. They were having cockfights while the bands were playing, and there was always trouble in there. People would be walking around with roosters in their arms. But, I'll tell you what, everybody played there: Asleep at the Wheel, Clifton Chenier, the

Thunderbirds . . . I mean, it was *the* place. It was the kind of place where they might not even shut the doors until after it was time for the sun to come up. And people are there to dance. Really get up and dance. It's not like around here [Durham, North Carolina], where you're playing and everybody is sitting down. People may be nodding their heads a little bit but around here there's not much dancing going on. When you get down to Louisiana, people are on their feet. And Lafayette had a bunch of clubs. All those towns had zydeco clubs, honky-tonks, and dance clubs. It was exciting. Lafayette had a place called the Grant Street Dance Hall, a huge warehouse they turned into a music club. We opened up for Ray Charles there. Bonnie Raitt played there a lot. The Neville Brothers. B. B. King. We were the house band there so we got some plum gigs.

"Another great place was Tabby's Blues Box in Baton Rouge. I think we were the first white band to ever play there and we used to play there regularly. That was Tabby Thomas's place.[7]

"The thing about Louisiana is that every weekend there was going to be dancing, there was going to be drinking, there was going to be eating, and maybe some fighting—whether it's in a club or at a bar or in somebody's house or whatever. I was making a lot more money in Louisiana because there you had . . . what we used to call the 'Crawfish Circuit' . . . every night. Here's the thing, man, back then and even now, going out to listen to live music is part of the Cajun culture for adults. A lot of times the children are there but they've got people watching them to make sure the kids don't get in any trouble . . . the *fais do-do,* which means 'go to sleep' in French. What they do is at some point in the evening they just lay out these pallets on the floor in the back room and all the kids would go in there and go to sleep. Somebody would watch after them.

"When I went down to Louisiana and started playing music, I would get booked. You would be playing in front of the docks and people came out to dance to that music . . . you could go play music every night of the week and come home with some money in your pockets."

Mark "Buddyro" Harrison: A Motel Lounge with Boxing

Mark "Buddyro" Harrison is a vocalist and a guitar player from Thomasville, North Carolina, who has played with the band the Fairlanes for more than

6.4. Mark "Buddyro" Harrison. Courtesy Doug Mokaren.

thirty years.[8] *He also plays in the band the Medicine Men. Mark explains that his first paid gig was in a motel lounge that also featured live boxing.*

"I didn't start playing guitar until I was well out of high school. I was about twenty. I had gotten to a point . . . well, my high school years were a lot of turmoil, in the middle of the Vietnam era. We're all thinking, we graduate and we're gone. But they quit drafting before I graduated. Anyway, I was always a great air-guitar player, one of the best. I was Pete Townshend on the air guitar. Once you graduate high school and you see all your buddies, going off to school somewhere. You see they're moving on. They're going to get some education and hopefully a career one day, but here I am pushing a board through a saw or something. I'm thinking, 'I ain't gonna be doing this forever, am I?'

"I did have a couple of close friends that didn't go off to college and we hung around. They bought acoustic guitars, and they just sat around and played. I said, 'That looks like fun. I think I'm gonna do that.' I left the factory job and enrolled in Davis County Community College . . . for one year. That year the college was having some kind of event in the student union, and they wanted somebody to play. I got hooked up with that. I had a friend I really enjoyed playing music with who knew all this

Bob Dylan music. He wanted to *be* Bob Dylan. I asked him to help me out with this little gig. So we start practicing, but about a week before it's time to play, I couldn't get in touch with him. He wasn't around. I ended up having to get another friend to come play, Delk Mendenhall—'Delco'—and he saved my butt. Unfortunately, he passed away this past January [January 8, 2014]. I told Delco, 'Dude, I should of just got you to begin with,' because he'd been playing music all his life. That gig was our triumph. So then we say, 'Let's start us a band' . . . we got a drummer and a bass player. Delco actually lined up this gig. It was at this motel on Business 85. It's been torn down long ago now. But it was a little motel that had a small bar right off the office area. In the back they had this boxing ring. They actually had boxing out there on certain nights.

"So it was like, 'Well, it's not boxing at the motel that night, that's good. Let's just go play music.' So we showed up to play the gig. I had no clue what was going to happen. The guy I was playing with, Delco, wore this shirt, and he thought it was cool. It was an old Thomasville Police Department shirt, like what a patrolman wears in the Thomasville Police. I'll never forget it. The first thing that the woman said when we walked in there to set up, she looked at Delco and said, 'Boy, you ain't going to be too popular in here with that shirt.'

"Anyway, we played, and we made it through the night. End of the night, we started packing up and I realized that I hadn't even plugged in one of the PA speakers. We had two speakers, and we played through one of them all night, just as happy as we could be. That was my first time playing a professional gig; I learned.

"For years, I'd drive down that same highway commuting for work. Every day I'd see that motel. I'd laugh about that little gig. It finally grew up all around there so you couldn't see the building. They widened the highway and tore the motel down. But yeah, that was a memorable start."

Several of Mark's stories came from later in his career with the Fairlanes, after Kenny Graham and Chip Click were in the band and they made the decision to play gigs closer to home so players could get to the gig and back in time for the day job. One of these was in a predominantly black bar in Virginia where the owners fed the band homemade barbeque chicken after the bar closed for the night.

"I don't remember the name of the place, but it was in the middle of the country, up near Danville, Virginia. It was like an old grocery store. It was in a big room, but they had the place kind of cut up into sections. But real nice people were running the place. They seemed to like what we were doing. It was mainly a black crowd, but it was country people, you know? At the end of the night, they'd say, 'We want to make you some barbecue chicken.' They would feed us.

"I said, 'That sounds good, man. I'm all over it.'

"And so they go back to the kitchen to make this chicken, and it was weird to me, I've never seen this before. The guy would fry chicken, and then he'd just pour barbecue sauce on it. But it was good. It was about three o'clock in the morning and you're damn right. It was great! But it was like . . . the one guy would be in there doing the chicken, and then the other fella is in here getting the money for the band. Okay, it wasn't a tremendous amount of money. We're talking probably about four hundred dollars for the three of us. . . . And we went up there maybe three times to play at that place. But here's the weird thing. Every time we played there and the guy would come out with our payment, it would be in ones and fives. I think a few times we even got some rolls of quarters. . . . There had to have been some machines or something going on in that other section. There was never any problem for us about getting paid; it was just that we were always paid in *small* bills. I mean, there wouldn't even be a ten-dollar bill in the whole lot. Oh, there had to be something going on in there that involved a lot of small bills. I remember this very well because I was trying to count all these ones and fives. I'd be interrupted and damn, 'I got to count this shit again.' We'd be there counting small bills and the guy would bring us fried chicken with barbecue sauce. After they closed and about a year later, I walked into Boston Chicken down in Greensboro. And that place was fairly new at that point. It was still Boston Chicken, not Boston Market, I believe. And there he was . . . the guy who owned that bar in Virginia . . . or managed it. There the guy was right there with his rotisserie going, the very same guy. And I just remembered that fried chicken with that little bit of sauce poured on it and I thought, 'Well, here he is and he's moving on up in the chicken world.' . . .

"Oh yeah. We also used to go to Folly Beach to play, right outside Charleston. This was the early days, when Chris and Kevin were in the band and we traveled more. They loved Chris down there at Folly Beach. That was a rough kind of—kind of a biker area. A lot of people ask, 'How did you end up at Folly Beach?'

"'Well, this is just where I ran out of gas.'

"But it was laid back and this guy had the big honky-tonk there in town. It was called the Sand Dollar [Social Club]. And I think it's still there to this day. Richard [Weatherford] and his sons ran it. The first time we ever played there was after Hurricane Hugo. That happened in September [1989]. We played there the December after that hurricane hit. That place was still tore all to pieces, but the bar was open. They would put you up in the Holiday Inn across the street there. It was oceanfront. And the first two floors of the Holiday Inn were still closed, and that's how high the water got. Once the Sand Dollar reopened, the damage you saw was outside, but the devastation was all along that whole coastline. The Sand Dollar made it through that hurricane. But man, this crowd . . . that was your typical roadhouse rowdy crowd. I mean, when they got rowdy in there, we would see the bouncer just pick troublemakers up by the shirt and just throw them out. Yeah. This one bouncer in particular, I just remembered, it was just like watching a movie scene. He'd toss them out the door, dust his hands, and say, 'Another satisfied customer.' But they were the nicest people. They'd want to book you for a weekend, so you could play like three nights there. On Sundays, Rich would have you over to his house for a cookout. Oh, this was good low-country cooking, you know? Country cooking. . . . Rich told us, 'This is what I do. I pay you such-and-such. Then I get you rooms in this Holiday Inn. Then we cook for you on Sunday afternoons.' It was really nice that we got a room at the Holiday Inn. If you had to buy your own motel room, man, you could go home broke; you could go home *past* broke."

A. J. Diggs: The Big Speakers

A. J. Diggs is a bass player and vocalist from Philadelphia who has played with a variety of bands, including the Dreamlovers, the Blue Notes, and Bill Pinkney and the Drifters. A. J. moved to South Carolina in 1988, thinking it would be a better place to raise his son, but moved to North Carolina

6.5. A. J. Diggs. Courtesy Doug Mokaren.

ten years later. He now lives in Winston-Salem and plays with the band House of Dues. In 2012, House of Dues won the Piedmont Triad Blues Competition and went to Memphis to compete in the International Blues Challenge. I interviewed him on July 29, 2014, at a restaurant in Winston-Salem. A. J. said some of his most colorful drink house experiences happened in South Carolina.

"There were some real dives in South Carolina. One of them I ran across when I was playing country music, but most of them were those drink houses where they were wanting us to play blues. A lot of the blues spots were hole-in-the-walls, and hole-in-the-walls are usually those neighborhood spots where everybody knows everybody, and if there's any drama going on in the neighborhood, it came right to that spot. Yeah. I've seen some knockdown drag-outs where the management actually had to take people out and call the cops. Odds are, these people were going to be friends again the next night, but at that particular time and on that particular night, it was something that had to be taken care of and the fight was on.

"One of the worst fights I've seen was actually in North Carolina, in the Indian country. . . . It was a fight in this club near Lumberton. The guy I was playing with had this thing about old-school equipment. He had two sets of speakers stacked five high on each side, and they were big. These were some *big* speakers. I used to hate to gig with this guy, but I worked with him for ten years, hauling those big speakers around. They had to be loaded a certain way, they had to be unloaded a certain way, and they had to be set up a certain way. . . . Yeah. You get the idea. Anyway, the fight broke out and they knocked one of those stacks of speakers over. All I could do was stand there and pray that none of those speakers hit anybody, because if they did, that person would have been seriously hurt. Even the tweeter battery was the size of a table. It would have hurt you, and that fight knocked the whole stack over; it crushed the table that it fell on. Luckily, everybody got out of the way. They had to call the cops, because that was a serious fight. They were going to tear that spot up and the management wasn't having it, so here come the cops. But those speakers survived. Yes, they did. Everything they fell on didn't make it, but the speakers survived.

"That's another thing about paying a band. We have to move the equipment from where it is, transport it to where we're expected to perform, and put on a good show. We have to set all this stuff up; we have to make sure everything is working right. If something broke, we have to fix it. All that has to happen before we even play. They usually want an hour, at least an hour per show. . . . If the club owner has any kind of—how shall I put it—any kind of *finesse* about him as far as being a club owner, the band might get fed. If we were fed, it was supposed to be on the house. But the reality is that we've had to pay for our own meals most of the time.

"After the show, you catch a breath. That's when you might get a bite to eat, might get a soda on the house. Generally you'll pay for your own drinks. After that, you have to break the stuff down, have to load it back in the truck, and, depending on how far you have to drive, you might need to get a hotel room for the night. Again, if the club owner has any kind of finesse at all, you've been provided a place so you can at least rest before you hit the road. I've stayed in a few band houses[9] and they weren't all that bad. As a matter of fact, some are pretty decent, but you can generally tell if it was a house used by bands. It'll stink and shit. And people always leave stuff behind in those band houses."

Steve Kelly: The Sheriff Puts On a Show

Illegal drink houses and bars depended on moonshine and bootleg for a profitable operation. In more than one story there seemed to be a special relationship between the law and illegal liquor, where a lawman was a notable customer or even part of the moonshine or bootleg operation. The story here involves the private and public face of southern law enforcement when it came to homemade alcohol, which was a primary product for resale in pour houses. The city of Hartselle, in Morgan County, Alabama, was dry in the 1960s. Over the years, cities in dry counties have voted to go wet, but Hartselle remains Alabama's largest dry city as of this writing (2015). Steve Kelly narrates the story here, which deals with law enforcement's reaction to the discovery of an abandoned still and a performance orchestrated for the local news.

"When I was fifteen, a good friend of mine, Danny Thomas—oddly enough, he looked something like the Danny Thomas star on TV[10]—found a moonshine operation. He lived out in the country with his mom . . . back then we rode motorcycles together in the woods, joyriding and stuff. . . . We also played chess. . . . So, this happened one day in the middle of the summer when I was cruising out to play chess with him.

"When I got to his house, Danny said, 'Hey, let's put off the chess game. I got something I want to show you.'

"We hopped on the bikes and rode through the trails. They had a lot of land, maybe a hundred acres or something. I followed him off to a far spot. They had a shack there that they rented out occasionally. . . . We rode up to the shack and he said, 'Yeah, we rented this out to these guys. They're not here now, but let me show you.'

"He took me inside and there was a still, fifty-pound bags of sugar, barley, and—oh, there was all kinds of stuff. . . . We were just kids but we knew a still when we saw one. Danny said, 'I don't think they're here anymore. I don't think they're using it. I found it a couple days ago but I've been waiting to show it to you. So, now we can go back to the house and call the sheriff.' Cell phones didn't exist at the time; we had to get to a landline. We went back to his house. We called the sheriff and the sheriff said, 'Really? Well, are you sure it's a still?' We told him where to go and we met him at the road. Then we led him to the shack. He had a couple of deputies with him and everything. We showed him what was there and he said, 'Sure enough. You boys found a still and we're going to bust this thing up.'

"I said, 'All right, we're going to have us some fun now.'

"But the sheriff said, 'Hold on. We're not going to bust this thing up until tomorrow.' I asked him if he was waiting for the guys, the moonshiners, to come back. He said, 'Well, maybe.' We didn't think the moonshiners were coming back.

He was kind of noncommittal, but he told us, 'We're going to bust this thing up tomorrow. We're going to be back out here about nine in the morning. We'll bust this thing up and take care of it.'

"He didn't say that Danny and I could come watch, but of course we went back out there on our motorcycles the next morning. We were just waiting to see what all was going on and what kind of fun was happening and all that kind of stuff. When we got to the shack, there was a television news crew there from Decatur, the big city close to us. They had a small television station in Decatur. The sheriff was talking to reporters. We weren't talking to them; we were in the background. They weren't interviewing us. The sheriff wasn't really letting us be much of the picture but he allowed us to watch. The sheriff had a couple of more cars of deputies there at that time. He had the television guys set up and everything. Then he got his deputies all together and was pretending the whole time like it was an active still with the moonshiners still inside. The sheriff and his deputies had their guns out. They staged an attack on the cabin, complete with yelling to get the moonshiners to come out. Then the deputies rushed the shack. They did this whole thing knowing that no one was inside. They staged this whole thing for the news crew, a big story about how they had found a still and charged inside to arrest the guys. Of course, the guys are gone but they chopped the still up with their axes and put on this whole big show for the news crew. We knew the shack was empty. We knew there was nobody there. Probably hadn't been any moonshiners in there for days; it was only a show. We're just watching the whole thing and laughing."

Steve also mentioned that there were black-owned drink houses in both Wayne County, Tennessee, and near Hartselle, Alabama, that white people discussed, whispered about, but would not visit.

"I had heard the adults talking from time to time about moonshine and black juke joints. This is white people talking. White people would never go to those places, would never think that they were safe enough to go inside of if they wanted to, and would never want to in the first place. They talked about those clubs in a derogatory way. When I saw the juke joint in the movie *Color Purple*,[11] I was reminded of places I'd seen like that, both in Tennessee and in Alabama. The adults always talked about them like, 'There's a place I wouldn't be caught dead in, no telling what they're doing over there,' that kind of stuff. Of course, white people are drinking illegal liquor, too. But they whispered about what might be going on in *those* places like there was a big difference. That was just racism coming out or maybe ignorance, not knowing anything about black clubs, and so they had to be bad and scary."

CHAPTER 7

Roots: Music, Magic, and Myths from the Drink House

The drink house, juke joint, or bar is an environment where longings and frustrations can find temporary release through alcohol and dance as well as expression in music. Anxieties over financial frustrations, social relations, health concerns, and a lack of personal power might be briefly discharged or at least could find fleeting consolation here. If there was gambling going on at the drink house, a penniless player could hope for a reversal of fortune, if the cards or the dice roll in his favor. The lonely individual might discover a significant other, if the right person walked through the door. A sick or depressed person can wait it out while self-medicating with alcohol. The lyrics of some blues tunes suggest that one attempt to assert personal power over destiny was through the practices of hoodoo, a combination of folk medicine and magical customs, which had a foundation in African spiritual beliefs. In the United States, these beliefs evolved over time into a blending of traditions from African, European, and Native American sources.[1] Hoodoo was the attempt to influence capricious luck so that chance and opportunity would move in your favor. It offered the promise of control over money matters, health problems, love relations, and the larger injustices of life.

In *Blues and Evil*, Jon Michael Spencer explains that blues music has many references to hoodoo, although the folk practices the lyrics referenced were increasingly forgotten as the music became urbanized.[2] The lyrics created transgressive culture heroes: the "badman," the conjurer, and the trickster, who take the narrative beyond the familiar stories of tragedy and personal loss to construct a response to oppression. For white musicians and the white audiences listening to them, hoodoo references in the lyrics were "cool" and perhaps offered a satisfying if unlikely solution to their own troubles. If you were looking for a hoodoo practitioner, likely places to get hooked up would be in the barbershop, beauty shop, bar, or the drink house.

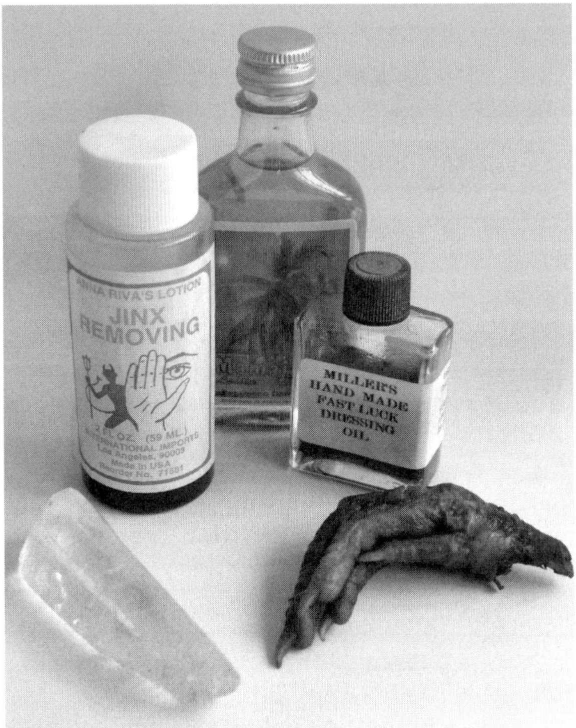

7.1. A variety of hoodoo products. Courtesy Doug Mokaren.

Although hoodoo references remain in the music and the drink-house stories about hoodoo have not completely disappeared, there seems to be more of a lingering fascination than a robust belief that hoodoo could produce actual results. For some storytellers, a hoodoo narrative simply makes for peculiar but interesting entertainment. As Debra Devi explains in *The Language of the Blues from Alcorub to Zuzu*, it isn't unusual still to find references to hoodoo in blues music even if beliefs have disappeared. "Just because blues musicians used hoodoo imagery in their songs to wonderful effect, it doesn't necessarily mean that they believed hoodoo really worked."[3] Similarly, audiences listening to the music may understand the hoodoo references and may even have hoodoo stories of their own, but retelling these stories can take on a "friend of a friend" or "story around the campfire" tone. The supernatural bar stories people share tend to extend through the spectrum of conviction, with actual confidence in the practices on one end, and skepticism and full-blown disbelief about practices on the other.

It is also important to note that alcohol has been a prime ingredient in hoodoo rituals. People generally think about hoodoo as connected to dried roots and bones, which the hoodoo practitioner used in charms and rituals. Roots are so important to these practices that conjuration is sometimes called *root work.* However, alcohol can be nearly as important as dried roots in traditional hoodoo. For example, ingredients for a conjure bag or mojo bag might be soaked in alcohol to give them concentrated power. Likewise, *tobys* or *hands* are small bundles of magical ingredients wrapped in brown paper on which the name of the person the spell should influence is written. The bundle is usually placed inside red flannel bags[4] and frequently "fed" with alcohol. For example, in *Hoodoo Mysteries*, Ray Malbrough advises that "all Tobys or Hands should, by tradition, be fed with Bourbon whiskey by placing them in a glass of whiskey . . . for twenty-four hours, then taken out and left to dry."[5]

In interviews with Robert Palmer, Muddy Waters discussed "mojo hands" at length, describing them as little red flannel bags that smelled of oils and perfumes.[6] Muddy doesn't mention the use of alcohol in the context of hoodoo, but alcohol was often a key element. Knotting threads wrapped around roots, hair, or other ingredients made strong magic, but spitting whiskey on the knots for the mojo would keep the devil from crawling through.[7] If not actually used in the rituals, alcohol might be part of an offering or a special gift brought to the root doctor. Alcohol also freed the mind in ways that helped make the magic appear possible.

Music, magic, and alcohol are traditional survival tools. Hazzard-Donald explains that among slaves in the American colonies, the use of song was an important element of resistance and hope and was united with conjure or hoodoo for protection.[8] Alcohol provided a form of self-medication, both physical and social. The drink house is not a genuine shelter from those things that make life painful, but its veneer of intoxication and ecstasy might offer an interim escape. The southern environment of pervasive violence and exploitation was good reason for "clearing a space for pleasure, fantasizing about revenge—a way of bringing oneself and one's community back to life by getting loud, fierce and down."[9] There are good reasons that so many bluesmen drink and good reasons that lyrics with hoodoo references continue to surface well into the new millennium. Music, alcohol, and magic are capable of providing a temporary distraction from even the most modern of problems—or they can help cause them. The hoodoo practitioner (conjure doctor, root doctor, root worker, witch doctor, or witch) might be called upon to solve a problem that alcohol, music, or another conjure doctor helped to create.

Because both the illegal drink houses and the legal bars were sites where many frustrations fermented, they could quickly become dangerous places. What might begin as fun had potential to become a situation for which a person might need extra protection. After all, a famous drink house legend tells us that a man jealous of the attention his wife paid to bluesman Robert Johnson murdered Johnson with poison added to an open bottle of whiskey. One variant of the legend suggests that it was not poison in Johnson's whiskey, but that "roots" had been put on him, which caused him to suffer for days before dying, crawling around on his hands and knees and barking like a dog.[10]

Roots in Her Drink

In a similar story about whiskey tampered with at a drink house, a woman interviewed in 2003 told about a "lady" who had "roots put on her" while she was dancing in a bar. The victim in this case didn't fully succumb to the influence of the "bad roots" because another root doctor was able to detect the problem and destroy the curse. This is her cautionary tale about an unattended drink in a bar:

"There was this married lady I know who went to a bar where this lesbian woman saw her and wanted her. This was a place that everybody went to for a good time, all kinds of people. When the musicians started playing a song she liked, this woman went out on the dance floor and left her drink unattended. She just left it sitting there on the bar. The lesbian saw her out there dancing and took the opportunity to slip some drops of a spell or something like that into the woman's drink. Later on that same night, the woman left the bar with her husband. She was feeling irritable. After that night, the woman couldn't love her husband anymore. She couldn't stand for him to touch her in a sexual way. She couldn't stand for him to touch her breasts or anything. The husband couldn't comprehend it. Overnight his wife had become peculiar. She didn't feel like she loved her children anymore. She had yearnings for other women, which—until that time—such a thing would have been unnatural for her. Her life felt unbearable. The husband finally took his wife to see this adviser, a root doctor. The husband learned that the lesbian had spiked his wife's drink with powerful roots so she would fall in love with the lesbian. At first they couldn't believe it, but this person the root doctor talked about was a known lesbian. The root doctor told her husband all that he needed to do to get his wife back. The husband did everything that the root doctor told him. That was how the root doctor lifted the curse and the woman returned to her husband and a happy marriage."[11]

The story resonates with the complaint in the song by Walter Davis, "They put ashes in my whiskey and strychnine in my glass."[12] The advice to "watch your drink" while partying still stands today, although contemporary concerns tend to be more about date rape or predator drugs than root-doctor curses and murder.

Root Doctors and Blood-Stopping after the Bar Fight

Many root-doctor stories had their beginnings in a bar or a drink house, when love triangles, jealousies, gambling debts, or accusations of cheating erupted into fights. For example, in one story collected from 2003, a man was stabbed in a bar fight and received serious injuries that would not stop bleeding. The wounded man had also been slashed with a razor. He was bleeding so much that he fainted from the blood loss. His friends were afraid to take the bleeding man to a hospital, so they took their wounded friend to see a root doctor who specialized in blood-stopping. The root doctor combined Bible verses with his conjure ritual to stop the bleeding. In the ritual, the root doctor laid his hands on the largest wound, pressing down, and recited Ezekiel 16:6 from the Bible: "And when I passed by thee, and saw thee polluted in thine own blood, I said unto thee when thou wast in thy blood, Live; yea, I said unto thee when thou wast in thy blood, Live." The bleeding stopped and the injured man recovered without a trip to a hospital emergency room.[13] In a similar story, a man suffered a deep wound to his knee, but in this case, the blood-stopper was a grandmother who did not touch the wound, but hovered her hands over the wound Reiki style[14] and recited the same Bible verse. The granddaughter assisted her grandmother with the blood-stopping ritual.

"My cousin had a gash in his knee. They were trying to bandage it up so it would stop bleeding. But it wouldn't stop. My cousin was scared he would have to go to the hospital. My grandmother said to me, 'Sugar,'—she always called me Sugar—'go to my bedroom and get my Bible.' I walked to the bedroom and got her Bible. At the time it was hard for her to read. Her eyes were bad, so she told me to turn to Ezekiel 16:6 and she just started saying 'Jesus, Jesus, Jesus' while I opened to the passage. She stuck out her hand just to the point where she almost touched his knee, but she didn't touch it. Then she was able to read the passage and she continuously said that passage over and over until the blood stopped."[15]

Although neither of these root doctors used any commercial products in the blood-stopping rituals, several of the commercially packaged hoodoo products intended for healing also recommend reciting Bible verses in the directions for the product's use and these directions are usually printed on the product labels.

Commercial supply houses and curio shops that appeared at the beginning of the twentieth century separated the traditional root worker, who created his or her own supplies, from the urban practitioner, whose practice became infused with European and Native American customs and commercial items.[16] Commercial exploitation of hoodoo was less developed in the South after WWII than in other areas but the traditional root workers and conjure doctors were already becoming scarce. However, a new community of laypeople continued to address concerns of love, luck, protection, and justice.[17] A layperson could simply read the directions for the ritual on the product label. For example, Indian Spirit House Blessing is a yellow-colored bath and floor wash. It is one of many such products that can be purchased in specialty pharmacies or curio shops, from catalogs, or over the Internet. The ritual for using the product is printed on the back label and explains that the user should fill a tub with warm water for a bath ritual, pour in half the bottle, recite the Twenty-Third Psalm, and then bathe while concentrating on desires. Commercial hoodoo products include sachet powders, washes, incense, oils, and candles; many have directions that include reciting Bible verses.

A Jilted Lover and "Love Me Bath Oil"

A woman interviewed in 1992 used a commercial hoodoo bath wash in a ritual to get her ex-boyfriend to come back to her after he had left her for another woman whom the boyfriend had met at the bar they frequented. In this story there was no root doctor involved, only a commercial product that had initially been purchased as a joke, until, on an impulse, the woman decided to try it. This is her story:

"It was called 'Love Me Bath Oil' or something like that. I did everything just like it said on the label. I let the water run as hot as I could stand to touch it and poured the mixture into the water as it ran out of the faucet, like a bubble bath, only there weren't any bubbles. It smelled nice, clean but not flowery. I read one of the psalms; I forget which one, something about a wicked and ruthless man. I read it until the bathtub was full. Then I got in the tub in the hot water while I looked at a photograph of him, holding it out of the water just in front of me, where I could see it but it wouldn't get wet. I just stared at his picture while I soaked in the tub and stayed like that looking at him and concentrating until the water turned cold.

"The very next night I convinced some friends of mine to go with me to that bar he liked. I could just feel that the spell was working. I don't know how to explain it. It was just a feeling. I knew he was gonna be at the bar and sure enough, there he was. Plus, he was all by himself; the bitch was nowhere around. I laughed with my friends and ignored him, but I could sense that his eyes were on me and I felt really hot that night. I was dancing and my friends were telling me, 'You're on fire tonight.' Finally, he came over to the table where we were. He said he wanted to talk. He bought me a drink and he told me he wanted us to get back together. He was sorry we split up. He was all apologetic and nice. . . . So we got back together."[18]

Adam and Eve Oil

Another informant explained how to attract a specific lover when you are in a crowded bar. This informant recommends using a different commercial hoodoo product, which the user wears like a very potent perfume.

"You can use Adam and Eve oil and get close to the person you want so he can smell the oil on you. It might work but it might work on somebody else, too, which can be a problem if it's somebody you don't want to bother you. I've heard that a better way is to get something from the person you want to fall in love with you, a lock of his hair or a button off his shirt. Something that is a piece of him or that he touched. You wrap that in red flannel cloth and tuck it into your clothes or down into your shoe. Then, when you're in a crowded place, like a bar, he will see you and come to you. Nobody else will bother you but the one you want to love you and he won't notice anybody else but you. I have never tried it myself but I've been told it will work."[19]

Rob Baskerville and Penny Zamagni Sell Commercial Hoodoo Products

Rob Baskerville and Penny Zamagni tell several stories about how they became involved in selling hoodoo products in the late 1980s after Chicago Bob Nelson[20] took them to see a root shop. This particular shop was located in the back of Miller's Rexall Drug Store in Atlanta, Georgia.[21] Located on Broad Street in downtown Atlanta, the drugstore was an ordinary pharmacy when it opened in 1960, but became famous for selling hoodoo remedies as clients requested more and more of that type of product. The original owner of the drugstore, Donald Miller, began carrying hoodoo supplies because his largely African American customer base requested these items. Richard Miller, the nephew of Donald Miller, continues to carry commercial hoodoo products as of this writing. Miller's Rexall stocks a wide selection of folk medicines, love charms, good-luck soaps, jinx removers, and power candles. Although much of their product line is associated with hoodoo or the more strongly African American folk magic tradition, there are also products reflecting Santeria and more New Age spiritualist and homeopathic practices. Richard Miller explained that herbs are used both spiritually and medicinally, so the pharmacy was a natural place to carry this type of product: "The pharmacy has always been a place of helping people confidentially and sincerely with their problems." The Millers also had root doctors who visited or worked in the store and would consult with customers. Miller's

7.2. Rob "Hound Dog" Baskerville and Penny Zamagni. Courtesy Doug Mokaren.

Rexall was the inspiration for Paul McCartney's album *Run Devil Run* (1999) and the storefront was featured on the album cover.

Because of their encounters with hoodoo in both music lyrics and in the practices of some of the musicians they worked with, Rob Baskerville and Penny Zamagni became fascinated and decided to become dealers of commercial hoodoo products.

Penny: So we go in the Rexall Drugs in Atlanta. This was in 1987, so they took one look at me, laughing behind their hands, and say, "We've got some crystals for you." Man. Why does everybody think I'm a hippie? It's the hair. So, a white lady with long hair comes into the store, she must want crystals. I told them, "No. I want some bend-over oil."[22] They were like, "Huh?" They are surprised that I even know what bend-over oil is.

Rob: We got all the High John the Conqueror[23] roots and oils. Had our candles dressed and the whole thing.

Penny: So then we talked to them about getting a franchise. A root franchise so we could sell this kind of stuff, too.

Rob: We ended up at Sonny Boy Root Products in Birmingham, which, by the way, I still have some of those products, and we talked about getting a supply that we would sell as we toured around on the circuit. I think our main customer was Reverend Billy,[24] who came to one of our gigs, saw our products, and said to us, "I want in on this scam."

Penny: It did become very commercial and we sort of lost interest because we saw how commercial it was. It wasn't an indigenous thing anymore.

Rob: Yeah. As soon as we see there's good money to be made with something, we're outta there. But, I'll tell you, Chicago Bob traveled with an altar and all his Marie Laveau[25] paraphernalia. He would always have it set up in his motel room everywhere we went. So we were exposed to it pretty heavily.

Penny: Going back twenty-five years, there was a kind of interesting root doctor place we went to in Yemassee, South Carolina.

Rob: That was the real deal. There weren't any tourists going out there.

Penny: No. The root doctor looked pretty rough and she didn't doll herself up. She didn't expect anybody walking in—especially white people—in the middle of the day. This was more of a nighttime thing and who knows what it was a front for. Very low country. She acted like she didn't want to sell us anything. She was really suspicious of us.

Rob: If she didn't say it, it was pretty obvious that she thought we were the police, maybe under cover or something. Sonny Boy's in Birmingham was the best place for product though. We had to go through some rough areas of Birmingham to get to Sonny Boy. I actually still have some High John oil, High John crystals, and this, that, and the other. That's how we ended up with our little record label, High John Records . . . someone stole the name later. So we had to reinvent our label, but our record label was the original High John and it was based on those experiences we had on the circuit. The best thing was trying to get the

Sonny Boy franchise so we could buy root products in bulk. That was an interesting time."

◆ ◆ ◆

It is not uncommon to find root-doctor or hoodoo stories with connections to drink houses and bars. The root doctors featured in these stories were usually unnamed, shadowy figures, although some were reported to be associated with or students of James Spurgeon (Jim) Jordan (1871–1962), a successful conjure doctor from Maney's Neck Township in Herford County on the eastern side of North Carolina, or from Chief Two Trees (Kenneth Ray Cannon, 1927–95), a spiritual worker from Old Fort in McDowell County on the western side of the state. Malbrough explains that root working "falls within the field of magic done by men . . . a type of spell working that as a general rule is taught only to men, by men."[26] However, many of the stories I heard involved women who practiced hoodoo without claiming to have been descended from or had any special apprenticeship with a famous male root doctor.

Binding a Judge to Do Right

Mamma Roue is a root worker from Caswell County, North Carolina, whose rituals are a combination of traditional customs learned from her mother and intuitive practices she discovered for herself.[27] For example, she would cut up sweet potatoes to put on a sick child with a fever because the sweet potatoes have power in them that would "pull the fever out" and the child would soon be well.[28] Mamma Roue also cut up old socks and used the toe part of the sock as her own technique for making a healing mojo bag. She would fill the sock's toe with ginger, onions, garlic, and other herbs, depending on the need, sew the bag shut, and then have the sick person wear this sock bag around the neck on a string until cured. Traditional mojo bags are sewn out of red flannel or red silk.[29] However, the sock worked for Mamma Roue, who also saved the tops—the ankle and leg part of the sock—to use as a bandage so that no piece of the sock went to waste.[30] Mamma Roue told about one situation in which a sock or a sweet potato would have been ineffective. A young man had gone into a bar and gotten into some trouble having to do with "reciprocity," which resulted in "necessary violence." This young man was arrested and jailed for assault but was soon released.

"A few days after he got out from jail, this man he had fought with was found shot dead in a car. They said [he] did the murder but he was innocent. Police arrested him a second time and his mother went crazy with grief. She was sure her baby would go to the state penitentiary for murder. I told her she couldn't be thinking that way. We held hands and prayed. I told her to have positive thoughts, to imagine her boy free, enjoying his life. He is a young man who enjoys his good times. I told her to think about him that way. After his mother went home, I lit the candle. I knew who the judge was and I bound that judge to do the right thing. Sure enough, on the day of the trial, the judge let him go free for lack of evidence."

Mamma Roue's story does not shine with faith in the integrity of the American justice system. It is also a story that echoes the lyrics of Buddy Johnson's "Root Man Blues." On the 78 record, Geezil Minerve sings, "When I first came to town, you really brought me down / So I found myself a root man, now I'm the baddest bean[31] in town / . . . / Last night I got in trouble, they locked me up in jail / But I walked right out that door and didn't even pay no bail. / Can't you see, can't you see, Baby, you can't take me for a fool. / 'Cause you can't beat me and my root man, too."[32] Whether the client was guilty or not, a powerful root doctor might help a client escape the law. More frequently, the client might be looking for protection from a system that seemed to ignore real culpability. When justice is rarely on your side, hoodoo might help.

A Truck Driver and Foot Track Powder

Another root-doctor story with beginnings in a bar tells the story of "foot track magic"[33] and a jealous truck-driving husband who spent a lot of time on the road and away from home:

"I know this man, a truck driver, who was at this old bar, when he saw his wife making eyes with a stranger. Later on she danced with the man. He said it was almost like his wife knew the guy or something. The trucker convinced himself that his wife was cheating on him whenever he was out of town. It kept eating at him until finally he went to see a root doctor about it. He told the root doctor his concern and the root doctor said he would need something of hers so he could verify whether or not she was having an affair. The husband got some hair from his wife's hairbrush and took it back to the root doctor. The root doctor examined the hair and after a while he said, 'Yes. She's having an affair.' So then the root doctor mixed up a powder for the man and told him to put it over the doorway. When he was going to be going out of town, the trucker was supposed to sprinkle that powder over all the doorways, along the threshold of every doorway in their house that opened to the outside. So he did. When the wife's lover came to visit her, unbeknownst to him, the lover walked right through that powder. Immediately, he started having horrible pains in his feet. His feet and legs would swell up. . . . The poor guy didn't know what was going on. This went on for two or three more times. Every night that the trucker went out of town and his wife's lover came over to see her, the man would suffer terrible pains in his feet and legs, just about crippled him. The powder didn't bother anyone else, just the wife's lover. This happened every time he walked through her door. Finally, the man wouldn't come around her house anymore. That was how the root doctor forced the trucker's wife to be faithful."[34]

Clyde "Pop" Ferguson Explains the Black Cat Bone

Clyde "Pop" Ferguson is a traditional blues player from Lenoir, North Carolina, who learned to play blues music standing outside a Caldwell County drink house and listening to the music inside. Although his father was a Holiness preacher who didn't allow him to play drink house music, Pop would grow up to earn his living as a bluesman, playing blues using Vestapol guitar tuning[35] and later incorporating more electric and urban styles. Pop spent much of his life traveling across the United States to perform at juke joints and house parties, and even setting out his tip jar on street corners. On his 2009 CD, *Big Boss Man*, Clyde "Pop" Ferguson sings a traditional blues song about hoodoo magic called "Black Cat Bone."

"I know exactly what that song is about. It's about a girlfriend or a lady that's going with a guy and she pulls tricks on him or something like

7.3. Pop Ferguson. Courtesy Doug Mokaren.

that and she gets to do whatever she wants to because she got the black cat bone . . . so a black cat bone is a lot like a wishbone, something like that. But she would be using a black cat bone . . . for it's supposed to be a lucky bone. They tell you how you can get one. Okay. So you kill a black cat and cook it until nothing is left of it but the bones. Then you throw those bones in the river or you throw them down in the creek. And all the bones will go floating down the creek but one. The one bone that goes up creek against the current, the one that floats back towards you, that's the one you put in your pocket and carry around with you all the time. That's the good luck bone. That black cat bone will bring you good luck for the rest of your life, make everything go your way. But if your baby got a black cat bone then she can do anything she wants to you and you can't get out of it. That means she got the power. So yeah, I knew the woman in the song had a black cat bone because you can't resist her. And she . . . you would think she was a witch because she would get away with anything. Because that black cat bone . . . you're helpless against it. My daddy was a Holiness preacher; he wouldn't have liked that song."[36]

Pop added that if you go in a club and see someone who seems to have a pushy power over others, you might want to turn around and "ease on out the door . . . or at least keep a distance." He doesn't believe that such a person will have a black cat bone; he just warns that you don't want to get "messed up" with that kind.

Be Careful Where You Leave Your Stuff

A young woman told this story, which supports the idea that personal objects are important in hoodoo and can be used against a person.

"I've always been told that you need to be careful where you leave your hair combs, brushes, or clothes and things like that because people can put spells on you through that. If you're out at a bar or a public place and go into the restroom . . . if you comb your hair in the ladies' room, make sure you don't leave your hair in the sink. If they can get hold of your hair, people can compel you to do things you don't really want to do. They can make you have accidents, make you get sick, make your hair fall out, make you lose your money. All sorts of bad things can happen if people get hold of your hair or your personal stuff."[37]

Abe Reid and the Diamond Dust

Abe Reid is a vocalist and guitar and harmonica player from Statesville, North Carolina, who competed in the Piedmont Blues Preservation Society Blues Challenge in 1998, which he won, and then he proceeded to win the International Blues Challenge in Memphis in 1999 before the competition was separated into two categories: band challenge and single-duo challenge. Abe admitted that when he was playing harmonica and performing with Cootie Stark[38] on the *Sugar Man* CD, the lyrics to Stark's "Jigroo" baffled him. He had no idea what the song was about.

7.4. Abe Reid. Courtesy Doug Mokaren.

"The song goes: 'brush my teeth with some diamond dust.' Diamond dust? What does that mean? I asked Cootie and he said it was like a spell, like New Orleans voodoo kind of a spell. That's kind of neat, don't you think?"

Abe didn't know exactly what polishing teeth with diamond dust referred to other than it was a reference to magic and assumed that the song's title likewise conjured up some hoodoo ritual. The meaning of *jigroo* remains a mystery, but diamond dust is an important ingredient in several commercial hoodoo products designed to bring luck in money matters or to attract good luck in general. A jug band song recorded by Gus Cannon (1883–1979) and his Jug Stompers has a similar reference to diamond dust: "I polish my teeth-a with a-diamond dust / I don't care if the bank has bust." The lyrics suggest a fantasy about having money that never runs out even when the larger economy is in ruins.[39] Before going to the drink house to engage in a game of Georgia Skin or bid whist, diamond dust on the teeth supposedly turned luck in your direction. However, in the case of Cootie's song, Tim Duffy reminds us that diamond dust was an abrasive agent in some commercial toothpaste products. Cootie Stark could just as easily have been singing about good oral hygiene. "If you met Cootie, he was a great blind blues bard, who went around spreading joy and happiness. He had complete faith in the unseen world and Jesus Christ." As for the word *jigroo,* Tim said, "A lot of these great blues bards have certain key words that leave a question in people's mind. Cootie had many of them and *jigroo* was a great one."[40]

Mel Melton, Papa Mojo, and the Raccoon Penis Bone

Mel Melton's band, the Wicked Mojos, makes several references to hoodoo in their music. Mel explained that the head "root doctor" is called "Papa Mojo," which became his inspiration for a song, the name of his restaurant and bar (Papa Mojo's Roadhouse), and the name of his band (Mel Melton and the Wicked Mojos).[41] A *mojo* is a physical hoodoo charm that the root doctor infuses with spiritual power. The charm may be kept in a bag that a person wears for protection or for good luck. The word *mojo* can also refer to a person's sexual vitality or charisma.[42] The mysteries of Cajun culture inspired Mel's cooking and the lyrics of his music. It also inspired him to carry a raccoon penis bone, which he lightheartedly refers to as "Voodoo Viagra."

"I do have a raccoon penis bone, but a Cherokee Indian gave it to me because I've got Cherokee blood. My great-grandmother had reservation rights as a Cherokee Indian. I can't even remember the guy's name who gave it to me. I met him in Hillsborough at the powwow. I've had that thing for probably forty years. There's some Indian hoodoo mixed up in there. . . . Well, when you look at all the Indian culture in Louisiana, there's a lot of cultural mixing going on. The Choctaw Indians are a huge influence on the food. The Mardi Gras Indians—that's where a lot of that came from. Those African slaves escaped into the swamp and were taken into the Indian villages and shown how to survive the swamps. It's not surprising that these beliefs are all mixed together. . . .

"The coon dong or penis bone is a sex charm. I didn't need a sex charm when I was nineteen, but the guy just told me about it and I was like, 'Yeah, I'll take one of those.' It's funny, man. One year I was playing this big society Christmas ball at the Virginia Museum of Art and there were these ladies there who specialized in sterling silver jewelry of the coon bone. These sweet ladies had all these coon dongs coated in silver. They had necklaces and earrings and all these other things. I got to be

7.5. Mel Melton. Courtesy Doug Mokaren.

friends with them, so I showed them my coon bone. I keep mine in my harmonica case. . . .

"My first wife's uncle was what they call a *traiteur*, a Native Creole healer. That's someone who uses herbs and rituals to cure people. I had a guy that worked for me, an older Creole guy who was involved in voodoo, but I never got too involved in it."

Law Stay Away Powder

Another informant explained that he had heard of bootleggers and moonshiners using the hoodoo influence of a commercial product called "Law Stay Away Powder" to keep a sheriff away from a still, an illegal drink house, or a truck that was hauling bootleg: "Anytime you are doing something and don't need the law messing in your business, you might want some extra protection. There's a powder you can use just like you use bug spray to repel ants from your kitchen. It's called Law Stay Away Powder. In times gone by you could use it to keep the law from finding your still but even now people continue to use it. I heard about this guy selling crack in Georgia also used the Law Stay Away Powder and his crack house was never busted. This was not that long ago either, so there are some people out there that continue to use this stuff. I don't know if it really works. I'm not sure I believe it does. Maybe the guy was just lucky."[43]

Finding Power and Luck

Even if most audiences listening to Muddy Waters singing about John the Conqueror root could not believe in hoodoo magic or would never spend good money on the commercial products, there is something compelling about the idea of manipulating that kind of personal power. In the book *Deep Blues*, Muddy Waters tells the story of a stranger who seemed to have uncanny good luck in a "juke house" dice game and was suspected of having a mojo hand. The stranger's luck changed dramatically when Muddy and his friend managed to sprinkle salt around him and slip a pinch of chili pepper into the stranger's jacket. Salt and pepper were supposed to kill the power of a gambling hand. Muddy claimed, "We won the shoes off his feet." However, when Muddy bought a mojo hand for himself, the good luck seemed to escape him. After three years of carrying the mojo and going broke in a crap game, Muddy concluded that Louisiana mojo might have some power but Delta mojo was "bullshit."[44]

One warning about searching for hoodoo power gets echoed again and again in blues mythology. The film *Angel Heart* (1987) is a violent exaggeration of this myth, showing what happens to a singer named Johnny Favorite who exchanges everything for fame. It is a cautionary tale about too much ambition. The movie and the legend both imply that the most dangerous of devils is the musician's own ego.

In the book *Season of the Witch,* Peter Bebergal suggests there was a deeply racist subtext in the hostile responses to early rock music because it borrowed heavily from African American blues, gospel, and spirituals. Some Christian adults viewed this new music as "incarnations of the perceived barbarism and ungodliness of black Americans."[45] That instinct for the ecstatic and spiritual experience may have been what audiences sought in the combination of music, intoxication, and euphoric revelry. It is a forbidden form of spirituality discovered in the most profane of places, the bar or the drink house. Young white musicians rebelling against mainstream hypocrisy by singing songs like "Got My Mojo Workin'," "Black Dust Blues," or "The Mojo Boogie" could have the satisfaction of making their parents afraid and angry. Musicians singing this dark music were announcing that they were dangerous. In a world inhabited with spiritual influence, they were the activists. They were powerful bad boys and bad girls and that made them sexy.

One younger informant explained that a genuinely magical influence once existed in blues music. It was magic so powerful that white ears not only listened; they paid attention as well. "It's black man's power. Those white boys over in England could hear it. There's something more to it than just music; it is a kind of magic. It takes a man to admit his grief and his problems; it takes a man to survive. Blues was the power to survive, power to endure, and it was sexual power. We can't forget that."[46]

CHAPTER 8

Feeding the Music

Pat Freitag: The After Party

Pat Freitag is not a bar owner or a musician, although she grudgingly admitted to having taken piano lessons as a girl. "In fourth grade I wanted a bicycle," she told me, "and I got a piano." Pat is a cook, a crafter (she makes quilts out of old music-festival T-shirts), and an avid supporter of live music. I wanted to interview Pat because she featured so prominently in many of the memoirs of Piedmont-area musicians for her legendary house parties. Pat also often provided musicians a place to stay when they had a gig in the area. She served as a board member for the Piedmont Blues Preservation Society in charge of hospitality for the annual Carolina Blues Festival. This meant feeding musicians, stagehands, techies, PBPS board members and anyone with a backstage pass. Festival audiences bought their food from vendors in the area around the front of the stage, but backstage was all Pat. She was determined to bring some home cooking to musicians who are always on the road, eating fast food and bar food. When Pat wasn't feeding musicians, she was "keeping up" with them. She took an official "keeping-up" job for Pinetop Perkins in the mid-1990s, when he was having a bit of an alcohol problem. Pat invited me to her house for this interview on June 18, 2012. She died on Tuesday, May 27, 2014.

"I started in 1989 as a member of the board [of the Piedmont Blues Preservation Society], but before then I was always going to some of Bill Griffin's[1] clubs [in Greensboro, North Carolina]. Bill Griffin used to do Sunday-night shows. He would get the really famous artists that were traveling through and would book them on an early gig for a Sunday night at his club and he would also serve food. It might be hamburgers and hot dogs. It might be fried chicken. Who knew what he would serve any night? But it would be some kind of food. You paid like six or seven

8.1. Pat Freitag and Carey Bell. Courtesy Pat Freitag.

bucks to get in and you would get your food and a show. Well, Bill was never prepared. He was never ready, so I would jump in and start helping him set up the food or serving it or whatever he needed to get the show going.

"Bill Griffin had many clubs in this town. He passed away some time back [1999], but before he died he had quite a few clubs. He had a club called Castaways, which had been reopened in about three or four different places. Bill brought a lot of the older black bands into Greensboro in the eighties to play in his clubs. He had a club on Battleground Avenue right at the Battleground-Lawndale split that had a downstairs. He was doing shows upstairs there—many shows—but there was a shooting out in the parking lot of the place and that really hurt his business. But I saw Anson there, Anson Funderburgh,[2] right there at his club, and other good artists, too.

"Bill brought in some of the best talent around . . . he brought in a lot of blues acts and was doing this on Sundays for quite a while. He had a place over on Arnold Street in the sixties. I was underage, coming over from Lexington [North Carolina] and sneaking into that place. That's where he had the Tams and General Johnson[3]—you know. Some really big talent!

"I got out of high school in sixty-four. So the 'beach music' or the 'shag' was just getting big around here. That was when the crossover with the race music really started. See, they used to call it 'race music' even then. For the most part the 'shaggers' didn't know that they were dancing to blues music or black music. When they heard it on the radio, they couldn't see, they didn't know it was black people playing the music. So they were dancing to it and by the time it was such a hit, well, they were already dancing to it. Then the black bands would play at Myrtle Beach and they were already popular. There was an old club at Myrtle Beach[4] that would bring in the black bands, and the white 'shaggers' would dance to this music and they loved it. But Bill was the one bringing these bands to Greensboro. And I was constantly helping him serve food. The Blues Society noticed this and asked me to be on hospitality. After the Blues Society asked me to join the board, I find out that I'll have a two-hundred-dollar budget. I have to feed upward of a hundred people on this . . . anyone with a backstage pass gets to eat backstage. So I started cooking. With two hundred dollars, what could you buy and have it last eight hours for the entire festival, feeding all those people?"

The work of hospitality involved a lot of cooking, hauling, and quite a few unreimbursed expenses. Pat would stock up on meat when it was on sale, then she often cleaned out her own freezer when she started cooking for the festival. She cooked for the festival from 1989 until it moved to Tanglewood Park in Clemmons, North Carolina, in 2000, which was too far away for Pat to drive two vans and "haul everything" needed for the backstage party. I asked Pat why she invested so much of her time, energy, and her own resources into serving the festival this way for so many years.

"First of all, I like to cook. Which helps. But I wanted to be sure the musicians were happy. I felt that if the musicians had what they wanted to eat or drink, and if the backstage was a good experience for them, then they were going to put on a really good show for everybody else. You know, I think what started it was . . . well, years ago my parents were beautiful dancers and they used to go out dancing quite a bit. I would be the built-in babysitter for everybody's kids. Mother would call when the dance would be over . . . maybe around midnight or whenever it was. She

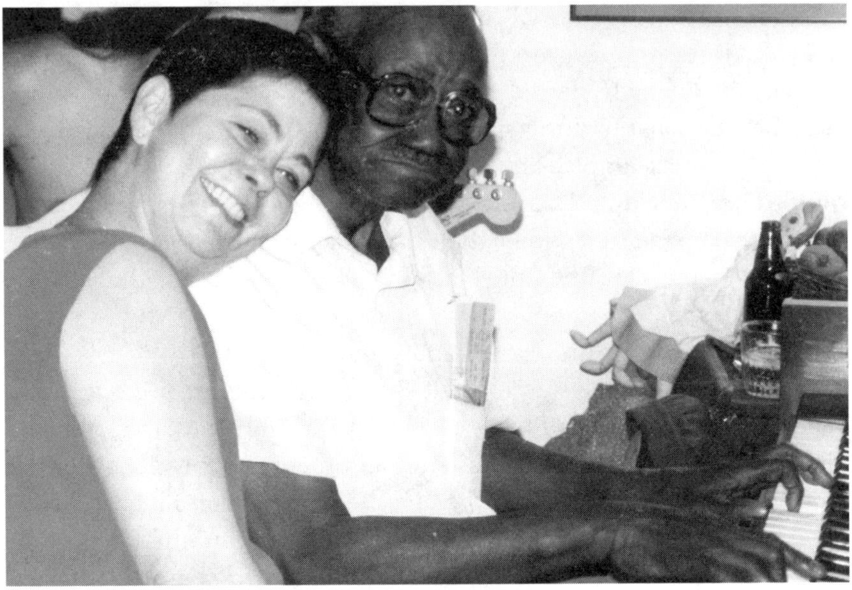

8.2. Pat Freitag and Pinetop Perkins. Courtesy Pat Freitag.

would call and say, 'I'm bringing some people over for breakfast. How about starting to cook some bacon.' So you could say Mother started me cooking this way, but she never had me doing all the elaborate things that I did for the festival. Still, I started out cooking breakfast really late at night for the friends Mother had been partying with and would bring on home to eat with us.

After she became involved with hospitality for the blues festival, Pat began having "after-festival parties" for musicians and their friends at her house. Older black musicians, who still didn't feel particularly comfortable in integrated hotels, spent the night at Pat's house.

"Yes, I brought musicians here. I did many a late-night breakfast here at my house. Even after the festival, I've had people here. I've had as many as thirty people sitting down for breakfast at three o'clock in the morning . . . and I've had musicians stay the night here. Pinetop always stayed here when he was in town . . . he would rather be in a house than a hotel. Of course, he'd sit up and play the piano half the night. I would have gone to bed and he would still be sitting in there playing the piano.

Pinetop was a hoot. They would usually have me pick Pinetop up at the airport. I'd always be sure I had my piano tuned the day he came. He liked the action on my piano."

At this point Pat began to relate her adventures as a "babysitter"—but now for Joseph William "Pinetop" Perkins (July 7, 1913–March 21, 2011), an elderly black piano player from Belzoni, Mississippi. At ninety-seven, Perkins won a Grammy Award for an album recorded with Willie "Big Eyes" Smith, making him the oldest musician to receive a Grammy. Pinetop was also in two feature films, *The Blues Brothers* (1980) and *Angel Heart* (1987), and featured in the film *Piano Blues,* which was part of the Martin Scorsese series *The Blues* (2003). Pinetop was in his eighties when he began staying with Pat. When Pinetop went on tour with the Muddy Waters Tribute Band,[5] Pat went with him. Pat's job on this tour was "keeping up with Pinetop."

"I was kind of 'looking after' Pinetop. Trying to keep up with him. In those days he was still drinking heavy and had a tendency to stray. It was a rough job to keep up with him. Also, he did not like the tour bus. He didn't want to ride in it, so I was driving him in my car and following the tour bus. It had another benefit because it gave the band a car. The band had a vehicle other than the bus, when we would be in one place for a couple of days. I remember one time we were at this gig, and . . . Pinetop had a really weak bladder, so right before he'd go on stage we'd try to make sure he had gone to the bathroom. So, this time in Texas, he came out of the bathroom and his pants were unzipped. I was trying to tell him that he needed to zip his pants. Pinetop was hard of hearing. He was getting ready to go on stage and I kept trying to tell him his pants were unzipped. He didn't hear me. He couldn't understand me and I repeated it three times. I finally just reached over to his zipper to zip him up and he says, 'Hell. What can't get up, can't get out." He says this and walks out on the stage. I believe that was in '94. He was still drinking at that time. Pinetop didn't quit drinking until he was in his late eighties. Before then he was drinking heavy. Heavy. But he was still able to play. He could drink a fifth of liquor and go on like it was nothing. He'd been drinking since he was eleven years old, so he had built up a tolerance. A couple of times we got into it when he was really, really drunk but that took a lot of liquor to truly get him so drunk it was noticeable. It sure did. I rarely saw him so thoroughly drunk he couldn't play. Some people can't drink and play, but drinking did not seem to affect Pinetop's playing at all. I don't believe Pinetop would ever have quit drinking but they put him on Antabuse treatment and he was locked up for six months. Antabuse . . . is a drug that if you drink when you're taking it, it will make you deathly ill. Deathly ill. But it's used for withdrawal from alcohol."

The US Food and Drug Administration approved Antabuse, also called Disulfiram, to treat alcoholism in 1951. The drug blocks the metabolism of alcohol. This increases the hangover symptoms of nausea, vomiting, headache, vertigo, and confusion to intolerable levels with even small amounts of alcohol. The intention is that an alcoholic will associate these terrible symptoms with drinking and will be less likely to drink. Pinetop's episode with Antabuse occurred while he was at his home in Chicago.

"I thought I was going to have to go and get him. They had arrested him for driving under the influence and took away his license. So we had looked into moving him down here to Greensboro. We wanted to get him away from there. . . . Where he lived was worse than a war zone. It just broke my heart to see the conditions he was living in, in Chicago. He had a much better life, the last few years of his life, once he got to Texas [Austin]. The Southside of Chicago was really rough. I went and picked him up from his place and took him to Buddy Guy's club one night.[6] I was really afraid to leave my car there [in Pinetop's neighborhood].

"I remember another time with Pinetop. We were headed to Mississippi. It was the day that they dedicated the Muddy Waters stamp.[7] That was at Greenwood, Mississippi. I don't remember who all they flew in for the dedication but it was a real big to-do. It was the day they put out the series of postage stamps and I was driving Pinetop from Texas into Mississippi. And, there it was again: Pinetop and his bladder. If he says to stop, you pull over and you stop. You don't waste any time—or else you keep a jug in the car for him to use. But he tells me to stop. So I pull over. We're out in the middle of nowhere in Mississippi. You know, just fields. He goes out in the field and it's a watermelon patch. And he goes out and finds a watermelon and brings it back, putting it in my car. He knew I was going to be coming back home the next day. He says to me, 'Now here, you take this watermelon back home to use.' So Pinetop stole me a watermelon in Mississippi. And I have to say, it was by far the best watermelon I ever ate. I don't know if it was because he picked it or what.

"I will say that on the B. B. King tour, when it was just Pinetop and me in my car, we were twenty feet or so behind the tour bus, going through Mississippi, and I got stopped. I looked immediately at my speedometer and I was not speeding. So I pull over and I get my license and registration out and I hand it to—it was a white cop—and I say, 'I wasn't speeding was I, officer?'

"And he says, 'No, ma'am. Is this your car?' and he is looking over at Pinetop.

"I say, 'I'm afraid to get away from the tour bus.' I told the cop we were part of the B. B. King tour and we were headed to wherever we were going but I didn't have the itinerary so I didn't have the address and I was afraid of getting lost from the bus.

"He said, 'Oh, they'll stop. I heard them on the radio. They'll stop right up there at the rest stop and wait on you.'

"But the only reason that cop stopped me was that I was white and Pinetop was black and he wanted to see what was going on. I told him that Pinetop was the piano player. Pine was at least eighty-five years old at the time.

"And the cop is questioning him. 'So you play the piano?'

"And Pine says, 'Well, I try to. The best I can.'

"Then the cop says to me, 'Well, you were a little too close to that bus. You keep your distance.'

"That was it. He let us go on, but I wasn't so close to that bus when he pulled us over. I could have . . . turned circles and not hit that bus. I was not right on the rear of that bus by any stretch. That cop had other reasons for stopping me."

This was not the only time when a young white woman driving an older black man around town caused a concern.

"I do remember this time when Snooky Pryor[8] was here for our festival and I think we had a festival-eve party at the Nightshade Café,[9] where somebody was playing. I went to pick him up to take him to the concert and he was afraid that it was going to be a problem for him to be alone with me because of race. I mean, here is this older black guy—and at that time I was forty pounds lighter, so I was looking better—and he was really worried that somebody would take offense at us being out together. This was 1990. I assured him it wasn't a problem at all. The next day at the festival everything is going fine and my son [Eric] is helping out. My son walks up to Snooky and says, 'I understand you spent the night with my mom last night.' He was just joking with Snooky, but my son said, if a black man could turn white, Snooky just about did. But then Eric handed him some German beer I had stashed away and Snooky was just fine after that."

In addition to Pinetop, other musicians stayed at Pat's house whenever they had a nearby gig.

"I've had lots of other musicians stay here and I fed them all. I've had Phillip Walker's[10] band to stay here for a week at a time when some gigs got canceled on 'em and they really couldn't afford to be staying in hotels for a week without any revenue. I had twin beds and a king. I've had them sleeping on the floor, on the sofa, on pallets, whatever. And I've cooked for them . . . now see—well, I've had Kenny [Neal][11] over here and he'd go across the street and go fishing in the pond—in the neighbor's pond. And he dug up grub worms in the yard to go fishing with. I've had Kenny Neal and all his family here—the band family. I guess they had come for breakfast before leaving town. Because I do late-night breakfasts and I do breakfasts in the mornings, too."

I asked Pat how she was able to stay up all night feeding everybody, host after-festival parties, and still be able to cook breakfast for musicians in the morning.

"Well, if I wasn't working, I could sleep later. I retired at forty for about ten years. I worked a little bit but for the most part I played, I read, I traveled a lot. Both of my parents died the year I turned forty. Less than six months before Daddy died, he told me not to wait until I was his age to do the things I wanted to do in life. He said to do them while I was still young enough. Well, he was sixty-six. Both of them were sixty-six when they died. And I thought, yeah, you're young, Daddy, what are you talking about? Now that I'm that age, I know what they were talking about. Of course, both of them were smokers, too. Both of them had a cigarette in their hand when they died. I smoked for forty-five years. This coming December the 12th [2012], it will be four years that I've quit. I didn't have much choice but to quit smoking if I wanted to live. And I still don't have but 50 percent lung function now and it'll never get any better than that."

Pat confessed that her smoking caused her to miss out on enjoying some of Pinetop's stories when they were on the B. B. King tour. Smoking had already caused her to experience uncomfortable symptoms of acute bronchitis.

"What I really hated was on that tour when we were driving across Mississippi, I had bronchitis so bad then—I was so sick that all I wanted to do was get the tour over with and come home to get some medicine. But Pinetop—he was telling me all these tales. Going up Highway 61, Pinetop is saying, 'Well, I was born over there. That was where the Stovall plantation[12] was. . . .' He is pointing out all this stuff and telling me things . . . here I am traveling with history, with him, and I was so sick I couldn't even comprehend it. I just couldn't even take it in . . . hardly."

Pat showed me a picture of Ike Turner that was autographed both to Pinetop and to Pat. Ike Turner (November 5, 1931–December 12, 2007) was both a guitarist and a piano player, perhaps best remembered for his work with Tina Turner in the 1960s and '70s. Pinetop had been Ike Turner's mentor, teaching him how to play piano.

"The date on this picture is May 4th of 2001. Pinetop had come in here and he had this picture Ike had just given him; he [Pinetop] had seen him [Ike] the day before. And Ike autographed this picture, and it says, 'To Pinetop. The man who learned me how to play. Love you, Ike Turner.' Well, Pinetop carried it to me. I went on the Blues Cruise [in 2006] and Ike was on the cruise so I took this picture to get Ike to autograph it again for me. So he writes, 'To Pat'—now he's trying to say, 'I'm gonna whip'—but he spells *whip* as *wipe*. W-I-P-E: 'I'm gonna wipe Pinetop for this.' He means he's gonna whip Pinetop for giving the picture away, and then he signs it to me. Then Ike died the next year. Ike was a Scorpio, too. Very intense . . . he was a fabulous musician and that band was top-notch. He really put on a show. You could hear Pinetop's influence in his music and he was constantly praising Pinetop."

Pat reflected on what she thought were the biggest changes she'd noticed in the music scene from the time she was sneaking into bars as a teenager through her years of feeding the bands to her more recent years.

"Maybe the biggest change in the music scene now is with the bars. There used to be a lot of really good clubs and bars that brought national touring acts into town. They're all gone now because people didn't support them enough for them to keep the doors open. Marcia Ball[13] is a prime example. When I talked to Marcia not too long ago, she was telling me how hard bands have to fight for the few gigs that are out there. It's bands of her caliber that don't travel anymore because, I mean—the festival is the best thing they got going, because they don't get the club gigs and the small venues or parties anymore. I don't know. Some of it is economic hard times. Some of it is people used to drink and go out a lot more. Marcia used to play the Double Door in Charlotte, North Carolina, twice a year. And I think losing Blues Harbor in Atlanta . . . when that bar closed, that really changed things. Blues Harbor used to bring in a band for a week at a time and they put the band up in an apartment for the week. That would get them going on the East Coast. So they would be at the Double Door and when Bill Griffin had the clubs going in this area, the bands would come on up here. For a while John Rudy had the Bluebird on High Point Road in Greensboro and they were doing the Sunday-night blues with national touring acts coming through. But you had to see it on a marquee to know if someone was playing because he wouldn't ever advertise and people wouldn't show up."

Pat believes tougher drinking-and-driving laws and sobriety checkpoints and roadblocks have discouraged people from going out as much or drinking as much as they used to even ten years ago. She believes we needed the stricter drinking-and-driving laws, but these laws may have had unintended negative effects on live music and the venues where musicians play. However, she also observed that when alcohol was less available to people because of dry counties or blue laws, it seemed, paradoxically, that people actually drank more. Former booking agent and Pat's longtime friend Nelson Penninger observed that when liquor laws changed in 1984 with the National Minimum Drinking Age Act, the new minimum age at which a person could purchase alcohol went from eighteen to twenty-one, altering the club scene considerably.

"Guilford County wasn't dry. Davison County was for a long time. Asheboro just recently has voted it in—in Randolph County. It used to be that in Guilford County on Sunday, you couldn't buy beer until the afternoon. Nowadays I think you can buy beer at seven o'clock in the morning if you want to. I know that when I lived in Burlington [North Carolina], you'd come to Greensboro on Sunday to get your beer.

"When I finally moved to Greensboro in 1986, somebody was telling me I needed to check out Bob Margolin at the Nightshade Café. So, I go on down to this dark dungeon down through the alley and in the basement underneath a Chinese restaurant. See if that can paint the kind of grimy picture of the place; I mean, it was just a nasty old bar. But I have heard some of the best music I have ever heard in that little place. But when I got in there that first time, I thought, what on earth is this? . . . But then Bob was back again at Nightshade Café and I went back and come to find out that Bob's manager was Nelson Penninger. I knew Nelson from my high school days. So Nelson started introducing me to everybody. That's where I really got involved with the Blues [Society]. Nelson introduced me to everybody in the Blues Society. Nelson would start telling me who to go see and where to go. That's how I became friends with Bob. And through Bob I met an untold number of people. I've been backstage with Bob at the Chicago Blues Festival with Pinetop and Jimmy Rogers[14] and all the family. I've had some incredible experiences."

Some of Pat's favorite memories are times spent with the Holmes Brothers,[15] Sherman and Wendell Holmes from Christchurch, Virginia. Pat traveled quite a bit with Sherman, Wendell, and Popsy and hung out with their brother Milton Holmes and, of course, put them up and fed them in her own house.

"One of the most favorite experiences for me was when I spent the night at the Holmes Brothers' parents' house after a festival in Virginia and woke up the next morning smelling bacon cooking and listening to the boys in there talking to their mama. The Holmes Brothers' music always just really touched my heart. They were one of the first bands I fed, I think. They were at one of the first festivals we did. They found out I could cook, and buddy, it was on after that. In fact, I fried chicken and carried it up there to Virginia to them that day. . . . The Holmes Brothers always showed so much love and respect for family. I've been around them and traveled with them quite a bit in years past and you'd always hear them every day calling home, talking to Mom and Dad.

"A number of years ago for Black History Month the Blues Society did a show at the Carolina Theater and had the Holmes Brothers come there. Sherman told me that back in the day when he came to that theater he would have to be up in the balcony, where the blacks were . . . that he couldn't come in the front door of that theater. Now here they were, walking through that front door and playing on that stage. I guess that's a good change. It's not an end to the story, but a nice change."

Chuck Cotton: Pat's Kitchen

Harold "Chuck" Cotton is a drummer who began his music career as a saxophone player but picked up the drums in the 1970s. Chuck has played with a long list of performers, including Pinetop Perkins, Roy Roberts, Johnny Rawls, Barbara Carr, Big Bill Morganfield, and Billy Boy Arnold, among others. He currently plays most often with the bands the Ladies Auxiliary and the House of Dues, and Bob Margolin. Chuck and Pat were tight friends, so Chuck attended many of her famous house parties.

"I think the first night I was talking to Pat, it was at the Walkers Which Way. I would see her at different places, but had never met her until I started playing with Bubba [Klinefelter]; I met her through playing with Bubba.[16] They started having blues shows, and I think it was with Bubba that I first went to her house after one of those shows. Yeah, I went to a bunch of Pat's parties. Eventually I started going to them all the time. When we would go to her house after one of the shows, like after the Blues Festival, that's when there was a real party, 'cause, man, there'd be Pinetop Perkins and the Holmes Brothers in the front room singing and playing like I don't know what. Bringing tears to your eyes. Then we'd be

8.3. Chuck Cotton. Courtesy Doug Mokaren.

in her kitchen eating, drinking, and everything else we do; those were great parties. I remember that she used to make those little-bitty ham biscuits. About the time we would get there, the table would just be so full of food and shrimp and grits and eggs and bacon piled high. Everybody just having a great time. That's where I met Earl King.[17] Yeah, I met Earl King at Pat's house, and I officially met the Holmes Brothers at her house. Yeah, over there with Pinetop and the Holmes Brothers . . . R. L. Burnside and just some of everybody, because she used to do that party after every festival. She'd leave the festival before it was all shut down and go home and get ready for the party. I'm telling you, 'cause she'd be like, 'I'm going home to get this stuff started,' and by the time we would get there, she'd have it all done . . . ham biscuits and all.

"Yeah. I met R. L. Burnside at Pat's house. He was nice. I played with him one time. He was one of those throwbacks, 'cause he's from Mississippi. Well, I say he was one of the throwbacks with the emotional timing thing. They didn't count off: two, three, four, one, two, three, four, and then go to the change. You sang and played and you did it your way. Back then, players like R. L. Burnside, they change when they want to. Whoever is playing the guitar would change when they wanted to. Or that's how it seemed to me. Now, they might have had some kind of count, but if you go back and listen to all that old stuff, like '40s, '30s, and stuff like that, them guys play and change off-count. R. L. Burnside played that same way. For a drummer, it's not that bad to follow, but anybody else that's playing along has to really watch what he's doing so they can change with him, so the music would sound right. He was a cool person, but I would always keep my eye on him for the changes when we were playing. I remember playing a gig, down in Key West, with Bob Margolin. We'd had a gig that afternoon and for some reason it didn't quite go right. At the end of the night, Bob was talking to us, he was telling us, 'You know, this thing is a quarter of a second thing. You gotta always be watching; you gotta always be listening. You never know, it may do something today that it's not going to do tomorrow, or didn't do yesterday.' When Burnside was doing that change, and I was kind of on it, but I could hear where everybody else would be maybe just a little hair behind him. That kind of thing. Like I say, he was one of those old guys that just change when they want to. I mean, those guys invented this music, migrating from Mississippi, the Delta, and all down in those areas and then going up to Chicago, by that time they had started getting electric. Different people are playing, and so it's easier to say one, two, three, four; we do it on the four, or we do it on the one. We do the change whatever the count is instead of just winging it, you know, instead of changing whenever. Yeah, change when you feel like it. That's what it sounds like to me. But I'm sure there's a system to it. I just didn't come up in that era, but I hear it on all the old records I listen to.

"I met Pinetop with Pat in his older years. He was just a real nice guy, kind of grandfatherly kind of guy, you know. I met him while he was still drinking. He was real nice, real nice. He was getting older, when I started being around him the most. I remember a story about him driving, and I think Pinetop was still drinking, and a train hit him. It took his car down the tracks, but Pinetop didn't get hurt. He may have stopped drinking after that."

Naomi Alexander: Supper for James Brown

One of Pat Freitag's close friends was Naomi Alexander, who died April 4, 2012, of stomach cancer. She was seventy-one. Naomi was the life of the party. Even when she was in the hospital undergoing chemotherapy, she was still the life of the party. Once when we were visiting Naomi in the hospital, she was propped up in the bed wearing a T-shirt with the slogan "Cancer, You Picked the Wrong Bitch." A nurse put her head in the door to ask Naomi if she could get her anything. Without hesitation and with heavily suggestive undertones, Naomi answered, "A man. You can get me a man."

Before she died, Naomi and I spoke informally about her father's juke joint. Her father ran a drink house in Guilford County, and by the time she was barely a teenager, Naomi told me she had already learned to drink corn liquor, roll her own cigarettes, and help her father bootleg whiskey to his juke joint.

"There was one of the times when I helped Daddy take some liquor back to his place and I was pregnant. I was expecting my daughter. We were driving along and saw the cops put on the light. They were going to pull us over. Daddy didn't want them to find the liquor he had so he said for me to act like I was having pains. So I faked labor pains. Instead of being busted for hauling moonshine, we had a police escort all the way into town, but not all the way to the hospital. . . . The police just left us once we got to the edge of town, so we just went on our way."[18]

The story about James Brown[19] and stealing her mama's cornbread was a story Naomi told more than once. When she was about fourteen years old, Naomi sneaked backstage one Saturday night when James Brown and his band were playing in Greensboro at the Bell Bar Cafe. Naomi worked in the kitchen but she had to see James Brown and her determination got her face to face with the idolized entertainer. Brown complained to Naomi that he was hungry. So Naomi went home and got a

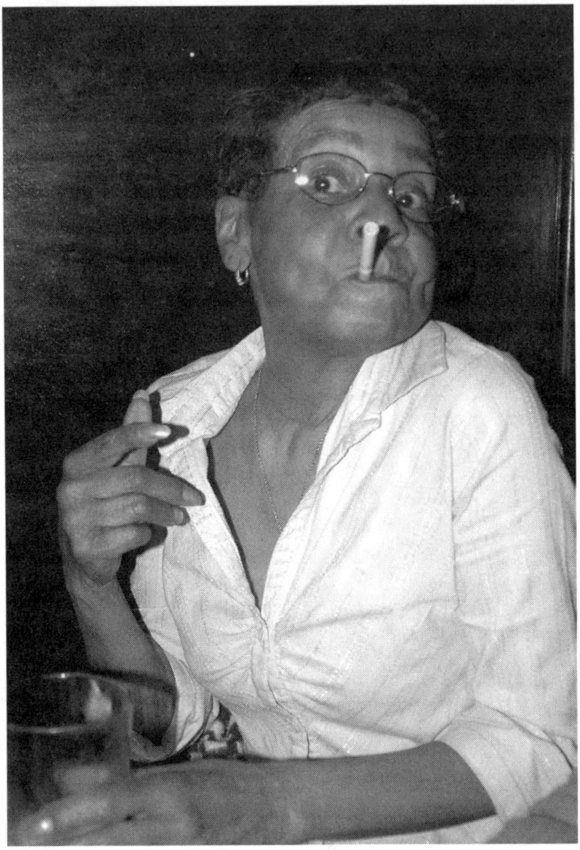

8.4. Naomi Alexander. Courtesy Doug Mokaren.

pot of her mom's pinto beans and a pan of her cornbread, the food her mother had cooked the night before in preparation for Sunday dinner, and brought the food back to James Brown and the band. On Sunday, after everybody got back home from church and her mother was putting the Sunday dinner out, she made the discovery that food was missing. Someone had not just gotten hungry and could not wait for dinner, because not only was the food missing, but the pots, pans, and serving spoons as well—everything was gone.

"I was found out and punished. My mother whipped me a new one. She didn't care who James Brown was; she wasn't impressed at all with musicians."

Naomi also told stories about going to events with live blues music held in tobacco barns in the late 1950s. There would be a rope partitioning the audience into two sections. One side of the rope would be for whites and the other side was for blacks. She said that once the liquor was flowing and dancing became enthusiastic, the rope would be on the floor underfoot and no one was paying attention to where they were dancing. Toward the end of the night, the crowd was really happy and pretty well churned up.

"Nothing nasty ever happened."

◆ ◆ ◆

In many different communities, the music scene has people who are important—not because they are on stage or because they own a bar, but because they bring something special to the party. Looking after the music can be as straightforward as driving an aging musician to a gig or making special cookies and little ham biscuits for the folks backstage. It might be providing a traveling musician with a safe place to stay. Some people also feed the scene with their energy. They truly love the party and want everyone else around them to enjoy it as much as they do.

CHAPTER 9

Piedmont Personalities

The Piedmont has its fair share of colorful personalities who were key figures in more than one story. There are many, many Piedmont personalities, but storytellers offered particularly colorful and poignant stories about these three: Guitar Slim, Guitar Gabriel, and "Sweet Daddy" Ray Burnett. These three men were very different, but musicians considered all three to be mentors. They were featured personalities at local bars and were known to "rip out" a Piedmont style.

Logie Meachum: Guitar Slim and the Paddy Rollers

James "Guitar Slim" Stephens (1915–89) was from South Carolina but moved to Greensboro in 1953, where he became a local celebrity. He began playing organ and piano as a child but the guitar became his instrument by the time he was a young teen. His professional career began when he started playing with the John Henry Davis Medicine Show to draw a crowd.[1] *Logie Meachum was Guitar Slim's Greensboro neighbor and had these stories to share about Slim.*

"I had been living next door to Slim for three years. I would take him downtown. He would drink Relska vodka and I would just drive him around. We would get in his Dodge slant-6 Valiant station wagon and go to town. People would buy him whiskey so he would play guitar. He would go to the Nightshade bar and on to Angel's place on the corner of Mendenhall Street and Spring Garden [Greensboro]. I called it Angel's place so much, I can't remember the real name of it. The owner was named Angel. He was witty and bright and nasty and mean. I loved that guy. Cussed, mean, long blond hair. You wonder why people patronized him. On certain nights Angel would have live music. Slim and I would

9.1. Lorenzo "Logie" Meachum. Courtesy Doug Mokaren.

play and David Bolton would play, too. Then sometimes I would take Slim to the liquor house on Cherry Street [Winston-Salem]. He was a pretty good picker, but Slim like to talk more than he liked to play so he would do more of that than anything. Both Gabe and Slim could tell the bawdiest, dirtiest stories. When Slim would sing songs, he tried to stick pretty much to the lyrics but he would embellish a little bit. Slim would tell these wild old tales. He was good at telling stories. I can come up with some good ones myself. I, God. Mine are true, though.

"I, God. I tell you that was it. That was Slim's favorite phrase: 'I, God. I, God.' I have interpreted that phrase nine hundred million different ways over the years that I've heard him say it. When he says it. How he says it. He says, 'I, God,' but he'll add it to anything. The way I was raised,

I was very reluctant to use a phrase like that. I had been raised in the staunch tradition of you don't wake God up unnecessarily. You don't call his name in vain and I believe that, so I don't say 'goddamned.' . . .

"Anyway, one time I was at my house downtown and I had cooked. Slim came to my house that night and he sat all evening long. We went and got a bottle of Relska and he told me about traveling with a girlfriend in West Virginia. He said, 'I, God, boy, them paddy rollers got after us.' 'Paddy rollers' was what he called the sheriff and deputies.[2] He said, 'I've never been so embarrassed in my life. They beat me in front of her.' He just got so mad. They caught him on the train; his new wife was with him. The paddy rollers had sticks and garden hoses nailed to the sticks and that's what they beat him with. They came on the train and caught him and beat him. He said, 'Boy, you could hear that thing whizzing through the air. Pow! Doo-whop-pow. Boy, they'd tear your ass a new one.' And it upset him that they beat him in front of his wife. . . .

"Slim had a friend that we called Reverend Do-me-dirty. Yeah, Reverend Do-me-dirty. Yeah. Slim and Do-me-dirty and Lotion. L. T. Scott they nicknamed Lotion. He used to say, 'I'm so smooth the women calls me Lotion.' Those guys were Slim's cut buddies.[3] Reverend Do-me-dirty and Lotion sat around and listened to Slim play guitar."

David Bolton: Guitar Slim and "Ghosting"

Logie mentioned David Bolton as someone who accompanied him with Guitar Slim as they roamed around to Piedmont-area drink houses. David Bolton is a therapist at Triad Behavioral Resources but has played guitar since he was fourteen and continues to play guitar with the House of Dues. He has vivid memories of meeting Guitar Slim when he was still in college and traveling around town with Slim and Logie to jam at drink houses or play for tips at local bars.

"I met Slim through Logie Meachum. Logie and I met playing music out in Guilford College at a bar out there. They had an open jam and we started playing acoustic guitar together. Logie lived around the corner from Slim, so when I would go to Logie's house, he'd say, 'Come on, let's go over to Slim's house.' We'd walk around the corner to Slim's house.

9.2. David Bolton. Courtesy Doug Mokaren.

This was in the late '70s, early '80s, when I knew Slim and we were messing around with him. It was the period just before and after I had gotten out of college.

"I remember the first time we went in Slim's house; it was in the wintertime and Slim had a wood stove going. He had a pot that was boiling and he had a possum in that pot. It was just a god-awful smell in there. He was just boiling that possum and the fat was gurgling up on the top of the pot. It just stunk. Slim was old school. So we'd pull out the guitars and Slim would pull out the cheap vodka he had. We'd always take something down there to him, too. We'd just sit around and tell lies and listen to Slim talk about the old days playing and jamming.

"In the '20s and '30s, Slim kind of went around with the carnies playing in the carnival scene. He played stride piano[4] and he was a really good piano player, but he was known all around here for guitar playing. One night we were playing down at the Nightshade Café down on Tate Street and Johnny Hammond Jr. was in there.[5] We took Slim down there because Johnny played a lot of old bottleneck and National steel guitar and Slim was great on steel. We took Slim down there, and he kept hollering out because he was getting kind of drunk. At the end of the night, after the show was over, we went in the back, into the kitchen,

9.3. Guitar Slim. Courtesy David Bolton.

and Johnny was really sweet. He said, 'Well, come on, Slim. Here, play my guitar.' So Slim picked up Jonny's guitar and he started to play this unbelievable version of 'Come On in My Kitchen,' since we were actually back there in the kitchen.

"Slim would do this thing they call 'ghosting.' Ghosting is like when you play a single note line but he wouldn't be singing along with the note. Like he'd sing, 'I want you to come on . . . ' and then he would play the rest of the line, but he wouldn't sing the lyric. Everybody knew the lyric was, 'in my kitchen.' But Slim would ghost it. He'd play it on the steel. And then follow with the lyric, ''Cause it's goin' to be—outdoors.' You know, he wouldn't sing the whole lyric. It was one of the most amazing moments I can remember playing with Slim and listening to him play. It was remarkable. I mean, he was just amazing. The thing about Slim, too, is he had these hands that were just huge. The fingers were . . . I mean . . . you'd shake hands with him and the fingers would wrap all around. It was unbelievable. His fingers were out two or three inches longer than mine, it seemed like. And his thumb, when he played guitar, his thumb would reach around the back of the neck of the guitar and he would chord with his thumb, which was really an old style. He played what they call Vestapol. It was Vestapol tuning. It was open tuning. It can be open D, G, E, but

I think Slim played in open G. He'd stick that thumb around there and he'd chord on the neck with his thumb. He was amazing, really.

"We'd get with him, get him out of his house, and take him around different places and he would just astonish people. If he wasn't too drunk, he was amazing. He would also tell us stories about playing stride piano in the old carnivals back in the '20s and '30s and that's how he made his living for a while. He would tour around with the carnies and he would play stride piano for the carnival music. One of the things Slim told me about roaming around as a musician in the 1920s was you'd get a meal by going around to the back of white-owned houses where there was a black cook and the cook would bring out a 'smothered plate,' that would be a plate smothered in food. This was Jim Crow era. A black man couldn't just go sit down in a restaurant so this would be one of the things you did to get by while you were out on the road.

"By the time I knew him, Slim was in his seventies. Man, he was a jack-of-all-trades. He could run a plow and a tractor. You'd see him out there. We'd drive by and he'd be out on the tractor cutting up the ground out there. You'd see him around town. He had an old truck he used to drive. You'd see him out driving and everybody'd go, 'Oh, watch out! Slim's out on the road,' because he'd be half drunk all the time he was driving that truck around. . . .

"In the 1980s we had a little band called the Half-Assed Blues Band. We would go down there to College Hill and play in the College Hill Sundries, which is a bar down on the corner of Spring Garden Street. We'd get Slim down there. It would be Slim, Logie, and me—and Logie's brother-in-law and another guy named Natural Brown, a harmonica player and a great singer who is now deceased. We'd bring Slim down there and he'd play with us, and we'd all sing four-part harmony. Jim Angel was the owner of the bar. He is now since deceased, too. He ran the place for a long time. He'd get us in there and he'd take beer-bottle boxes and we'd stack them up and sit on them. Close the front door and we'd sit right there and play in front. It was all acoustic. We didn't use any PA system or anything. Everybody was just singing, playing harmonica.

"We would play with Slim in little places, in the little drink houses all around here. Billy Ransom or Billy Ransom Hobbs played with us, too.[6] You may know his story. Billy Hobbs used to play with Slim a lot. He knew Slim well. Billy was kind of a busker and a gypsy kind of a guy. He was around town. He played all over the place. Wonderful guy. About four or five years ago now, he was murdered in a house on Summit Avenue, the old Summit Avenue house. They called it the old castle. He was in there and some guy followed them back from a bar or something. The guy came in and set the house on fire. Shot and killed Billy and beat up his friend—the girl he was with—he beat them up and left them both there to die. Billy Ransom Hobbs. I wrote a song about him and recorded it.[7] Police caught the guy who did the murder, but they had to let the guy go because of the way they collected the evidence. They extradited him from Florida and brought him up here and everything, then the police had to turn around and let him go; they couldn't keep him. Yeah. Billy was in that period when really all he did was wander around and play music. When Billy and Slim played together, that was a memorable time."

Interestingly enough, New Orleans has a Guitar Slim (Eddie Jones, 1926–59) as well as a Guitar Gable (b. 1937), who should not be confused with the equally colorful Piedmont personalities. Thomas "Guitar" Gabriel (1925–96), known as Guitar Gabriel or Guitar Gabe, was born in Georgia but moved to Durham, North Carolina, as a boy. Some people knew him as Nyles Jones. He was a street musician in North Carolina before he traveled with medicine shows. He recorded an album, *My South, My Blues,* and a hit single, "Welfare Blues." However, he never saw the royalties from his work. Gabe returned to North Carolina to the streets, clubs, and drink houses of Winston-Salem to play his music. Both Gabe and Slim were primarily local street personalities until Tim Duffy (the Music Maker Relief Foundation) rediscovered them in the early 1990s. Tim was recording Guitar Slim for the Southern Folklife Collection at the University of North Carolina at Chapel Hill when Slim counseled him to find Guitar Gabriel.

Tim Duffy: Guitar Slim and Guitar Gabe

"I was studying blues with a guy named James 'Guitar Slim' Stephens out of Greensboro, a first-generation blues artist. Before he succumbed to cancer [1989], he taught me a lot. In school they told me there was no more blues, or it wasn't happening. I met Slim and he introduced me to all these people in Greensboro that still played old blues. But the folklorists, the record purveyors of culture, have their sense of time and when their time is out of it [no longer extremely popular], they think it's all ended. I don't believe that. . . . Slim said if I want to continue my studies to meet Guitar Gabriel. So it was through Slim that I learned about Guitar Gabe.

"No one would take me to Winston, or to the east side as it was called. None of my southern friends would take me. No one wanted to go over there. . . . Gabe was a tough guy to get to know. When I was substitute teaching in Winston-Salem and I asked my homeroom students about Guitar Gabriel, one said he was burned up in a house fire. Others said he was dead. Another gave me a map to a drink house. She called it a 'drink house.'

Tim went to the drink house and people there thought he might be "the man," but he explained that Guitar Slim had sent him, so that was his pass.

"They took me over to Piedmont Circle, a little housing project in Winston, and they introduced me to Guitar Gabriel. I spent two or three years, everyday basically, with the guy. We just became best of buddies. He had been on that drink house circuit since 1970, playing. . . . It was '91 when I met him. He had been making his spare change for twenty-one years at these places. I came along well into his career, but I got a chance to see all this stuff. We performed together. If we weren't traveling and performing, we were street musicians playing on the street or playing in drink houses. We played every day. That's what we were doing for a living.

"If you follow any popular music throughout the world and you come back to its roots, you stand squarely in the South. You find yourself in the working-class communities like these drink houses in Winston, where working-class men and women invented blues, jazz, and gospel music traditions on Friday and Saturday nights. Very little of it was ever recorded. The stuff that we do know about . . . we're thankful that the folklorists and the record companies found and recorded it. But there were lots of people that played it around here and there still are. Those are the people that the drink house was ground zero for meeting. I believe Gabe was born and raised in one of those places. His father was a blues artist, Sonny Jones. Gabe grew up on this stuff.

"We founded Music Maker because Gabe introduced me to lots of musicians: Macavine Hays, Preston Fulp, Mr. Q, Willie Mae Buckner.[8] They're all dead broke and they're all living in dire poverty. I mean poverty of three to seven thousand dollars a year. It was apparent that the music industry never worked for these guys. Never. Touring wasn't an option because they were so old now. We decided to do Music Maker through a friend of mine, Mark Levinson, a brilliant audio engineer who came up with the name the Music Maker Relief Foundation. He fell in love with Gabe. Gabe attracted a lot of attention 'cause he was just a great artist. People took him seriously and it opened a lot of doors. We started a sustenance program, where we could help people buy their Ensure. Gabe had a stricture in his throat and couldn't take solid food anymore. We would buy Ensure and help with utility bills. We started a microgrant of $100 or $200 a month. If you were living off of $400 a month or $600 a month, an extra $100 would really help. That little extra might keep the guitar out of the pawn shop."

Big Ron Hunter: Guitar Gabe Pleases the Judge

Big Ron Hunter honed his acoustic guitar style as a young man playing with Gabe in drink houses. In 2006 we were at an outdoor café on Fourth Street in Winston-Salem when he told these stories.

"I can tell you a little story about Guitar Gabriel that happened right across the street there one day. The Speak Easy Jazz building wasn't there—it was something else then—but I saw him right there on the street, right where that place is now. So Gabe had told me he had to go to court that day. He always carried his guitar on his back—so he goes to court and I met him coming from court—right across the street there. I asked him how did everything go in court.

"Gabe said, 'Oh, Ronnie, it went real well.' He said he played his guitar for the judge and the judge let him off. He gave that little laugh like he always did and says, 'The judge liked it.' Gabe played his guitar for the

9.4. Big Ron Hunter. Courtesy Doug Mokaren.

judge and the judge liked his guitar playing. So, Gabe played his way out of jail that day.

"Gabe and I used to play a place called the Town Lounge. So we'd play there, Thursday and Fridays. It was over there near the curve below the Baptist Hospital in Winston-Salem. I was playing with a band but Gabe and I would do the intermissions. And after we played the club we'd go do the liquor houses, your drink houses up on Cherry Street and play there. Gabe would say, 'Come on, Ronnie, let's go.' And we'd go play the liquor houses and the clubs. The first place we'd stop would be this little one-room club on North West Boulevard called the Black Velvet Lounge. It was a one-room club back then, the Black Velvet Lounge. It's still there. It expanded, but in those days it was just one room. We'd set up in the middle of the floor in that one room and they'd let us play. We played for the fun of it and for the tips. Gabe knew everybody. And they were happy to have us come in and play.

"Gabe used to tell me, he would say, 'Ronnie, can't nobody else play like you.' See, he would always play and sing and I would back him up. I would play the lead parts. Back then—my style—I was into B. B. King—so on acoustic guitar—I could play that style of guitar. He would love to hear that, that moaning style, that crying style, that pushing up on the strings, twisting them around. He really liked that and he played the rhythm. After a while I got married and joined the church. And so I never came out to the liquor houses after that.

"A time passed and the next time I saw Gabe, he was playing at Ziggy's club and had been overseas playing his guitar and everything, but I was so into the church by that time that I didn't go to the clubs or drink houses. This was in the 1990s. Then the last time I saw him, I was playing at this old theater called the Rich Theater—this building is still standing, too. Rich Theater. I was in a choir there. I played guitar for them. And Gabe came in with these five guys that called themselves the Harmonizers. The Five Harmonizers. And they played and I saw Gabe outside and I was talking with him and he says, 'Hey, Ronnie, I got to go around the building right quick.'

"Gabe always had a little small bottle of wine he kept with him. And he says, 'Yeah, Ronnie, I got to have me a little nip.'

"I had my wife with me and she asks me if Gabe was going to go in there and try to play after he'd been drinking. I told her not to worry, that Gabe could handle it. He could. Gabe could handle his liquor. And they brought the house down that day. They turned the place out. The Harmonizers just had voices and Gabe on the guitar. That's all they needed. And it was just awesome."

Mike Bennett: Guitar Gabe and the Walking Stick

Music teacher and owner of the B String, Michael Bennett shared these Guitar Gabriel stories when I interviewed him at his shop in 2006.

"Back when I worked at another shop—this was a music shop across town and Gabe would come in there. Gabe was real popular back in the '40s and '50s but then kinda got screwed out of his money—caught up in a bad contract or something like that and he just dropped out of things. Gabe was a character. He was the real thing. Once when he saw me playing, Gabe stopped me and said, 'Boy, you don't need all that in there.' I started playing again and he stopped me and said, 'You don't need all that.'

"What he meant was that I was playing too many notes. So when I started playing again, I played fewer notes and he said, 'There you go.

9.5. Michael Bennett. Courtesy Doug Mokaren.

That's how you do it.' He didn't want me playing all up and down the guitar. It's like what B. B. King says: 'It's not what you play; it's what you don't play.' I was trying too hard to get in a lot of notes, as many as I could, to be impressive. It took me getting over the '80s and being in cover bands where we shredded the guitar before I could follow Gabe's advice. Gabe was the real deal. His kind of music is less flash and more expressed. He was more of a personality, a real showman.

"Music Makers bought Gabe a really nice Gibson guitar but Gabe didn't like it. He was used to cheap guitars, the kind where you really had to mash down hard on the strings to make the chords. So I took Gabe's new Gibson and fixed it so that Gibson would play the way he liked to play. Basically, I ruined that guitar. But Gabe was happier to have it play like the guitars he was used to playing. He had to mash harder to make the notes and that was how he got his style. Those old bluesmen played cheap guitars. There's a distinct tone to them, a raw sound.

"But there was one repair I did for Gabe that made him happier than anything and it wasn't on a guitar. Gabe used to carry this walking stick with—I think it was a lion's head on the top. The stick was hollow. You screwed the lion's head off and there was a test tube down inside about seven inches long that would hold three or four shots of liquor. You screwed the lion's head off and the tube was supposed to pop up, but it wasn't working right anymore. Gabe complained about it, he would say, 'It's just like me; it don't pop up much anymore.' He would have to turn the cane over, upside down, and try to beat it to tap out that liquor tube but the tube would get stuck.

"So I said, 'Here, let me see what I can do to fix it.'

"So I took his cane into the back of the guitar shop and unscrewed the top of the cane and looked to see why it wasn't working. I saw where it was supposed to have a little spring down in the bottom that would push the tube up. The spring was worn out. So I took a little high hat spring and fit it down in the bottom of the cane and put the test tube back in, screwed the head back on, and took it back to Gabe. He unscrewed the head and that tube popped out and you would have thought I'd given him a hundred-dollar bill. I fixed his drinking cane and he was very happy with that.

"You know. These old guys get to drinking and well—you got to control the alcohol. Bonnie Raitt's first job was to manage the liquor for some of the older blues musicians. You got to control the alcohol. But Gabe sure liked to have a drink. I don't know if Gabe would have been Gabe without all the alcohol."

Abe Reid: Guitar Gabe's Little Roadie

Abe Reid is a harmonica and guitar player and vocalist from Statesville, North Carolina. It was early June in 2014 and Abe had just picked strawberries when I interviewed him at his home. Abe explained that he had learned to love blues music from his mother's boyfriend, Tim Bridges. His interest in the music eventually led him to a friendship with Guitar Gabriel.

9.6. Abe Reid. Courtesy Doug Mokaren.

"I loved Elvis Presley. My mom's boyfriend when I was growing up, Tim Bridges—Timothy Dane Bridges—bought me a guitar, bought me a motorcycle, spanked my bottom, hugged on me. Tim helped raise me up. When I was loving on Elvis Presley, Tim kind of made fun of it like Elvis Presley was a cartoon character or something. So he started giving me Brownie McGhee and Sonny Terry albums.[9] Blues albums. Big Joe Williams[10] . . . stuff like that, because Tim wanted me to understand who Elvis had listened to so he could sound the way he did. I didn't listen to those records . . . back then I was into the Grateful Dead. So I had met this guy that lived up the street from us. He was going through my record collection. I was really into the Grateful Dead and I had this album called *Bear's Choice*.[11] It had a song on it called 'Katie Mae Blues,' which is a Lightnin' Hopkins song. I had Lightnin' Hopkins records in my collection but had never put them on the table. I knew they were cool old killer-looking records, but I'd never listened to them. I was doing the San Francisco thing then with Big Brother and the Holding Company, Jefferson Airplane, Grateful Dead, Ten Years After. I loved all that stuff. . . . I was playing that Grateful Dead record and I loved that song ['Katie Mae Blues']. I kept playing it over and over.

"My friend said, 'That's the blues.'

"I was like, '*That's* the blues?' . . . I thought the bluesmen were all dead. I thought, God, man, could you imagine being alive while there were still bluesmen walking this planet? I was positive they were all dead, but we decided we'd try going to a blues festival anyway. We went to the one advertised at the old train depot in Greensboro.

"I had a kid. I was sixteen or seventeen years old, but I already had a little boy, Caleb. We left Caleb with my mother and went to the festival. And there was freaking Snooky Pryor and the Holmes Brothers and all those guys.[12] That's where I met Tim Duffy. He sat behind me and he said, 'Man, shoot. You got to meet this guy, Guitar Gabriel.' Then sometime after that, Gabe was playing right across the street from where the old Ziggy's used to be. There was an old sports bar there, where he played. That's the first time I met Guitar Gabriel. My mom watched my little boy and we drove down from Statesville and I got to meet Guitar Gabriel. We were friends after that.

"He was always like, 'How my little roadie?' He called me his little roadie.

"I remember one night after Gabe had played and I was following him around carrying his stuff, we stopped by the Blind Tiger when it was across the street from the old Wild Magnolias because Bob Margolin was playing there. I wasn't old enough to get in but Tim Duffy was with us and vouched for me. I promised I wouldn't drink anything. I'm forty-two now so that had to be at least twenty-two years ago. Then I didn't know who Bob Margolin was. I knew he played with Muddy Waters, but I figured there was maybe three thousand people on the planet that could say they had played with Muddy Waters. I didn't really understand. Well, they let me in, and Gabe came in and Bob made eye contact with Gabe and they smiled at each other. Bob finished the song and they brought Gabe up. Mookie Brill[13] was playing harmonica and bass with

9.7. Guitar Gabriel. Courtesy Gaile Welker.

them that night. Bob Margolin just gave Gabe his guitar. He turned his band over to Gabe.

"Gabe played Statesville one time. I was so excited; I got him booked in Statesville. You know how it is when you book a band and you get them to come to your hometown? You're so proud. . . . Max Drake stopped by to see him. Max grew up with my dad and his brothers. They call him the 'Great Maxi Pad.' They'd say, 'If you could buy Max for what he was worth and sell him for what he thought he was worth, you'd be a millionaire.' They're full of all these little funny sayings. Really, they're all just guys that played music together, but while they're all swinging hammers now, Max has continued with music. Anyway, Max came in and got Gabe's wine bottle off the stage to put in his case of things from all his bluesmen that he's played with. Max said that Gabe was dirty. Then, I loved Gabe so much—and I'd never heard Gabe be dirty—so that just tore me up when Max said that, but I'd never heard the 'Over 21 Song.' Max was right. It's filthy.[14]

"We used to go to Sam's Drink House with Gabe—this was a different Sam, not Sam 'the Dot Man' McMillan but another one.[15] Now, Sam the Dot Man, he would go to the Goodwill and buy a suit and cover it all over in dots. He'd just paint little dots all over suits, hats, ties, and even shoes. Sam would paint polka dots on everything. Gabe wore one of his dotted-up suits once to play a gig. And Gabe usually wore that tall, ugly hat. He wore that hat because he thought people would remember him if he wore it. He was right. It was distinctive. That hat got washed and messed up, which is why you see Gabe in different versions of that fluffy hat . . . and he wore one of Sam the Dot Man's polka-dot suits. But now I'm talking about a different Sam with a drink house in East Winston. This was Sam Red. We would go out to Sam's house and we'd go into the kitchen and there'd be a lady sitting in there next to the door so no one could slip in there and help themselves to something. She had all these little cups like you rinse and spit with when you go to the dentist. . . . You'd go up to the kitchen and pay her and she'd pour you out a shot in one of her little dentist cups. . . .

"I used to go to Gabe's house in East Winston and in the front yard there'd be lighters on the ground everywhere. Just everywhere. Like autumn leaves fallen off of the trees.[16] This was the time when crack cocaine was getting popular. So there'd be lighters all over the place outside in the yard. Inside the house, there'd be lighters lined up like decorations across the mantel . . . eight blue ones, eight red ones, eight yellow ones, and then eight more blue ones. Just like that, all across the mantle and on the tables like in a spiraling design. We tried some of them out once, didn't none of them work. I don't know why Gabe lined them up like that. He was very superstitious."[17]

Rob Slater: Sweet Daddy's Two-Dollar Bill

"Sweet Daddy" Ray Burnett (1949–2012) was born in Snow Camp, North Carolina, and became widely known as a guitarist for numerous bands in the Piedmont area. He was the front man for the band Sophisticated Blues, which traveled extensively up and down the East Coast. Ray was a familiar personality in the Triad jam scene, sometimes as a host and other

9.8. Rob Slater. Courtesy Doug Mokaren.

times as a player, where he was recognized as a "sharp-dressed man," usually wearing a suit, hat, and tie when he was on stage.

Rob Slater is a guitar player who met Ray Burnett later, after he discovered the jams, in particular jams at bars like the Flat Iron, the Zion Bar and Grille, and Summit Station in Greensboro, all of which are closed now. This is Rob's story about playing the Piedmont jam scene with Sweet Daddy Ray Burnett.

"I played in bands for a while, doing the music thing in the '70s. One thing led to another and I quit teaching and worked with Mitch Easter and those guys. It was mostly rock and roll and pop. I played in this band that was one of the first promo, do-it-yourself, pop acts to come out of North Carolina in the mid-'70s with Chris Stamey, Mitch Easter, and Will Rigby, who has been playing drums with Steve Earle off and on forever.[18] I did that kind of thing for a while. Then my wife was pregnant and so it was time to come back home and be with her, to quit messing around with this music thing and to get a real job. So I went back to teaching around 1983. I didn't play any music for a long time. Then I discovered the jams.

"A bar will host a jam along with a local band or professional musician who will run the jam and organize players into sets. Usually there's a sign-up sheet. I went to the jams in the legal bars. I didn't go to the house-party jams; the jams I went to were legit.

"When I got involved in the jams, I soon realized that there were personalities involved. You'd see a lot of the same people over and over again. There are different jams at different bars, but a lot of the same players. There's also a hierarchy there and as a player, you come up through that hierarchy. The first few times you show up at a jam, you're persona non grata and you get the shitty set with the shitty players. If you're persistent enough, then eventually things will work out to where you'll catch a good set every once in a while. There's usually a surfeit of guitar players, so you wait your turn.

"The guitar is an instrument that's very easy to play badly. Nobody wants to play in the set with that bad player. Nobody wants to have that bad set, but somebody gets it. The more you hang around at the jams and the more you support the scene, the more of a contribution you make to it, then the more likely you are to get the good sets. It's a sort of . . . I hate to use this term because it doesn't do it justice, but it's a 'dues paying' sort of thing. If you support the scene, if you come and hang, and if you do the right thing, then eventually you work your way up to the good sets. A lot of people at jams don't support the scene. The right thing to do is buy a couple of drinks, tip the waitress generously, and just support the thing. Too many guys just blow in and sit there, hoping to get a decent set. As soon as they play, they're gone because they've got to go to work the next day. If you're consistent and faithful to the scene and support it with your presence and you continue to work on your playing, it's just this graduated progression. You occasionally get a good set, and then occasionally get a better set. If you're a really good boy, you'll get either the first set, which is usually the one where they try to put the bar a little

9.9. Ray Burnett. Courtesy Doug Mokaren.

higher, or the last set, which was the Ray [Burnett] thing. Eventually, if you're lucky, you get the good set. If you go to a jam and Ray Burnett is there, you aspire to play his set. That would be *the* good set.

"Ray was a great teacher. He was a great role model. He was a great guy and gentleman and a good player. He knew his craft. I noticed after a long time of going to the jams, that in the last set of the night a lot of the best players got up with Ray. In honor of Ray, to do Ray justice, Ray was being supported with good players. Whoever was running the jam would get a good band up for Ray to do his thing. For me, watching this for a long time, it just seemed like, wow, the ultimate gig here at the jam is to get the Ray set at the end of the night. . . . As I was watching this, it seemed like this is where this jam thing leads to: the last set of the night when Ray Burnett is on stage. That's what to aspire to: we all used to call it the 'Ray set.' For me, if I got the Ray set, if I was able to be on stage with Ray and participate in the Ray set, I had a buzz that was good for the rest of the week. If it happened on Sunday night, that buzz would carry me through work and everything else for the week.

"Normally there weren't a whole lot of people left by the last set of the Sunday-night jam or the Thursday-night jam, where people had to go to work the next day. Many people were gone by the last set. In some ways that was really cool. The musicians were playing for themselves and Ray. Rather than getting up there and jerking off on your guitar for twenty minutes, the Ray set became where the music really wants to go: these tunes, played well with dynamics and feeling. It was most purely about the music.

"If you got the Ray set, there was a decorum. You watched Ray and you listened to Ray and you learned his cues. He taught us all stagecraft. He taught us how to play. He taught us when to get quiet. He taught us how not to be too loud and to be enthusiastic and to follow . . . it's just good musical decorum. Even in the goofy jam late Sunday evening at eleven o'clock, there was a professionalism. Ray brought that to the jam. It was kind of unusual. There are some people around here, Shiela Klinefelter[19] is one, who understand how these things are; how they can be good and bad. You can cultivate something really good depending on how attentive you are.

"We were really lucky to have Ray around because he was so respected. I think going back to the 1970s, he hosted jams out at SomeWhere Else Tavern. So Ray has been in the local jam scene forever. Ray started out as a horn player and gravitated towards guitar. He didn't know categories. He played everything . . . jazz . . . blues. He was that way with people, too. No categories. I think it was one of the reasons he had such respect. But you had to mind your Ps and Qs when you played with him. If you were too loud, you got *the look*. Ray had a look. He would give a look that shot across the stage. If you weren't reading that look the right way, that might be the last time that you would get the Ray set. You minded your business. That's what I mean when I talk about Ray teaching. He taught by example this whole notion of stagecraft. There's a time to support other players and then there's the time when you get your moment to step out front. You take your lead and you were allowed your creative voice. There are certain boundaries within which you should probably stay, volume being premier among them. Don't play bad. Don't play loud. If you get a solo and you're soloing, don't overstay your welcome. These all really, really good lessons that every player should know. Some guys who don't get to play out regularly become overly eager at the jam. It's like, 'Oh boy, this is my big chance.' Those guys might go on and on when they got their lead, but Ray would let them know. There was *the look*. Time to get out of it. If you didn't interpret the look properly, then Ray would come back in with a verse or there would be a musical cue, kind of like, 'You're done. We're going back to the tune now.' Whoever was running the jam, for example if it was Shiela, she knew Ray would not tolerate those guys who could not learn the lesson; she would not put those players up with Ray.

"But Ray also acknowledged when you did something good musically. Usually, Ray was always listening. There was this kind of Darwinian joke, a complicated and paradoxical joke. I don't know where or when it started. I remember the first time I experienced it was at Zion [Bar and Grille]. It was kind of a compliment with a nod and a wink. Wherever Ray was in the room, he was listening. If you played something particularly tasty or really, really heartfelt or slightly musically dangerous, if you took a chance, if you went out on the catwalk and managed not to fall off, and Ray was in a good mood or in a particularly good mood—it wasn't this thing that happened often, which is what made it so special—he would saunter over slowly to the front of the stage and he had a dollar bill. Sometimes he'd walk up on the stage. It was almost like tipping a stripper at a club. If you had a shirt-front pocket, he would tuck that dollar bill into your pocket, look at you with this shit-eating grin, and then just turn and walk away. It was also a means of putting you in your place. At least that's how I interpreted it. He'd put this dollar bill in your pocket; it was like a caution and a benediction and a nod. It was also a 'mind your manners' kind of thing. That dollar bill slipped in your pocket had numerous meanings. The joke involved a few of us. It was a thing where the players who enjoyed the joke would do it. We were all careful not to wear it out. Once every two or three months this might happen. Ray would come up and tuck a dollar in your pocket. We would do that to each other, too. It seems like when somebody played something that was unusually good, the dollar bill would come out. It was a really big treat. It said that the players were all listening.

"The ultimate, ultimate was one night . . . I don't know what I did, but Ray came out and he tossed the dollar. I picked the dollar up but it was a two-dollar bill.[20] A two-dollar bill was really, absurdly wonderful. The two-dollar bill was like a papal benediction and a middle finger, both at the same time. It really was the ultimate. I think I've still got two of them in a picture frame at the house. . . . I cherish those two-dollar bills as much as I do anything.

"After Ray died and there was going to be the funeral . . . we were all wanting to hear people testify and go into the church and hear what Ray's home church had to offer up and all that. I don't know what possessed me, but I thought, you know, it's going to be my last chance to lay a two-dollar bill on Ray. I thought about it beforehand. I thought, on the one hand, I should not do this. It might be considered disrespectful. Then I thought, the hell with that. This is it, my last shot. I got a two-dollar bill at the bank before Ray's service. I tucked it into my pocket and I made a point of getting to the church early. You know, the southern tradition of going to the church for the viewing. There's Ray's body in the coffin with the crisp velour interior and the custom-car appoints that they had. I thought, this is just between Ray and me. I had the two-dollar bill folded small and neat. I had it in my pocket. I got there early. My plan was just to wait until there was a hole in the crowd and there wasn't anybody by the coffin. I walked up and I just had a chuckle. Ray was always turned out. So of course he was dressed really fine in this blue suit. I pulled the two-dollar bill out of my pocket all folded up nice and tight, and I just tucked it inside his coat pocket, his breast pocket. Again, it was this whole notion of, 'Well played. Watch yourself,' the paradoxical nature of the whole two-dollar bill thing. I got to tuck that into his jacket pocket.

"Ray was special to all of us. If there is anybody on the planet who would have appreciated that two-dollar bill and would have gotten pissed off that he wasn't able to return the favor in kind, it would have been Ray Burnett. Ray knew what it was to try some kind of dangerous solo where he went to the edge and danced along it and pulled it off. It was my way of saying, 'Wow. Spectacular.' He taught me to listen. I had the greatest respect and admiration for Ray Burnett. As a player, sure, but just as a human being he was a great man. I'd be willing to bet he started the whole two-dollar bill thing. I'm absolutely willing to bet that he was the one who started it. I bet he was the first one to crumple up a bill and throw it at somebody. That's just a Ray thing to do. Like I said, it had a multiplicity of meanings. That was what Ray was all about . . . depth of meaning."

◆ ◆ ◆

The Piedmont is home to a fair number of colorful personalities. There are far more stories and personalities than the few shared here. What the stories about these three personalities reveal is the rich insider dynamics of a robust, roaming musical jam from a drink house, to the more organized bar jam, to the tip jar on the sidewalk out front, back to the drink house. When one bar closed or a drink house got shut down, the jam would move somewhere else. These three personalities in particular were like gurus to younger white musicians and fans, but gurus with an edge. The lessons they taught their protégés were notable ones: support the scene, don't overplay, don't overstay, don't be too loud, don't be too proud, wait your turn, tell your story (even your lies), truly enjoy the occasion when it's your moment to shine, and—finally—let the good times roll.

CHAPTER 10

Even Chocolate Cowboys Get the Blues

Roy Roberts

Roy Roberts is best known as a blues musician, vocalist, guitar player, and record producer. He was born in Livingston, Tennessee, in 1942 but spent his early years in Park City, Kentucky, before he moved to Greensboro, North Carolina, in 1960, where he met R&B artist Solomon Burke (1940–2010). Burke adopted Roy as his musical protégé and took him on tour as his guitarist. Roy has since played gigs with the likes of Eddie Floyd, Stevie Wonder, Dee Clark, and Otis Redding. His own band, the Roy Roberts Experience, became popular in clubs across the South and particularly on the beach circuit. Roy began cutting records in the 1960s and did session work for other artists as well as recording some of his own material. In the early 1990s, Roy built a recording studio, Rock House Records, in Greensboro, where he has produced artists like Lou Pride, Chick Willis, Skeeter Brandon, and Priscilla Price. However, in the 1980s, Roy's career took an unusual turn toward country, when he followed the example of O. B. McClinton[1] and became a "chocolate cowboy." For years Roy performed country music in some scary southern honky-tonks before he made his return to blues. Roy said the motivation to try country music belongs to disco.

"I was playing in all the R&B clubs. I had over 300 clubs I was playing in, and during a period of thirty days, nearly everybody called and canceled. The disco had arrived. When disco came to town, it put all the bands out of business. All these clubs that had been booking live bands started booking the DJs with the disco. It started in '77 or '78. And then in '79, it just blossomed. No one is listening to live music.

"I'm sitting at the house, worried up, don't know what I'm going to do, so I called a buddy of mine, Arthur Smith[2] in Charlotte. I was talking to

10.1. Roy Roberts. Courtesy Doug Mokaren.

him about it and Arthur says, 'Well, you can always come down here and do bluegrass with me.'

"I said to him, 'You must be out of your mind, man. I can't mess around with no bluegrass.'

"He was laughing. He said to me, 'No, Roy. You ought to consider going into country music.'

"I said, 'That's just—well that's just bad, man. You know good and well they ain't going to let no black man play country music around here in the clubs.'

"He told me, 'I wouldn't tell anybody else to do it, but I'm telling you to do it because the attitude that you have, and the way you get along with people, you can pull it off.' He said, 'Write a couple songs and bring them over, and I'm going to produce them for you.' During that time, Arthur had shows on fifty-two radio stations. I went over there. He cut the songs, pressed it up, and put it out on his radio shows. Then I came back over to Greensboro and was hanging around waiting on something to happen.

"I had this guy, black guy, that was a manager, Ed Luther. Ed Luther was a chef. They call him Chef Eddy here in town, and he had a restaurant called Chef Eddy's. Oh, he had several restaurants. They were just little small restaurants, not clubs, strictly restaurants. Had one downtown, and then he had one over here off of Bessemer, I think it is. That's how I met him, by going into his restaurant. When I'd go in there, if he wasn't real busy, he'd come sit down and talk to me and everything. One time he was talking to me he said, 'Man, you know with your voice and everything, you'd be great in country music.' He said, 'You ever want to get into country music you need to come with me, and I'm going to help you to produce this stuff.' Ed Luther loved country music. It was really wild, man, just how much he loved country.

"So we heard that Ernest Tubb was up in Madison playing at this big club. I told him, I said, 'Hey, Ed, let's go up there and check it out.'

"He said, 'Man, you must be crazy going up there. You know how redneck that part of the country is.'

"This is Madison, North Carolina, right up the road on 220. We went on up, walked in the door, and it was full. I guess there was probably about 500 people in there. Everybody started looking at us. All eyes was on us, the only two black guys in the whole club: me and Ed Luther. Oh no. He was scared to death.

"I said, 'Man, ain't no sense to be scared. They going to think two things: either we're the ABC officers or we crazy.'

"Ed said, 'Yeah. You are just that damn crazy.'

"I said, 'Let's go on in there.'

"So we went in. Everybody, man, I mean everybody just stopped what they was doing. All eyes was on us. We two were the only black people in the place. We just walked on over to the bar. I started talking to the bartender and the lady that owned the club; she was behind the bar. Some of the guys that was in the band that was playing in there knew me from the beach days and everything. When they came off the stage they came straight to me and shouted, 'Roy Roberts! Roy Roberts is in the house!'

"Now everybody's looking around. They want to see who is this Roy Roberts.

"The boys in the band came up to me said, 'Hey, Roy, you going to sit in and sing a couple songs with us tonight?'

"I told them, 'Yeah. If y'all don't mind. I'll sing a couple of songs.'

"They said, 'Okay, when we go back we'll play a couple and then we're going to bring you on up.'

"They brought me up, and I did my thing on Elvis Presley, my imitation of Elvis Presley, and a couple of other songs. Man, everybody was just clapping and hollering out. Everybody was into that. When I came off the stage, people were coming up to me, saying, 'Man, you were just great.'

"About two weeks later we went to Burlington to a club there. I forget the name of it now. So we went to this club, walked in to talk to the lady that owned it. She said, 'You know, I heard about this black guy that was up in Madison last week; he just set the club on fire with a couple of songs.' She said, 'I'd love to bring you in but I don't think it would work down here. I don't think the people would accept it.'

"I knew what I could do. I told her, 'I tell you what. If you let me come in and do a show, you don't have to pay me a dime.' I said, 'But if I come in here, and we turn this club out, you pay me double of what I was going to charge you.'

"She said, 'You've got a deal.'

"We went in there and set that club on fire. There wasn't that much publicity either. You just had the radio and the newspaper. That's what you did back then. She advertised on the radio and people knew they were coming to hear this all-black band. We worked up country music songs. I was doing all kinds of stuff: Elvis Presley, Waylon Jennings, George Jones, just all of those guys. It wasn't hard. The reason why it wasn't so hard is because a lot of that stuff—like I did some old Hank Williams and stuff like that—that music was familiar to me. I grew up out in Kentucky, so that's all you could hear most of the time unless you stayed up late at night to listen to WLAC[3] or something like that. But all during the day was the little country radio stations. I knew everything that all the country artists were doing as a young boy growing up. When I decided to try and get into the country music, I still remembered the words to a lot of those songs. We didn't have the twang. This was going to be country soul—or country with soul. Picture Ray Charles doing country. You know how soulful that was when he did 'I Can't Stop Loving You' and stuff like that. That's the way our music was. That's what set us apart from all the other country-western bands. I didn't have a steel guitar or banjos. We just had the guitars: two guitars, a bass, drums, and a keyboard.

"In the country music scene we played for all-white audiences. All the time. And some of the worst places you've ever wanted to go to, we went there. One of them was in Lillington, North Carolina. The Klan was active there. Okay. We were actually playing for one of the head guys in the Klan; we were playing right in his club. I don't remember the name of the club now, but it had Klan pictures up on the walls and everything, pictures of crosses burning. Well, we were so popular that other white people were going to the Klan boss and telling him, 'You got to book this band in here. This is the baddest country band you ever want to hear.'

"The old guy said, 'Okay. I'll give it a shot.'

"Sure enough, he hired us and we went in and turned that place out. People were as happy as they could be. He was, too. He started bringing me in like every six or seven weeks. He would bring me back to play in that club, right in Lillington where the Klan was in full force even then. Later we moved on over to Selma [North Carolina], which wasn't much better as far as the Klan, but they also liked our music.

"Out of all of them, probably the most memorable country music bar was when we were playing in that Klan club. When I go in this club with those Klan pictures all around the wall of crosses burning and all of this stuff, I'm looking around, I'm thinking, 'Oh, *hell*, I'm in the wrong place. But I done got booked in here, so let me go and take care of business.' Man, that turned out to be one of the best clubs I ever played in. I'll tell you why. What happened was this white guy came up to me one night, and he said, 'Roy Roberts.'

"I said, 'Yeah, buddy. What's going on?'

"He said, 'You know what I just can't stand, a G-D nigger.'

"I'm thinking, 'Oh man. This cat's getting ready to get knocked out or something.' I got mad . . . but I'm thinking I can't lose my cool because I'll lose my job and look where I am.' So I busted out and started laughing.

"This confused him. He said, 'What the hell are you laughing about?'

"I said, 'I'm just like you. I can't stand a'—I didn't use God's name, but I said, 'I can't stand a nigger neither.'[4]

"He started laughing then. He said, 'You know one thing, Roy Roberts. You crazy as hell.' And then he said, 'I like you. Anything that you boys want, just go over to the bar and y'all get it and put it on my tab.'

"From then on, every show that I played down in that area, he was there. He was there and was acting like my best friend. He was my biggest fan. But if I would have done what I wanted to do in my heart—and that would have been to knock him out—if I had done that, I'd have messed up everything. Lillington, Selma, and Smithfield, all of these little towns are all around each other, and I'm playing the clubs in all of these towns. If I'd of knocked that guy out, I would have blown everything that I was trying do. So I was just real cool about it. From then on, every time I would play anywhere around Lillington, he was there. Lot of times he would be the first one at the club. I made a fan and a friend. It's all in knowing what to do in a situation. Just like Arthur Smith told me from the beginning. Arthur said to me, 'I wouldn't tell anybody else around here to go into country music like that,' but he said, 'You. You're totally different. I've known you for years, and I know you can go out there and you can pull it off, and you can handle whatever comes along.'

"I think I handled that one real well."

I asked Roy if he started wearing a cowboy hat and jeans for his country gigs like Charley Pride or Clarence "Gatemouth" Brown did when they played country music.

"No. I did it only one time. The girl who ran the bar in Burlington, she said, 'Look, if you're going to be playing country music and everything, you got to get the boots, you got to get the jeans, you got to have the cowboy hat.' I told her—I don't remember her name, but I told her, I said, 'Look. I have never been comfortable with going on stage with jeans on.' We were playing there Friday and Saturday nights. I said, 'I'll tell you what I'm going to do. I'm going to try it on a Friday night, and if I'm not comfortable, I'm going to have to go back to my regular dress.'

"She said, 'Okay. That's the deal.'

"I went in there, and I felt like I was undressed with all the cowboy stuff on. Yeah. I felt undressed. Just like I wasn't dressed at all because that wasn't what I was used to doing. I was used to dress clothes all the time. Suits and stuff like that.

"We went on in the next night. She said, 'Well, I see you didn't enjoy it last night with the clothes you had on.' She said, 'But you looked real good.'

"I said, 'I can't help that. It just wasn't my style.'

"She said, 'Okay. I ain't going to mess with it.'

"So I started wearing regular clothes again. My regular stage clothes. I may have been a chocolate cowboy, but I didn't wear the jeans."

We discussed the cowboy stage presence for a bit. Roy explained that his R&B experience taught him that stage presence required a nice suit. You might see an occasional picture of Solomon Burke wearing a cowboy hat, but he almost always has on a suit and tie. Roy explained that the strategy was to open up the first set with country music, but his band's second set reverted to soul and R&B. A suit worked better or felt better for the R&B portion of his country gigs. It wasn't until the last few years that Roy felt comfortable playing a gig in jeans or without a suit coat. Even when he was booked as a country band, Roy knew he would end the night with R&B.

"What was happening there is because the white people in the club, they love black music. They love the funk and soul music and everything. Looking at us being black guys, they knew that we could play that stuff. When I opened up the show, I did strictly country covers: Hank Williams, George Jones, all of them guys. I'm doing that. Then when we take our break, I'd have people start coming up to us asking, 'Can you do the 'Ladies Night?' Can you do 'Brick House?' Can you do this or that?'

"I said, 'Oh yeah. Yeah. We can do all that.'

"Then I go back on stage and I say, 'Special request. These people want to hear this and that.' Then we just go into our bag and then really kill them. They were doing line dancing to R&B. It was a sight. Some trying to do whatever they could do. They were in the groove with the funk we were playing. Most were line dancing, two-step, whatever you want to call it, and slow dance. You couldn't do too much two-stepping to R&B, but there's some songs that you can. It's just according to how the tempo is being set and everything.

"I did the country scene from 1980 to about 1989. What happened was in '87 was . . . Then, well, O. B. McClinton, the black country signer out in Nashville, he and I were real close like brothers. We had been doing some stuff on the road together, and the last show we did . . . I think we were in Wilson [North Carolina] or someplace down in there. That night he came out, he just didn't perform hardly at all to where it was any good. It was clear that he was just trying to get through the show. He made it through the show, and then he went to the hospital. They patched him up and sent him on back to Nashville. When he got to Nashville, he had another sick attack. He went to the hospital, and when he went in there, they examined him and took X-rays and everything. They told him that he had cancer. The cancer that he had, he had one year to live. Sure enough, he lived exactly one year.

10.2. Roy Roberts. Courtesy Doug Mokaren.

"I was just . . . I was kind of devastated over that. I was also just burned out because I never had a break in the music. I'd been playing straight since 1962. It was New Year's Eve, and we were playing down at Lake Royale. I just turned to the band at the end of the show, and I told everybody go get your job with somebody else, I'm through.

"I brought all my equipment back home. Locked it up. Went on over to Virginia in 1989. Bought me a little recording studio over there and I moved over to Virginia away from everybody: family and everything. I didn't want to be bothered by nobody. I just wanted to be by myself to get myself together for a while. I went over to Danville and was screwing around in my studio. It was doing pretty good. I produced some gospel artists, did a gospel record. Then one day I heard Robert Cray[5] on the radio. When that happened, listening to Robert Cray, the old blues bug bit me again, fired me up.

"I said, 'Man. This cat is out there.' Because we both got kind of the same style playing, I thought, 'Here's this cat; we got the same style and he's out there making money and I'm setting up here in this studio.'

"So, I went and wrote me a couple of blues songs. When my engineer came in, I told him about it. I said, 'Man, I got these songs. I want to cut these blues songs. I'm going back into the blues.'

"The engineer calls a couple of boys over. They came in and we cut the songs.

"Then I had a friend in Nashville. Guy named Ed Crowley. They had a little record label. Went out there talked to him about it. He said, 'Well, bring it out here, Roy. We can't promise whether we going to have a hit or not, but hey, I can put it out on my label, and we can see what it will do.'

"I did that. Then after I did that, this guy down in Cary called me one day and wanted to produce an album on me. That's in '93 I think it was. That was the album *Introducing Roy Roberts*.[6] That was my first blues album. Yeah. I went down and recorded with him and come to find out he wasn't nothing but a big crook. Man, he was messing over Skeeter Brandon[7] too. When I found out what he was doing, and he wouldn't pay nobody any royalties, I went in this studio of a friend of mine over here in Kernersville. I went into his studio, and I recut the album because I couldn't use that other production without getting sued. It's my music, and my songs, so I went back in the studio and did it over. I recut that album and made it identical to that first one. Then I put it out and no sooner than I put that thing out, I got a call from New York wanting me to come to Harlem. They said, 'Hey, man. You did something nice here.' From then on I just kept on in the blues."

Roy admitted to me that he had a fascination for the cowboy as well as the Western, which helped to make the idea of country music more attractive to him. I asked him to explain the mystique of the cowboy.

"My granddad was the first man to have a television in our hometown. That was back in the early '50s, or somewhere like that, when TVs first came out. Every Saturday they would have these Western movies coming on. *The Lone Ranger* [1949–57] and *The Rifleman* [1958–63], all of these cowboy shows were on the television. I loved that stuff. It's just something about the Westerns and the history of it. When you go back into the history of Jesse James and all of those guys. The outlaws and stuff like that. I just always loved that history of the cowboy and the Indian. But I don't like the hat. Well, I'm wearing jeans now. Yeah. I started wearing jeans. I guess for probably about six or seven years now, I been wearing jeans. And I love horses.

"I used to live on a farm. Where we lived there was a farm. I used to break horses and everything. The guy, the white guy that owned the farm, he'd go out and he'd buy horses and stuff and couldn't nobody ride them. I'd get out there and catch them. Get them in the barn and mess around, get a saddle on 'em and everything. I'd jump on. Got thrown off a few times. I got a few bruises. I guess you could say I broke horses. I was sixteen or seventeen, I guess. I was young. This was in Kentucky. I broke five horses for that guy. He was always getting those horses that couldn't nobody else ride them but me. One time the guy went and he bought a real pretty little pony for his kids. When he got it back home, the pony wouldn't let the kids ride it. He came to me, said, 'I got these kids a pony, and they can't ride it because he won't let them ride. You got to break this pony for them.' I took the pony out. Kept him about four or five days. Sure enough I broke that pony, made him gentle to where anybody could ride him.

"That's my history of me being a real cowboy."

We chatted about black cowboys on the American frontier and about how those stories were largely missing from mainstream American movies and television. Roy had a similar talent for taming horses that made Nate Love (Deadwood Dick) become a cowboy. Nate Love's ability to tame or "break" a wild horse landed him a job with a trail boss. We had a brief discussion about Cleavon Little's role as a black sheriff in the satire comedy film *Blazing Saddles* (1974) before the conversation circled back around to playing country music in southern bars.

"The other country music story I have was here in Greensboro at a motel that I was playing at downtown. Club was full of white people. This one black guy came in the club. When I took a break he came over to me and started requesting songs and all of that. I told him, 'Man, I can't do that type of stuff right now.' I said, 'I'm in here doing country music and everything. I have a job to do.'

"Then he started getting nasty with me.

"I said, 'Man, you don't know who you messing with. Best thing for you to do is get the hell out of my face before they carry you out of here.'

"The guard heard what was happening. He came over and he took that cat out. The man says to me, 'I'm going to wait for you outside.'

"I said, 'That's good. I want you to wait for me outside because when I come outside, I'm going to beat the hell out of you and go on home.'

"When I left the club, he was gone. Yeah.

"I still like country music. It's the lyrics. It's still a form of blues to me. . . . The market now for distributing music is strictly on the Internet. I can release a country album on the Internet and don't even have to let them know who it is. I just put it out there on the Internet, sit back, and see what will happen. Nobody knew who Charley Pride was until after he done cut all those big hits, done made millions of dollars. Then all of a sudden they bring him out on a show. I think Conway Twitty or somebody had him on a show. They brought him out on a show. They said you could have heard a damn pin drop in the floor—a feather. Said everybody was just spellbound when they looked up and see who Charley Pride really was. Then he said something to the people and started singing. Everybody was fine after that.

"Today, far as the blues that I'm doing, there's not much difference from doing the country music because I'm still playing to mostly all the white crowds. You don't see many blacks in the audience for blues anymore . . . and country music came from the blues. That's the basics. You listen to country music, it's like listening to a blues song. Only difference is you're going to hear fiddles and steel guitars playing the music. If you pull that out, then put a keyboard in there, bass and drums and everything, it's a whole different ball game. That same song that was country, now it's a blues song just by the way the instrumentation is. There's a song of mine called 'Tonight Your Love Belongs to Me.' I wrote it. When I wrote that song, I was still doing country music. Another song I wrote, 'I Truly Love Ya,' I wrote that back in the '80s. You can take any song and make whatever style you want to out of that song. You want it to be a country song; you can make it country. You want it to be blues; you can make it blues. It's the instrumentation that you're using on the music. I might cut me another country album. I like country music. I got some real good country songs."

Although Roy would not play for tips in a place that he recognized as a drink house, he did book his band into some pretty rugged honky-tonks when he was playing country music as well as a few "dives" while he was playing R&B.

"I went down in the woods out in the back woods, down dirt roads to old country-and-western clubs and stuff. I'd go around. Yeah. I'd drive around to the different bars to do all my booking, driving down these dirt roads with tractors and stuff out in the middle of nowhere. Places outside of Selma and all down through that way like going to Morehead City and all down through there. I'd go in there by myself to book shows. Walk in the club and everybody looking at you. I said, 'Lord have mercy. Lord please keep these people straight because I got six bullets in my gun, and I'm going to take six of them with me, and I know the others going to get me in the end, but I'm going to get six, and I'm going to take them with me.'

"So I go in there. The next thing you know, I walk up to the bar, somebody would say, 'Hey, buddy, you want a drink or something?'

"I would say, 'No. I don't drink. Maybe I'll drink a coke or something like that.' I start talking to the guy. Next thing you know, I'm in the house. If I heard of some new club some places, I'd jump in my car, and I'd go because I'd want to see what the club was all about. . . . But the country bars weren't the worst. The worst dive I played in was probably when I was playing the old-school R&B and stuff, and you might be down in South Carolina in some old beat-up shack or something out in the woods. Playing the blues and R&B, stuff like that, I was playing some bad dives down in there, when it come to clubs, man. They were black clubs. You didn't see white people going down to them clubs.

"Everything that I've done in the music business, I took it as an experience and always try to make something good come out of it. It's about knowing how to deal with people. The average guy . . . well, a lot of people can't deal with different kinds of people. I can get along with anybody if you give me a halfway chance. I'll tell you why. I was born in Tennessee. Livingston, Tennessee. You know the Klan originated in Tennessee.

Okay. The Klan migrated into Alabama and all around in Mississippi and Georgia, but it originated in Tennessee.[8] My grandfather owned a service station in the '30s right in downtown Livingston, Tennessee, on the square. The building is still there today. The majority of the people that came to his station were white. They looked at him like he was some kind of hero or something because he could fix anything. Any problems anybody had, they come to Roy McKinney, so Old Man Roy, he would help them with their problems, fix things, and stuff like that.

"When he sold that place, he went up to Park City, Kentucky, and bought almost one hundred acres of land. If you've heard of the Mammoth Cave National Park, that mountain and part of that cave is running up under some of his land. He bought all that land down the whole strip of that highway. Built another service station and little restaurant beside that with tourist cottages in the back. Then he had his house and everything. When he gets to Kentucky, it's the same situation. Everybody's coming to Roy McKinney. This man can fix anything. Only black guy anywhere around that's got a service station. That was unheard of. So I didn't know what prejudice was because back there on the farmland—he had a couple of houses back there—the people that lived in his houses were white people. They worked the farm. He didn't care nothing about prejudice. If you came through and you didn't have no place to stay, and the house was empty, you go on up there. You got a roof over your head. That's the way my granddad was.

"Being raised up in that type of environment, I didn't know nothing about prejudice. I didn't know none of that stuff 'til I came here in 1960. I mean, I heard stuff. We might be listening to the radio or something. Heard about Emmett Till when he was killed down there in Mississippi.[9] Stuff like that. You would hear of hangings and all that in Mississippi and Alabama and stuff. You'd hear about that on the radio or after he got a television. You would see some of that stuff in the news and everything, but up there where we were, black and white were together on Saturday nights. Friday and Saturday nights both. You couldn't get in the restaurant hardly because it'd be jam-packed—black and white. They're watching that TV. He's the only man got a TV, and everybody's excited over that TV. It's like going to the movies. If you wanted a little nip, a little drink of something, he has these little liquors and stuff in there. Some old white lightning. He had a little bit of that in there. Granddad had a jukebox in the restaurant with all kind of blues because he loved blues, too. He had all kinds of blues music on it and some country music, too. People would just eat and set around. Every once in a while somebody might want to get up on the floor and try to dance a little bit. It was funny."

"My granddad used to tell us as kids when I was growing up, he'd say, 'Son, you see that smoke way up down there in the mountain?'

"I'd say, 'Yeah, Granddad. What is that?'

"He said, 'Don't you ever go up there because the Indians are up there, and if you go up there they will kill ya and cook ya,' and all this stuff. He had me scared to death of Indians.

"I said, 'Well, I ain't going up there in the mountains.'

"Come to find out as I started growing up that my granddad was selling some old white lightning. This white guy came in the station one day with these two big gallon jugs looking like they had water in them, and it's white lightning. Granddad was in with the white guys that had the moonshine still back up there in the mountain, right there back there of his place, you know. You'd see all this smoke going up. Yeah. Way over here would be some smoke going up but it wasn't Indians. It'd be the smoke from the moonshine stills."

Before our conversation was over, Roy shared a note about a Greensboro man, Dockery Lewis, who Roy believes was instrumental in the careers of a number of African America musicians, providing a place to stay and helping with bookings in the early stages of a career.

"James Brown, Joe Tex,[10] Little Willie John.[11] They all stayed here in Greensboro because there was a man lived over on Market Street who was their manager, Dockery Lewis. Everybody called him Duck for short. Duck was the one that got James Brown started, Joe Tex, Little Willie John. He helped all these guys. All those guys came, stayed at his house, and everything. Do you know when everybody got famous, made all that money, they didn't pay him no attention? The old man died, and there wasn't nobody at his funeral. I was out of town on a gig when it happened, but when I came back and found out he had died, people told me there wasn't nobody at his funeral. He did a lot for those people. Buy them old cars and book gigs for them and stuff like that.

He was like their manager, trying to help them get started and it was a shame, because once they started getting on their feet with hit records, with record companies, attention and everything, they didn't come back to give Duck a dime or nothing like that. Yeah. The old man died and nothing honored him. He was the one to help them get started. You probably heard of a club here called the ABA club.[12] That's where James Brown played. It was a pretty good-size place. I guess you could get about 400 people up in there back in the day. Whenever James Brown was coming here, hanging around here in Greensboro, Ducky would book him in there."

Although Roy had a successful run as a chocolate cowboy, and has written a few country tunes, he is better known for blues. He explained that he could find inspiration for his music just about anywhere.

"My inspirations for lyrics can be a lot of different things. I'll be in a nightclub and I'll see somebody make some kind of a statement—and that little phrase sounds good to me. And I'll say, 'Hmmm, there's a song in that.' So, you know, I'll take that phrase and I'll write the song. Just like my song 'Daylight with a Flashlight,' for instance. I'm in Mississippi, Jackson Mississippi, performing, and we had been on stage playing. There was a lady in there named Jackie Bell,[13] who was an entertainer herself. She was a singer who worked there with the house band for the club. So that night I'm performing. I come off the stage and the women are going wild and everything. She comes over to me.

"She says, 'Roy Roberts, ain't no way in hell I'm going to get tied up with you, because if I did you'd have me running around in the daylight with a flashlight trying to find you with all these women up in here liking you, you know.'

"So in my mind I get tickled and I'm thinking about this. Say, 'Man, that's the perfect song right there.' So, I hold that in mind 'til I get to the hotel room. Then I pull my guitar out and I write the song that night—or the next morning, actually. After we left the club. Yeah. So, that's how I write a lot of stuff. There's another little song called 'Show Me What You Got,' for instance. We were playing here down on Greene Street, I think it was—at a club down there one night. They booked me in as a blues band and got all these young people in there that's into the hip-hop. So while the hip-hop DJ is playing, I mean the floor is just *full* of people. When we start playing, there's just a few people that'll come out and dance. So I told the band, 'We got a problem tonight. Here we are, a blues band, trying to play for these young people and they're into the hip-hop music.' If the DJ had been playing blues that night, it would have worked. But it's hard to go in a hip-hop club and then you put a blues band in there; it don't work. It's just a hard night.

"So, we took a break and my mind is thinking and I said, 'Man, when we go back up there we got to get these people on the dance floor.' So when we went back, that's when I told my band what we would do. I told the drummer, 'You play this beat. And you play this line on the bass.' And I told the keyboard player, 'You play this.' And I said, 'We'll turn this joint out when we come back.' And sure enough, we came back, kicked the funky beat off, and I started saying, 'Show me what you got; show me what you got. Show me what you got down there.' That's what happened with that song. When we started doing that with the hip-hop beat to it, the dance floor filled up. . . .

"But young people—they're just not into traditional blues. Because of the new trends and also because they think of blues as slavery music. My generation—everybody's dying. I'm not ready for it but it's true.

"I'll tell you how the rapper became famous. . . . It's because this new music gets embedded in young people's minds. They look at Ludacris[14] and they're thinking, 'I want to be like him. So if I do this nasty song, and I do this type of stuff, then I'll be big like him.' Well, Ludacris got lucky and had somebody working for him. What happens with a lot of those people in those early days of the rap, they had the record companies looking to make money. They don't care what you said, what you did, or anything like that. All these dudes sitting back up here in the record company are going, 'We want to make money. So we get down here on the street in the ghetto and we pull this dude out—and he can rap and he can rhyme, you know, so let's put him in the studio, put a good beat behind him.' They don't care how the voice sounds. Somebody picks the dude up, takes 'em in the studio, puts this beat behind 'em—a good beat that the young people are into—and then they put it out. Then they *pushed* it. They put a lot of money behind it. You can cut any kind of record and if you've got enough money to push that record, it'll be a hit for you. That's publicity. So when they release a record on one of them guys . . . you talking about two or three million dollars behind that record. Put enough money behind it so it can't be nothing but big. Anytime you turn a hip-hop radio station on, you gonna hear that artist. But the rap music is gonna run its course and it's chilled out some already.

"I'll tell you what, I played the country music. I played a little of all of it. Yes, I did. But, I'm gonna keep playing the blues 'til I die."

CHAPTER 11

Traveling Blues: Road Stories and Odd Venues

A fair number of musician stories were about traveling from one venue to the next, hoping for a decent-paying gig but typically finding more adventure than money. Festivals are favorite venues for musicians because the money is usually better and the crowds are often more appreciative than they are in a bar, where the musician may be competing with sports playing on multiple television sets and other activities. Festivals brought the party outdoors. Another venue with an appreciative audience was the prison gig; the audiences may not have easy access to alcohol (with the possible exception of a bit of foul-tasting pruno or prison wine) but were still grateful for the music and the gig was interesting, whether you were a prisoner or a visitor.

These are a few stories about people, odd venues, and situations encountered away from home.

Pop Ferguson: Finding a Place to Stay

After he left the army, where he played guitar in the special services, Clyde "Pop" Ferguson spent much of his life on the road, traveling without an itinerary or a destination gig. Although his travels took him to quite a few different drink houses or juke joints, they could also put him down on a street corner without a dollar in his pocket or any companion other than his guitar. But he explained that his guitar always came through for him.

"When I went in the army, I was eighteen years old. I stayed in there with the USO because of my guitar playing . . . and I played for special services sitting out there and I could just pick up on something. I stayed right up in the army and I started back to school and then I got a little band started. Yeah, I played around the area, in North Carolina,

11.1. Pop Ferguson. Courtesy Doug Mokaren.

for dances and things. Mostly played for dances and was not ever in no stationary place. I just moved all around. I never had one place to stay.

"Then for a time it was just me traveling with my guitar. I played Vestapol. My guitar and I played all kinds of places. . . . And I went to places where I did not have enough money to go. I didn't know what I would be able to do when I got there. I would just go and get off the bus, pick up my guitar, and get that ole tin can, find me something to sit on and get on my guitar and start playing. First thing I know, I'd have two people listening. Then I'd have three people. Then I'd have a little crowd before long. When I got through playing, that's when I had to find somewhere to stay. I said to people in the crowd, 'I'm not going to have nowhere to stay. I don't know what I'm going to do.' And sure enough, someone would offer, 'Well, you can come stay with me.' That was my way to travel. I knew that somebody would say, 'Come on, stay with me.'

"Somebody out there always has a place to stay. I would stay all night; sometimes I'd stay for a day or so. But you know, I would play so hard, work so hard for maybe two or four or five dollars, something like that.

"I was always on the road. I met a lot of nice people, you know. But I gather one thing. I learned to separate the bad from the good. I know the secret. The way you do that, you—well, you can have a conversation with anybody . . . certain ones you can find out who they are from their talk. You know them from what they're talking about, what they're most interested in. If they're down home, you want to tag along with them but if they're looking for something wrong-headed, looking for a lie, if they are mean and misrepresent, then I just walk away. If it's no more than just one day that you got to put up with that kind, then you can tolerate them maybe, if you have to. Sometime you may have to. But you got to learn to separate the bad from the good and not get taken in by the bad. If somebody is just down home, they're okay. If they tell lies and like that, then you just walk away. Most folks are nice, but I also know when I need to ease away."

Mark "Buddyro" Harrison: Blood Money

Mark "Buddyro" Harrison of the Medicine Men and the Fairlanes explained that when he first set out to be a musician, he got the money to record an LP because of a decision to move to Florida and drink a beer on the way to meet some girls.

"We made a record, an album, full-length LP that I actually paid for, because I moved to Florida for about a year. This would have been in 1977. Anyway, I got in some trouble and lost my driver's license, and said, 'Screw it, man, I'm moving out of North Carolina.' So I moved to Fort Lauderdale, Florida, of all places. Godforsaken, God help us all. I moved down there, this little country boy moved down there and like, 'Oh my God, man,' it was a big city to me. I thought this is going to be quite an experience. And it was.

"I ended up getting beaten up by this cop.

11.2. Mark "Buddyro" Harrison. Courtesy Doug Mokaren.

"Me and one of my best buddies down there, we didn't have any way to get around. No car. So we had to take a bus and walk, you know. We were going to see these two ladies that I actually worked with in the restaurant where I had gotten a job. We were going to go to their place, and then we were going out on the town or whatever. So we take a bus over to their neighborhood, and we get off at the bus stop. And we walk into the 7-11 and buy some beers to take over to their apartment. We start walking down into their neighborhood. But it was dark. We're walking around with this bag of beer, and we decided we were going to crack one open, drink one as we're walking. So we were walking along, and I kind of notice a little—it's a residential area, and I heard a couple that kind of sounded like they were arguing a little bit, out on this porch. But we just kept on walking. Heard a couple of door slams, you know, and heard a guy get in his car. And he backs out of his driveway. I'll never forget that car; it was a 1974 Buick Riviera. Big old car. Anyhow, he comes flying out of that driveway. He was backing up, and he didn't see us. We both just jumped out of the way.

"And I said, 'Whoa, whoa, look out man.' And then he stopped and pulled up. He rolled down the car window, and I see this patch on him, it says: 'Fort Lauderdale Police.' And there we were, just a couple of little skinny redneck boys, standing there, each with a Miller beer. Oh man.

"The guy got out of his car. Man, he was about the biggest man I ever seen in my life at that time. Scary looking.

"He says to me, 'What are you talking about?'

"I said, 'Well, sir, I don't think you saw us. We were right behind you when you came screaming out of your driveway.'

"I can't remember what was said at that point, because he confronted me and kicked me on that bone in my ankle. So I go straight down. Then he jumps on top of me, starts pounding me. I'm laying there, and he's pounding. And by that point there's blood everywhere, it's getting nasty.

"Neighbors were coming out and screaming at him, 'Stop! Stop! Stop!'

"And then my buddy that was with me says to him, 'Man, you gotta stop. Man, you're going to kill him!'

"And then the cop jumps up and he told my buddy, 'You're under arrest too.'

"He cuffs us, and he's taking us downtown. They took me to the hospital first, because I was bleeding. I've still got the scars. I was cut here and all the way back down here [pointing to his face and neck], so they had to sew me up. It was weird. 'Cause I was in this little emergency room. I remember all these police standing around while they're sewing me up. The only thing I could say to them was, 'My leg is killing me.' I had these cowboy boots on. I said, 'I can't get my boot off, but my right ankle is just throbbing.' It *was* killing me.

"All they said was, 'Shut up. Ain't nothing wrong with you. We're going to sew you up and take you to jail.'

"They sewed me up, took me to jail. This was Friday night. Finally, by Sunday, some of the guys in the jail there . . . were able to help me get the boot off. By then the ankle was just green and swollen. The next morning, they handcuffed me to some crutches and take me back to the doctor. He wraps it up. Of course, it's too swollen for a cast. And then they take me back to the jail.

"My friend finally got his parents to bail him out. They didn't want to get him out for a while; they wanted to teach him a lesson. And he . . . after about three or four more days, he talked his parents into getting me out. I never got to use the phone. I had no family down there in Fort Lauderdale. All my family was back up here in North Carolina. So my friend's parents finally helped get me out of jail, but I did stay in jail for about a week. Once the swelling went back down on my ankle, I had to go get a hard cast, and the ankle was broken. I couldn't work. I lived in an upstairs apartment. And that's when I said to myself, 'Screw it.' I had to come back home again. So I did get an attorney, because everybody said to me, 'You have to sue those people, this is crazy.' So I got an attorney, and it was like tit for tat. This, that, and the other, then, after a couple of years go by, I ended up getting three thousand dollars or something like that. That's the money I used to help pay for that record that I made. Yeah, that was blood money. But we enjoyed making and having that record. That was kind of the goal in those days: make an album."

In the early 1980s, Mark met the drummer from the Swamp Cats, Gary Collins. Gary introduced Mark to "a bass player, this kid from Stokesdale," Chris Carroll, who was hanging out at Logan's Pool Hall (later to become the Blind Tiger). Chris would go there to play pool. They formed the Fairlanes with Chris Carroll (bass) and Kevin Wilson (keyboards). Gary came up with the name of their band.

"And I hated the name. I hated it for years, and I always meant to change it. Then right where you'd get to a point where you were ready to change it, people would say to you, 'No, don't change it, nobody will know who you are.' So the name just stuck, but people would ask us if the name was about the Ford or a bowling alley.

"That first incarnation of the band, we might have played a half a dozen little gigs, with a woman singing. We tried another singer. That lasted six months, maybe. Then Gary left too. He wasn't into all that practicing and Swamp Cats were kind of busy. Chris was still with me. And we got another drummer. Then my daughter, Hally, was born, 1989. And Chris left. Then he came back, rejoined the band for a few months, then left again, to go back on the road. So Chris has quit the band twice. Before Chris left the Fairlanes, we were traveling the East Coast from the DC, Baltimore area down to Charleston and North Florida. Nowadays we don't travel to gigs any farther than we can get back in a day. But back when Chris was playing with us, we traveled. We all rode in the pickup truck together. We had a Chevrolet pickup truck with a camper top. For years, that was the tour bus."

It is hard to know the meaning behind some types of southern decor in a bar. A rebel flag or a photo of George Wallace might be visual satire or it could be an indication of a firmly held ideology. Such items can be even more disconcerting for an African American band member for whom the visual satire might be off course.

"Back when Chris was still with us and we were still traveling quite a bit, we used to go down to this place way down in South Carolina. It was called Jackson Station in Hodges, South Carolina.[1] It was an old train depot, right on this train track. It was very near the Georgia line, near Athens, Georgia. At that time, you maybe can still do this, but on Friday nights in South Carolina back then, you could sell booze all night. On Saturday night they had to stop at midnight, but on Fridays you could party all night long. Their main night was Friday night at Jackson Station.

"It was about a five-hour trip for us to get down there. We didn't start playing until at least midnight, but we played until about four thirty or five in the morning. I remember the first time Chris went with us, we told him, 'This place is different, man. They get a really good crowd.' And they did play some big slam all night long. But we went in there with Chris, and they had all this weird stuff. . . . Not only railroad memorabilia, but a lot of just roadside signs and stuff that they put in there to decorate the place. Just a bunch of old southern stuff. But they had this photograph of George Wallace that was blown up. And that photograph took up just almost a whole side of one of the walls; it was huge. So Chris walks in there and he sees this big photograph and says, 'Man, that's George Wallace, man. You know who he is?'

"'Yeah, man, it's all right, man. These people are cool.'

"But it freaked Chris slap out, initially, to see that picture of George Wallace. Chris thought he'd landed in Klan territory; he thought we were playing in some kind of Klan headquarters or something. But once he met the owner of the bar, and actually the owner of the place—his name was Gerald Jackson—he was gay. Sweet guy. And what happened to him was one night he was attacked. A bunch of guys beat him out in the parking lot of his own bar one night, and almost killed him. That was the end of that bar, because it like killed him. Gerald Jackson. But Jackson Station was a true drink house because Gerald kept it open all night. And they didn't pour shots there. You bought airplane bottles. It was a South Carolina thing. I don't know if it was a county-by-county thing. But it was just so far out from any town or anything, an old roadhouse in the middle of nowhere. It was just close enough to Athens, Georgia, where you'd get a bunch of college kids come piling up in there about two or three in the morning after the bars in Athens had shut down.

"A lot of players from around here know about Jackson Station. Gerald had to shut it down after he was beaten up. Somebody else took it over for a while and we did go back and play one or two more times, but it was never the same without Gerald."

Terry VunCannon: Agents, Tobacco Road, and the B&L Warehouse

Piedmont musician Terry VunCannon spent a good bit of his professional career on the road, traveling from one gig to the next. Currently, Terry plays guitar with the band Lawyers Guns & Money,[2] which won the PBPS Blues Challenge and went to Memphis to the International Blues Challenge in 2014. The year before, Lawyers Guns & Money won the Cape Fear Blues Society challenge, so Terry has spent two consecutive years competing in Memphis at the IBCs. This interview was recorded on July 4, 2013, on Oak Island, North Carolina. Terry had just married his wife and sometimes lyricist, Janice Gatton, when we had this conversation. He explains that as a younger musician, not all bars where he traveled were open to a racially mixed band.

"I can remember in Asheboro growing up, there were still some signs posted when I was a little boy when my grandfather would take me out to eat, there were still signs that said 'Colored Entrance Only.' And

11.3. Terry VunCannon. Courtesy Doug Mokaren.

'White Entrance' at Hop's Barbecue on Sunset Avenue. This was in 1965 or '66, many years past when you should have a sign like that still up. This was right about the time I was starting to play the guitar—in 1966. They left that sign up.

"My experiences with race and the music scene might not be the same as everybody else because I was kind of in the hippie crowd as well as the musician crowd. I had long hair, parted in the middle, hippie-type hair. In Asheboro, the black section of town was referred to as 'the Hill.' Over on 'the Hill.' My gang of guys was welcome to go to parties on the Hill. Being a hippie and a musician, I was able to cross over racial lines pretty easy, so easy that I didn't really even think about it much. The first time I ever had a problem with race was later on, when I was playing in traveling bands and going to different bars and clubs. I was in a band and we had lost a drummer and hired a different drummer. So for a while we had a black drummer. We'd been traveling six-nighters with that band. We booked with East Coast Entertainment out of Charlotte and played the whole East Coast. And word was coming in from the agents who would be telling us, 'You can't play in Anderson, South Carolina.'

"'Well, why can't we?'

"'Because you have a black drummer. You can't play the bars there.'

"I remember thinking, how strange is that? Why can't we play in Anderson with a black drummer? ''Cause there's some good ole boys down there that will beat the shit out of you in the parking lot if you show up with a black drummer.' This was a foreign concept to me.

"Back in those days—'70s and early '80s—music was good money. I laugh about my first gig in high school for two hundred dollars. I actually know bands that get paid two, three, or four hundred dollars now [2013]. I often say that the difference between a good thousand-dollar band twenty years ago and a good thousand-dollar band today is twenty years. Another thing is agents. . . . I've seen the time when 10 percent of the gross was a fair agent cut. I've seen that go to 15 percent. I've seen it go to 20 percent. I've also seen the more aggressive agents go to 35 and 40 percent. To me it's just a rip-off. Take a thousand-dollar gig and think that three or four hundred of it goes to the agent and you have three or four guys splitting the five or six hundred that's left over. . . . I actually know of a couple of big agencies, which behind closed doors they use terms like 'shooting the net.' The way these agents work is to call a band up and ask, 'What do you have to get to do a show?'

"And the band might say, 'I need a thousand dollars to do a show.'

"The agent would then call a customer and say, 'I've got a really good band that I can get you for two thousand dollars.' The agent would confirm the job for two thousand dollars and call the band back: 'I've got a thousand-dollar gig for you.' That's 'shooting the net.' They net the same amount that the act nets. The band may never learn what the gross was. . . . It's an unethical way for an agent to behave. Now, I think an agent deserves to get paid if he does his job. A lot of bands are not great businesspeople. They're not great on the phone. They're not great in promotion. If you're not a good businessperson, you can make the choice to struggle around, playing once or twice a month. Or you can get an agent and play every weekend. An agent can work for you. I'd rather make 85 percent of four or five jobs than make 100 percent of one job. So, I see the good in agents. But I also think the agent owes it to the act to be straight up about the gross and percentages, but unfortunately that's not always the case. . . .

"When we were out on the road, we were always working from nine [p.m.] to one [a.m.] and . . . down in Alabama, Georgia, Florida, there were these 'after-hours' places. You would have these after-hours clubs and drink houses down in Georgia or Alabama that didn't open until midnight or one o'clock. When the regular clubs shut down at one o'clock, there was another club or two in every town that would go on until sunup and you could be partying or drinking until four or five o'clock in the morning. With some of these clubs, the wildest things that would happen would be people coming up and—on especially good nights where people were wide open and dancing—people would come up and be stuffing joints in our pockets or little bags of hashish or pills. It was crazy. . . .

"We used to play up in the mountains of North Carolina, North Wilkesboro, in a club called Tobacco Road.[3] Out in the middle of nowhere. You'd ride down the road forever and then come up on this little club. One night we saw a guy drop a baggie full of Quaaludes [methaqualone, a sedative-hypnotic drug] on the dance floor. The bag hits the floor and these white pills just go every direction. As quick as he was trying to pick them up and put them back in the baggie, all these other people were picking them up and eating them. That night got really weird by the end of the night. Really weird. I knew that those pills were around. We used to call them 'biscuits' in those days because of the way they looked. They were big pills. When that baggie of Quaaludes hit the floor that night—smack! Those pills went every direction. I remember playing guitar and watching people picking them up and throwing them in their mouths. An hour later the whole club was a mess—a sloppy, stumbling-all-over, crazy-dancing, girls-stripping-on-the-dance-floor kind of a mess. We saw one guy get up on a table dancing and a girl got up with him and as he lifted her up to dip her, the both of them came down hard. But they came jumping right up off the floor like they were uninjured, too. Quaaludes made people bounce.

"Tobacco Road was a unique club. We played there Wednesday through Saturday nights. It was so far out in the middle of nowhere that there were no motels or hotels anywhere near this place. Their way of dealing with that was at the end of the night, they would clean up, close the bar, and they would lock the band inside the bar. We brought sleeping bags and stuff like that to camp—to sleep right there in the bar. They said, 'Ya'll just make yourselves at home.' So we slept in the bar because there was no place else anywhere nearby to stay."

Terry told stories of playing at a club called the B&L Warehouse in Athens, Georgia, in the 1970s. The club was a beer club located on Oconee Street, which evolved into a big music venue by the end of the decade. The club changed names in the 1980s and later became a band practice space and a place for keg parties. The fire marshal shut down the warehouse in the late 1990s.

"I used to love this place in Athens, Georgia, called the B&L Warehouse, which was an old tobacco warehouse. It had literally two stages in this huge warehouse—one at one end and one at the other end. They always booked two bands for the week and you would alternate hour sets. . . . One of the first times we were in Athens we were teamed up with this guy that was wide open back then and may qualify as one of the strangest things I've ever seen, T. Graham Brown. He later became a country singer, but back then he was more southern rock—Lynyrd Skynyrd style. When T. Graham hit the stage, he was high-energy, southern rock. He would walk to the front of the stage, pull out a fifth of bourbon, unscrew the top, turn his back to the crowd, and throw the top away, and then proceed to drink that entire bottle during a performance. He was wide open. He was one of the local, popular guys in Athens, Georgia.

"The first time we played the B&L Warehouse, we had moved up in the world and had gotten rid of our little van and U-Haul trailer and had bought a motor home. So, we actually had a shower in the motor home while we were traveling. That felt very good because a lot of the time you'd travel all day and didn't have time but to set up and play. With a motor home, you could take a shower going down the highway and by the time you hit the club, you'd be fresh—or fresher. But this night, we had finished playing our set and T. Graham Brown was especially wide open. The club could hold two thousand people. . . . The crowds were fun back in those days. Really, it was a lot more drinking, a lot more dancing, clapping, and yelling. People were more high energy. Well, T. Graham had gotten just ripped this one particular night and at the end of his set, he stood at the edge of the stage and had about two inches of bourbon left in that Jack Daniels. He walked to the edge of the stage with his microphone in one hand and that bottle in the other. He turned up and bubbled the remainder of that bottle and then yelled at the crowd, 'That's it! I'm outta here.'

"And then he turned and walked to the side door of the club, knocked the doors open, and left. . . . We started playing at one o'clock and played until two in the morning. When we finished, T. Graham's band was still trying to find him. T. Graham had knocked the doors to the club open and made his big exit. Now his band didn't know where he was.

"So the night was over and we loaded up in the motor home and headed back to our hotel where we were going to stay, which was the hotel the club had booked for us. We're driving down the road, laughing about the night. 'Aw. I can't believe T. Graham did that. He was wide open.' The guy that was driving the motor home suddenly screamed and slammed on the brakes. He yelled, 'There's a body in the road!' We squealed to a halt and came running out of the motor home. The body—there was somebody in the middle of the road. He sat up and started laughing. It was T. Graham Brown, saying, 'Oh, I really got you guys this time.'

He had just left the club and started walking, and then had suddenly realized in his drunk stupor that he was miles away. He started walking back toward the club and he saw our motor home coming down the street. So he thought he'd lay down in the street and stop us. If Reese, the guy driving our motor home, hadn't been paying attention, we would have driven over him. But he would do wild stuff like that. He'd drop his jeans to his ankles—flash the crowd. Yep, T. Graham Brown on stage was something to see. Later he had a pretty big career as a country music star.

"We did play this really rough bar in Fayetteville, North Carolina, near the marine base. It was a little place called Shorty's. This would have been 1976 or '77 and this was a legal bar. They had their liquor license and everything. We actually saw several fights at Shorty's. Shorty, the guy who ran the club, was an ex–drill sergeant. About five foot four. Tough man. Cigar in his mouth. He used to say, 'I'll kick your goddamn ass.' He actually said that all the time. You'd see these tall guys get in a fight and here would come Shorty across the dance floor. He'd reach up and grab them. He was so strong he could grab these tall men, and he'd walk them to the door and throw them out. This one time when we played there, we were going to be the opening band for Steppenwolf. We were booked Monday through Saturday and on Friday night, Steppenwolf was going to come in. A big deal. . . . Anyway, Shorty had advertised Steppenwolf for two shows.

"Back when you had a name act like that come through, they'd usually do two shows. The opening band would do a quick thirty-five- or forty-minute set, and then your big-name band, like Steppenwolf, would come on. That set would be over maybe by ten o'clock. Then they would clear the club for the second show. Name bands would play two shows in one night. Well, Steppenwolf showed up and I remember they didn't want to play but one show. They were Steppenwolf. One show, that's it. Shorty called them into the office to talk about it.

"Once they got in his office he said, 'Ya'll aren't getting out of this office until you agree to play two shows.' And then he locked them in from the outside. Their manager is in there banging away on the door. Shorty opened the door and he says, 'I'm not picking.[4] You boys are playing two shows. I'll whip every goddamn one of you's goddamned ass, but you're going to play two shows,' and he locked them in a second time. We're all standing around like—oh my God. But Steppenwolf played two shows that night. That was a memorable place—Shorty's Club in Fayetteville."

Melva Houston: Studios, Horse Farms, and Asparagus Fields

Melva Houston is a vocalist originally from Memphis, Tennessee, who got her public start in music at twelve years old as a "Teen Town Singer," which was a group of young people from across the city who got together on Tuesdays and Thursdays for rehearsals for a one-hour radio show on WDIA on Saturday mornings. By the time she was fifteen, Melva was a background singer for Stax Records; before her next birthday, she was singing for Isaac Hayes. Melva was such a popular background singer that she made numerous recordings with stars like Wilson Pickett, Otis Redding, the duo Sam and Dave, and other celebrities on Stax Records. Since 1999, Melva has been performing at festivals internationally.

11.4. Melva Houston. Courtesy Doug Mokaren.

"I started out with A. C. Williams, who was one of the DJ promoters there at the radio station, WDIA.[5] He formed this group years and years before I even got in it, and I used to hear it on the air every Saturday morning—I would get to the radio to try to hear the group. We called him 'Big Daddy.' Big Daddy was a person that, as far as I was concerned, led us in directions that, had it not been for him, maybe some of us would have been out on the streets, whatever. He was a loving person—if you didn't show up on Tuesday for rehearsal . . . he was calling your house. If you didn't show up for Thursday . . . if you decided that a bunch of kids, like we used to do, we used to play hooky, and shoot . . . if you didn't show up for rehearsal, by the time you got home, all your parents, and the neighborhood, knew about it. Back in those days, the neighborhood took care of the kids in the neighborhood for the parents.

"I am the baby of seven. I graduated high school in 1967. Before I graduated, '66, '67, and '68, that's the times that I was at Stax Records. That was way before they had bought Stax out. But anyway, I was on the road with Sam and Dave,[6] and the experiences that I had then taught me a lot about the music business. When I was fifteen and sixteen years old, I sang background for Isaac Hayes. Isaac would always pick me up from school and take me to the studio. But at sixteen, one of the situations that happened to me that was—well, the wife that he had at the time was in my class at school. But he was sneaking with somebody else. He told me—I will never forget this—he said, 'If Emily asks you'—her name was Emily Watson—Tuna, we called her. . . . He said, 'If Emily asks you, tell her that it was you in the car yesterday afternoon. You tell her that I came and got you, I picked you up at four,' because Isaac had his windows tinted on all his cars to where he could see out, but nobody could really see in. And sure enough, the next day at school, his wife asked me if I did any sessions. I lied and told her I did.

"Anyway, that was Stax. And after going into Stax, and I guess, coming out of Stax, I got out of music and went into the medicine thing. So, at about twenty-one, twenty-two, I was working in medicine, and married the first time.

"What really turned me off of music—and you will not believe it but it was the same identical thing that I hear musicians say today—people treat musicians like they are some oddity that comes from outer space or something. We don't have the respect as human beings, and we're human. We have hearts, we have souls, we eat, we drink, we do all that. . . . We're human! And people have a tendency to treat musicians like they're nothing, you know? They're like, 'Oh, well, yeah, we can hire them. Yeah, well, put them over in the corner right there,' or, 'Yeah, well, move this table out of the way and let them set up there.' And the thing that really grabs my ass is the fact that musicians accept this type of treatment, just to make that little bit of money. And, believe me, it's not that much money! And I hear it all the time. They'll say, 'Well, Melva, some money is better than no money.' Not when as soon as the hell you get it, you so stressed out that it's gone and you got to try to go back out there to do it all over again, taking the same old crap. So, I started putting things in my contract: I want food for me, I want food for my musicians, I want a place to change clothes. If you cannot supply those, just those little necessities, then you might need to call somebody else. . . .

"Moving from Memphis to Mount Airy is like going from Memphis to Maui. I lived in Georgia for a period, and I had a cousin who was stationed in the military, so of course, family, I am hanging around his house. He would tell me about the gentleman who lived next door, and I really didn't care at the time. Eventually, I spoke to him and he kind of started a conversation, and then . . . at that time, I had gone into medicine, because I had gotten out of music, because of frustration and aggravation and all the other issues that go along there. . . . I had gotten out of music, and actually went into private nursing. So, his aunt was his only living relative and she was getting up in age and couldn't take care of herself. She was living up here [Mount Airy]. So he was having to try to get from the base back here to find someone that was suitable to take care of her. I was kind of having a little hard time, and I decided I would try it. So I came here, and I have been here ever since. That was June 1979. Anyway, I met my husband in Georgia, and I came here and I started taking care of his aunt. I was here in 1981 . . . and he said, 'We need to get married.'

"And I said, 'I am not going to be staying up here!'

"He said, 'No, we need to get married,' and so we got married on July 4, 1981. And then a friend of mine asked me if I would come and join the group that he was with because their lead singer was getting ready to leave. The group was an R&B beach band called Stormy out of North Wilkesboro. For about three years, I was on the road with Stormy. Those were some very nice gigs, because we did a lot of the horseshow-type things, and those were gigs that paid money. The whole thing dealt with horses and the breeding of horses, and how they raise horses, and then they would have these parties, and they would hire bands to play all night long. We played back up in here in the mountains, and all around Nashville, Black Mountain, everywhere where there were big horse ranches, they had parties, and they hired our band. They put us up very well, I mean . . . *very* well. The horse people knew how to treat musicians.

"But, child, I did the chitlin circuit, too. I don't even think of it as the chitlin circuit anymore, I just think of it as the fat part of the hog. You play these gigs and when you get through playing, you know there's at least fifty people in that place, but the man tells you, 'Well, I can only be out twenty-five dollars apiece,' and here you've done sung for four hours. . . . My biggest thing is that, as I got older, I liked the festivals more. With the festivals, you didn't have to go out there and actually promote yourself, plus sell these other people tickets. Plus, sometimes they don't even want to pay you once you sell the place out. So, with the festivals, you get a set fee; whether people show up or not or it rains, the fee is already down. I much prefer the festival to an old bar or the chitlin circuit type of thing. I am too old to play for fifty dollars. I played for fifty dollars fifty years ago when fifty dollars was actually worth fifty dollars.

"When I was working with Stormy, we worked in this one place called Tobacco Road way out in North Wilkesboro. We didn't have to sleep inside the bar, though. We would always go back to the drummer's house. He lived in North Wilkesboro, so everybody would crash at the drummer's house. But I was there in Tobacco Road when . . . the "N" word came up in a crowd of people, and I am talking a *crowd* of people, and when that word came out. . . . Seriously, it was like the waters parted, because everybody but the person who said it spread away from him. This was—let's see, that had to be 1984 or '85. Somewhere in that area it had to be. The "N" word came out and everybody just backed up. And we were on the stage, performing. And the guy says, 'Get that N—— up off that stage,' just like that. And I am standing there, and it was like the water parting, with that one man standing in the center. And my guitar player, Benny—I have no idea where he is to this day—Benny Holbrook. Benny started off that stage with a razor in his hand, and I was begging him, begging and begging, 'Leave the man alone. Leave the man alone. He's drunk, don't do it, he is drunk, he is drunk, he is drunk,' . . . and that subdued that. I never had one problem after that incident.

"Now let me tell you, I am going to give a nice example of a truly great gig on the back of a wagon. I played in an asparagus field, in Germany, in the middle—and I have photos to prove it—in the middle of this huge asparagus field, where the people came and parked all around . . . and when I say 'wagon,' the wagon was hitched onto a tractor. That's how they brought the wagon out into the field. And all around the whole area was where the people parked. They sat in their chairs in front of the stage of a wagon in the middle of this asparagus field. That was a good gig! It was a fun gig in that, I just could not get over it, but a little farther over, just off to the side, I see these people bent down, because they are picking asparagus while we're doing jazz. But yeah, it was a good gig. It turned out to be a great gig."

Eric Gales (a.k.a. Raw Dawg): Romancing the Festival and the Prison Gig

Eric "Raw Dawg" Gales was born October 29, 1974, in Memphis, Tennessee. He picked up the guitar at age four. His older siblings, Eugene and Manuel, continued his guitar lessons and protected him from the drink house environment, yet he spent some time in prison. Eric is right-handed and plays a right-handed guitar "upside down" with the E-bass string on the bottom, mimicking his older left-handed brother. In 2008, Eric Gales was part of a touring Jimi Hendrix tribute called Experience Hendrix. I interviewed Eric in Greensboro on July 22, 2013. He was intending to move to Greensboro and he and his new wife LaDonna had been house hunting. Except for a brief period playing a jailhouse gig, Eric's career has largely been devoted to the festival circuit, which is how he met LaDonna.

"I'm the youngest of five brothers. We all come up in a musical household. Music was very prominent even before me coming along. My next-older brother is ten years older than me. Ten years later my mama and dad decided to go back in the sack again and here I come—another little guy. My mom and dad and grandfather were very devout church people, like *heavy* church people, and there wasn't really room for any worldly music to be played at all in the household. To get around listening to it, we had to wait for my Mom to go to church and my brothers would play, you know, old blues and rock 'n' roll, stuff like that. When Mom was at church, they'd crank it up. That's how I got turned on to it so early. Four years old, I just picked up the guitar and I picked it up left-handed, upside down and backwards, and I figured—I said to myself, I really kinda like this thing. All my brothers play guitar that way. One of them is truly left-handed. But me and my oldest brother both write right-handed. I got two other brothers. One was Simon Gales, he passed at thirty-seven, and Little Jimmy, who is the godson of Albert King, and he passed at thirty-nine. Rest their souls. Yeah, but everybody had some

11.5. Eric Gales. Courtesy Doug Mokaren.

sort of musical inclination. My mom and pop didn't play but my uncles, cousins, nieces—music was just all over the place. Just all over. My brothers started noticing me progressing on guitar. My oldest brother, Eugene, started mentoring me along, showing me the dos and don'ts. . . . My first real gig was at eleven years old at this thing called the Ambrose Jam. My brother asked me, he said, 'I'm going to take you out in front of an audience and see how you do with an audience. See if you're nervous or if you'll be okay.'

"I looked at him and said, 'I'm cool.'

"He took me out there and it was the loudest sound I ever heard. People were just yelling and clapping. They seemed like they were just blown away to see this eleven-year-old kid with a guitar bigger than him up there. . . . A story about it went in the papers and all that. I didn't play again like that until two years later in this thing called the Battle of the Bands [in Memphis, 1988]. We got in the competition and that particular year we got third place. We came back the next year and we won both days of competition [1989]."[7]

On the day of this conversation, Eric was complaining about a toothache. Eric blames drug use for the tooth decay and his other dental problems. Although his brothers tried to protect Eric, drugs eventually found him. He was in the Shelby County Detention Center for three years on drug charges and after his release, he was busted again for Xanax and cocaine. Once he finally left prison, Eric was determined to have his teeth fixed because he told me he was too young to look that way.

"I am thirty-eight years old. I still got some 'young' in me. There was no way possible I should be looking like that. I said when I get out [of prison], I'll get my teeth fixed . . . after all this playing around, God spared me . . . when I was one sniff away from killing myself and didn't care. And nights I went to bed with my heart beating so fast that it sounded like a subwoofer going down the street—or parked in my driveway—or even sitting right there in my bedroom. Life just came around. . . . And then I started hanging out in the street life and I got glamorized by it—the drug life. I tried cocaine for the first time on a dare. I was just being infatuated with the street life and how those guys 'kicked it.' You know what I'm saying? I saw them doing it and I'm like, 'What's that?'

"And this one guy tries to prevent me, saying, 'This ain't what you do.'

"And I lied and said, 'Yes, it is. Let me buy one.'

"Worst decision I ever made in my life. It took me through some years . . . ten, twelve years strong. I can count less than two months or three months out of five years that I wasn't high. I was living with 'death on the installment plan.'

"You know what? There's a really unorthodox—excuse my French—fucked-up trade-off. I'm not gonna sit here and tell you that I don't miss the days of being zonked out of my mind. When I say, 'zonked out of my mind,' the best recipe for me was coke and Xanax. For the record, I've never smoked crack or anything like that. . . . I've just always had a problem with snorting—toot. You get started on that and there ain't no stopping it. It wasn't something that the music industry influenced me to do, either. It was from trying to fit in with all the boys in the neighborhood. I was just trying to fit in. I did it on a dare. Worst decision I ever made. I can't say that I won't ever smoke ganja again—weed, the universal peace pipe—but I got to be careful. It's not worth risking the recidivism of going back to jail. . . . I am just grateful that all my opportunities haven't been taken away from me."

Eric found romance and stability when he played the Carolina Blues Festival in Greensboro in 2012. The Eric Gales Band was supposed to perform following E. G. Kight, the Chicago guitarist, vocalist, and songwriter, but instead followed Smokin' Joe Kubek and Bnois King, who were originally scheduled to be the last band of the day. The Eric Gales Band was lucky to arrive at all. Eric explains what happened.

"I got in trouble the night before in New York and went to jail. That's how I missed my flight. So that's how I went on after Smokin' Joe Kubek and Bnois King that night. So, I got caught outside this place. . . . I was waiting on a limo, smoking a joint across the street.

"Some plainclothes cop comes up and says, 'Drop the joint. You're going to jail.'

"I spent all night trying to get out of jail. I missed the first flight that morning and finally caught another one. It got me in later. So I played the show, but I played last. It turned out to be a great gig, an epic gig. Saw LaDonna in the audience. She was with her friend standing there and I thought, wow. Her head was just bobbing back and forth and I saw it. Wow. I thought, 'You're feeling what I got going on.' I saw it, but I thought the guy she was with was her boyfriend and I didn't want to be too forward about the situation. Then later on they were standing in line to meet the band when I was signing CDs. When I found out that he wasn't her boyfriend, it just blew my mind. It was that powerful. I said to her, 'You just wait right there for a minute. Once I'm done here, we're going over to the Marriot and chill, have a drink, and talk.' That's what we did. So, I missed my flight again the next day to fly out. . . . I didn't have another gig, but the flight I was booked on, I missed it. We had done talked the whole night through. . . .

"I told her, 'I'm on the road constantly. I'm not staying anywhere, really.'

"She said, 'If you ever need to come by my place, my place is yours.' So, I took her up on that offer the next day because I missed my flight. I went to her place.

"I said, 'You remember, you told me I could come by.' . . .

"After that we talked over the phone for like a month. Then I came back [to Greensboro] about two months later and we got married. It was just that fast. Couldn't help it. When I say I couldn't help it, I really mean I couldn't help it.

"Since all that happened, the whole turnaround has been way different. I ain't on probation. I ain't been in any trouble. Things have been going good. Got my passport back. I'm about to get a new house. All of the old me is out the door—all the way out. Now, music is the main priority. . . . Anybody that asks to have the life of someone in my shoes, really do your research about it before you wish for something like that, because you just—you know—you may not make it through. I'm one of the lucky ones. I've been through a whole lot of things. Seeing someone die in my arms and things like that. Somebody you with one moment to the next moment you get a phone call saying that they've just got killed. Things like that—I don't miss that life at all, I really don't. . . .

"Back when I was in jail, I got a knock on my dorm door. It was the warden. He said to me, 'I know who you are and I think you can help change this jail around.' He said, 'I want to start a band in this jail.' And he put me in charge of his prison band. We were out playing for the mayor, the councilmen, and all that kinda stuff. Not stuff that you get paid for but we got all kinds of equipment, privileges, and getting to see our families more times a week *and* they could come to the events and bring us 'free-world' food. Sometimes you were so excited you couldn't get to sleep knowing that the next day you would get 'free-world' food. You know, food like—well, anything that's not prison food. So, I definitely didn't have the life of someone who had to do hard time for three years. So, I'm thankful for that. There are privileges that come with talent.

"People mention Johnny Cash and Folsom Prison and all that but I don't think he was locked up while he was playing. I was incarcerated while I was going from prison to prison and playing, but it was a perfect outlet for me. Prisoners make good audiences. They don't have nothing else to look forward to and they get as excited as anybody else. They're more excited because they don't see no excitement in their lives—for some of them, they don't see no excitement for years. And that's where they've been in a cell half the size of this porch we're on with a 'dormie' [cellmate] and all they get to see is the chow hall and the gym for years, decades. So to have the warden tell them, 'We got a show coming here to play for ya'll,' that's their only chance to let loose. In the prison you see girls with girls. Guys with guys. You see the obvious relationships that's going on out there, but that's how jail life is. . . .

"Before, when I was wrapped up in street life, I didn't play as many gigs as I do now . . . but now—now I'm booked up. I'm on the road a lot. I will tell you this one little road story before I go. One time we pulled over in Arkansas and my tech was driving. I got out to do 'the ritual.' He forgot that I was out there. He gets his business done, gets in, and pulls off. He was gonna leave me. I was running behind the truck with my stuff hanging out. In Arkansas . . . think about that. Aw, he was apologetic. It was night and I'm running down the street with my family jewels: 'Hey, man. Wait up. Wait! Wait! Wait! Wait!' I guess there's not a moral to this story. You can't say, 'Don't do the ritual.' But that was one of the oddest things to happen to me between gigs."

Mike "Wezo" Wesolowski: Wezo Gigs in Prisons

Harmonica player Mike "Wezo" Wesolowski had the experience one summer of playing prison gigs in all the eastern prisons of North Carolina with the band Blues with a Feeling.[8] *Ralph R. Speas had helped the band receive a grant through the Durham Arts Council to tour prisons and entertain inmates.*

"We're doing this series of prison gigs all throughout the east, all the eastern prisons in North Carolina. We did this whole summer full of these gigs. Well, they booked three bands on every show. The first show we did was with this gospel group called the Void Brothers.[9] It was a guy named Landy Void. That was his actual name. Fucking awesome fucking singer. He had a great gospel band. So that first show, okay, it was us, we

11.6. Mike "Wezo" Wesolowski. Courtesy Doug Mokaren.

were a blues band; the Void Brothers, which are a gospel group, and the third group was called Southern Culture on the Skids.[10] . . . It was really avant-garde stuff. . . .

"One time we were at this prison farm way down east in North Carolina, where everything's flat. This was a maximum-security prison. Maximum. The most maximum that you can get and it's also the prison farm. They raise vegetables and stuff that get sent to all the other prisons. It's so flat where this place is, and it's out in the swamps too, flat area. You can see everything driving up to it . . . from about two miles away. No trees or nothing around it for miles. You drive up, and the first thing you notice is these rows of twelve-by-twelve cages, square cages, on both sides of the road as you're coming into this place. Well, that's where the maximum-security guys get their hour of outside exercise, in these twelve-by-twelve cells. They're shackled at the hands, shackled at the feet, so they're like this for an hour a day going around this twelve-by-twelve thing. That's their exercise. There's other maximum-security guys who are less maximum, who get work release to farm and that sort of thing, but this is a place where they keep all these baddest of the bad motherfuckers who have killed lots of people in a vicious way and are not sorry about it.

"So, we're playing at this maximum-security prison, and we're set up at the back of the cafeteria. Ten to twelve feet away from us, there's a big security fence, ten feet tall with razor wire with the things that go up towards us, and then there's a ten-foot alleyway kind of thing, and then another security fence where the prisoners are. So there's two fences in between us and the prisoners, plus another ten feet in the middle. These are some bad motherfuckers. We never got advance notice of actually who was on this gig. We found out when we got there. Besides us, it was the Voids, the gospel group, and Billy Wirtz. The Reverend Billy Wirtz. I'm telling you what, man. He comes out and . . . oh my God.

"Well, Reverend Billy Wirtz, he's a one-man thing, and he does all this parody shit, and he's got this lightning-quick delivery of these one-liners. He's a badass piano player. I mean, he's funny and he calls himself the 'King of Polyester.' He wears like a lime-green polyester leisure suit, and he's got tattoos all over him. At the time, he had really long hair in a mullet kind of thing. He's wearing these alligator wing tips usually with these cool nylon socks that came up. But this one particular time he's not wearing his socks. He's doing his spiel and the prisoners do not get his humor. They can't follow it. You could see these one-liners going over their heads, and they don't dig any of it until he started singing. Then he started playing piano with his foot; you could see all these tattoos on his ankles. After his show, those prisoners were just interested in the tattoos. It was just, 'Hey, man, let me see that one on your elbow.' You know? They're showing him their tattoos. This one says MOM or something. These are all prison tattoos, but Billy Wirtz has got the real thing. They were fixated on these tattoos. They didn't care about anything else. All they wanted to do was talk tattoos from twenty feet away behind these two security fences."

Wezo continued to play prison gigs with a reconfiguration of his band, now the Ministers of Sinister.[11] The irony of his next story is the request from a prisoner, a proud member of the Aryan Nations,[12] to sit in and play guitar with a blues band playing predominantly black music.

"In most of these less-maximum facilities we went to, we actually ate lunch with the prisoners. We'd eat in the cafeteria because they'd feed us. They give you prison food, which is usually a meat and two sides. It's usually Salisbury steak about the consistency of shoe leather. Then some creamed corn and maybe some macaroni and cheese. To drink, they've got endless vats of Kool-Aid. Endless vats. At every facility we went to, 'You want something to drink?' 'Yeah, just give me the Kool-Aid.' I mean . . . it's always cherry or grape. You get cherry or grape.

"One year, I'm with the band the Ministers of Sinister and we're playing at the Raleigh State Prison. They've got maximum-security guys there, too, but we don't have the security fences. We're playing in this very small auditorium. It's their little place where the prison band could go practice and stuff like that. It's right next to the weight room where they lift weights. Okay, so we're in there, and we're setting up, and we're meeting these prisoners who are coming up. There's at least five different guys who came up and said, 'Hey, man, you ever let anybody sit in?'

"Max said, 'Nah, not usually.'

"They tell us, 'Man, we got this fucking awesome goddamn fucking guitar player. He's the best guitar player in prison. His name is Snake. Man, I mean, he's the best guitar player in here, and he's in our band.'

"They've got a little rock 'n' roll band in this prison with donated instruments and a piece-of-shit drum set, piece-of-shit bass, piece-of-shit guitars, and here we are with all our gear. About five people say to us, 'Man, you need to get Snake on here. You're going to see this place go wild.'

"Finally Max says, 'Tell Snake to come up and talk to me.'

"So here comes this guy, this big biker-looking guy, and he's in the Aryan Nations. He's killed six people. He'll never get out of prison—ever. Life without parole. He comes up, and he's one of the nicest, most polite guys we've ever talked to. Snake was a 1-percenter. The 1-percenters are murderers. The deal is, if you've got a spiderweb on your elbow, that means that you have done the deed and killed somebody. He had them on both elbows and on both his knees. He killed about six people.

"He asks Max, 'Hey man, what kind of guitar is that, man?'

"Max tells him, 'Oh, this is a '67 Strat.'

"Snake's impressed. He tells us, 'Man, I've never held a real guitar. What I got over there is some serious piece of shit from Goodwill or something.'

"Max says, 'You want to sit in?'

"Snake says, 'Hell, yeah, I'll sit in.'

"Man, when Snake got up there to play, he was really rudimentary. I mean . . . he was basic as you could get and ever be. Minimal. But that place was going crazy. I mean, the guards were starting to gather at the door. In this prison, the prisoners can walk in and out of the room if they wanted. If they wanted to go to the weight room, they could go in there and hang out. If they want to hang in the auditorium, they could come in there and hang out. It wasn't really very restricted at this particular prison, but the guards were starting to gather at the door because they heard all this commotion. The commotion was Snake up there playing with us."

Max Drake: The Broken String

Here is Max Drake's memory about playing that same series of prison gigs.

"We played, I think, basically most of the prisons in the state. We played at a women's prison [North Carolina Institution for Women] right after the inmates had killed somebody. They had a riot and they all killed an older guard. So then we show up to play. It was a terrible gig. I broke a string during that gig. Immediately when the show was over, the warden came over hunting for that string. She's anxious about it.

"We're looking around and I say, 'Oh, there it is on the floor.'

"She said, "Let me have that."

"I said, 'What's the big deal?'

As soon as I asked, I realized.

"She told me, 'That can be used as a weapon to cut someone's throat.'

"Those gals in that prison weren't playing. They had killed a guard. They got into the toolshed and used the tools as weapons. There was an

11.7. Max Drake. Courtesy Doug Mokaren.

older guard who was about to retire. They had a riot and he was trying to get over the fence to get away from them. He just couldn't get up fast enough. They got him and they killed him. Somebody actually got the chair for that. So you don't want to leave a broken guitar string laying around on the floor of a prison."

Terry VunCannon: Dry County Cooler and Parachute Parties

"In 1973 in the tenth, eleventh, and twelfth grades I started playing school dances and after football games and an occasional party or two in Asheboro, North Carolina. . . . Asheboro was in a dry county and I remember in high school we had some bootleg places in town. Oh yeah,

11.8. Terry VunCannon. Courtesy Doug Mokaren.

there were bootleggers in Randolph County. During my eleventh- and twelfth-grade year—as a matter of fact, we used to brag about being able to go to this little place called Wimpy's that had a drive-through window just like a fast-food place. So we had whiskey sours 'to go' during fifth period of my senior year in high school. Nobody was checking your ID.

"There was this one place that went through several names. It was the Four Winds, and then it became the Mirage Club, and then later it became the Crow's Nest. It was a large place with a bar area on one side and a big room on the other side. . . . I played at the Mirage Club several times. When I was still in my early twenties, I decided to host an event for my band and do my own promotion. This was going to be a cooler party, BYOB. It was called a 'cooler party' because you couldn't legally sell beer. That was another way to get around the liquor laws. I rented the big room at the Mirage Club for a flat fee and hired a security guard. The Friday after Christmas—1977 or '78—I threw my own party. It was the first time I did my own promotion. I went around town putting up signs for a 'Day-After Christmas Cooler Party.' I charged five dollars a person and eight dollars for a couple. The parking lot was full and people were parked all up and down the highway. Literally there were cars parked on both sides of the highway, just lining the streets outside of the club. It drew so much attention that the owner of the bootleg place came up to me and said, 'Well, if they don't close me down after tonight, they never will.' We wound up that night with the band making close to two thousand dollars. I remember sitting in the back room with all this money . . . the most money the band had ever made.

"When I was in the Willie Boy Band,[13] the only places to play in Asheboro, where all of us were from, were bootleg places. We were on the road a lot. We never really played for our friends in Asheboro. We would have two or three days to come back, pay bills, do laundry, see people, see our girlfriends, and then head back out. A guy in our band had rented a house deep in the woods off of old Goat Hill Road. He was single, living in the house by himself, so we made his living room our practice area. That was the band house. When we had a weekend open, we had 'parachute parties.' We had this huge military parachute once used to drop jeeps and tanks. We would take that parachute in the front yard of the band house, spread it, tie ropes all the way around, and then throw these ropes over the trees to pull the parachute up like a tent. We would get four space heaters, turn those on, and the parachute would rise up like a big dome from the hot air inside. It was a beautiful thing. We would take our stage lights and point them up. So we had this huge dome with multicolored lights hitting this solid white, sheer material of the parachute. It formed a dome of multicolors. We'd have 'parachute parties' and charge five dollars a head. Bring your own beer. I guess it was an extension of the original party at the Mirage Club. Oh, we would pack it out. We'd have our parties on Saturday night . . . and on Sunday afternoons we'd still find people passed out in the pasture and the fields around the woods. When somebody would pass out in the yard and lay there, the next day when they would finally wake up, if they had been laying on their face, their backside would be soaking wet from the dew settling on them, dirt and leaves stuck to their face. We started noticing these guys come shuffling up to the house like zombies; they'd be half wet and half dry. We started calling them the 'half-dead.' So we had these huge parties and we would make pretty good money on a night off. All we were really doing is playing what we played on the road. Our friends from high school and friends from college, girlfriends, people that didn't get to see us play because we were gone on the road three or four weeks at a time could come and see us play in our own front yard."

Robin Stamps Doby Easter: Love at Smilefest

Robin Doby's favorite venue is also a festival. She has performed at FloydFest,[14] *at a grungefest at City Markets, and at July Fourth festival celebrations, but a favorite outdoor event was the Smilefest*[15] *at Pinnacle, North Carolina. When Robin's band played the last Smilefest in 2011, it was a family-oriented arts, music, and camping festival.*

"I heard about this but I had never experienced it. Yes. I spent the night in a tent and it was the first time. My friend Mel [Melanie Wallace] used to always say she wanted to take me camping. I told her, 'You're not taking me camping. I'm an inside girl.' But we went and it was fantastic. People were saying to me, 'Are you a hipster?' What? No, I'm not a hipster. They thought I must be by the way I dress. I like to wear the long stuff and long dreadlocks. But I'm like, 'No, I'm not a hipster.'

"After we performed we stayed for two days at Smilefest, sleeping at night where the music was right outside the tent. It didn't stop. It was fabulous. . . . This festival was such a pulse from the earth and the people were so loving. The people said to me later on, 'We heard you. What a great start to Smilefest.' It was mind-blowing just walking from where I was camping to other sites, seeing all the people. As a black female, I had never experienced anything like that. Not too many black people at Smilefest. But there was so much love, I think I would have overdosed if it had been any more of it. I felt like I was floating on it. I told my family when I got back, I said, 'I've witnessed such love and such—' I said, 'You guys just have got to go to a festival.'"

11.9. Robin Stamps Doby Easter. Courtesy Doug Mokaren.

Roy Roberts: The Agent and the Frat Party

In the process of collecting stories I also came across several mentions of southern fraternity parties with alcohol served in a dry community. Sometimes there would be a row of fraternity houses, with each fraternity trying to "out-party" the other. Christmas and New Year's fraternity parties were the best gigs. Dry-county frat parties might include moonshine as well as bootleg.

Roy Roberts tells about working with a booking agent for a time and this agency booked his band to play a white fraternity party in Georgia. The fraternity had requested a specific band, the Embers,[16] and paid the deposit, but the agent decided to book the Embers in a better-paying gig on that same date. Without telling anyone, the agent substituted Roy's band for the Embers. When Roy's band showed up to play the fraternity gig, Roy describes the scene as tense.

"The guy in charge comes marching out shouting, 'Ya'll aren't the Embers! We booked the Embers!'" Roy explained to the man that he didn't know anything about the switch. "All I do is show up and start playing." The situation was potentially volatile. The fraternity had already advertised the Embers and the frat boys were vocally disappointed. It was the early 1960s and clearly one R&B band is not necessarily interchangeable for another. However, the fraternity decided that the show must go on because it was too late to cancel. They allowed Roy's band to go ahead and play the gig and ultimately the partygoers seemed to appreciate the music, although the beginning of the night had been rocky.

The southern fraternity party might be viewed as a formalized and somewhat legitimized version of a house party, catering to a members-only audience. Like knowing which bars will welcome which patrons, fraternities had their own versions of exclusivity. You generally don't want to show up uninvited. Overall, musicians said that playing a fraternity party was a good gig. The frat boys paid at the end of the night, whereas a house party might not pay, even if there had been a cover charge. Although the white fraternity was unhappy with the switch from the Embers to Roy's band, Roy still got paid. However, after that incident, Roy decided to do all his own booking.

CHAPTER 12

Baby Boomer Blues: The Crossroads of Culture

Musicians and fans who admired the music of Elvis Presley, Jerry Lee Lewis, Carl Perkins, and the later British invasion looked backward for the musical influences of these artists and discovered southern black musicians and the venues where these artists performed: drink houses, liquor houses, bars, lounges, and juke joints. All crossroads circled backward to these sources and all roads led South.

The South has had a complicated relationship with music, alcohol, and social integration. The damp, royal blackness of a southern night sky bedazzled with stars and mystery has by and large been replaced with night skies awash in the pastel pinks from the light pollution of developing cities. For the musician who went searching for that genuine sound, the country juke joints and traditional drink houses that were "ground zero" for authentic music appeared to have shut down or evolved into social houses and after-hours clubs playing recorded music rather than encouraging a roaming jam. Long after the progressive boomer coming of age in the '70s felt that integration and social color-blindness should have been achieved, many southern bars continued to self-segregate.

Several of the storytellers contributing to this collection are boomers, born in the two decades after WWII. Looking back at experiences from the '70s, '80s, '90s, and the first decade of the new millennium, there have been a lot of changes. Forty years saw the slow disappearance of some liquor laws and the new appearance of others, altering the scene for live music. Some bars closed and some transformed; others became considerably tamer, possibly because of the rise in music tourism and the aging of blues artists and audiences.

In his book *Blues Music in the Sixties: A Story in Black and White*, Ulrich Adelt interpreted the whitening of the audience for blues music as a result of that "crossroads" of the civil rights movement and the burgeoning counterculture of the 1960s. White hippies, in their search for purity and authenticity, were starting to listen to blues music, while black boomers began moving toward newer musical forms. Adelt concludes that when Lee Atwater,[1] a skilled guitarist and arch-Republican, played blues music with Albert Collins at the 1989 inaugural gala for George H. W. Bush, the concert symbolized multiple ironies. The music that had once been the accompaniment for the temporary discharge of oppression in the drink house bacchanal, the music so connected to the struggle for civil rights, had become "the music at a party celebrating the highest member of the white male power structure."[2]

The ironies and the whitening (and graying) of the blues scene are not lost on the storytellers in this project. Although not all the white storytellers identified as hippies, many consistently championed the "genuine American values" of social equality, personal freedom, opportunity, and nonviolence. A few white storytellers even referred to themselves as "rednecks," though not in an association with hostile southern values, but as an economic identifier: "we were poor as red dirt." Coming of age in the '70s, they too rebelled against more tyrannical traditions of southern life and the meaningless commercialism of American life in general. They felt in blues music the unfiltered experience they wanted. Black communities might be beleaguered with poverty and crime but black friends appeared to be free of white, southern suppressive values and moral restraints. The virility and passion of black music and the rebellious celebrations of the drink house were the proof.

Adrianne Carageorge: Hippies at Smitty's Juke Joint

Adrianne Carageorge[3] is not a musician or bar owner but a media educator, teaching film- and video-production courses for the Rochester Institute of Technology. I came by her story quite by accident on August 9, 2012, when we were both in Chicago for a media convention. The conversation turned to music and drink houses and she told me a story about white college kids in the 1970s looking for psychedelic excitements and discovering a juke joint.

"I had moved from our family home in Pensacola, Florida, to go to Florida State University to finish up my degree. My friends at Florida

State were adventurers. And generally they were more adventuresome than I was—you know how friendships go. And part of my social group included musicians. They were always looking for somewhere to play and different kinds of people to play with. Of course there was the college drinking and getting high and all that going on back in the seventies. One of my friends, a guitar player, started telling us about this place called Smitty's. He told us that you had to kind of walk through the woods to get to it but there were these pastures near Smitty's that were full of cow patties, which were famous for growing psilocybin mushrooms. Tallahassee was like a lot of the Gulf Coast in summer; it had a regular period of rain every day. It would rain from about two in the afternoon to four thirty and then it would stop raining and get steamy and hot. It was after those rainy afternoons, after the daily steam bath set in, that you could go out into these pastures full of cow patties and find psilocybin mushrooms. And so everybody studied mushrooms to figure out which ones were the ones that you could eat. Some of us got pretty good at recognizing them. We would collect the mushrooms and cook them for the high. One day we went out to find the mushrooms, and there must have been six of us, driving away from the campus and then climbing through barbed-wire fences and secreting our way through cow pastures. But just beyond the pastures there was this juke joint we could go to. And they served beer and all kinds of people went there. This was in the daytime as the sun is going down and into the evening. So that's how we discovered Smitty's.[4]

"So . . . all kinds of people went to Smitty's. College students discovered it and would bring guitars in and just go and drink and play music and enjoy being there. There were black people and there were country farmer types, you know, those north Florida cracker types. Everybody got along. You never knew what kind of musicians would show up and what kind of music would happen. But everybody got along and there was never any strife that I knew about. We were also the legal age to drink. I'm talking beer, not anything more powerful, because we were more into getting high than getting drunk.

"Smitty's wasn't a house or a barn, really; it was just a building, as I remember it. A large building with a big open room with a simple bar and then there was a kind of elevated stage where the music happened. The guy who owned the place was an old black man who was really cool. He kept inviting us to come back because one of my friends was a pretty good guitar player and the rest of us were harmless. We were just people who would fill the room, buy the beer, and not cause any trouble. We would also talk to people who didn't come with us. We would mingle and there was dancing. Some people plainly came out there to dance. There was a wood dance floor. Black folks and white folks would dance together. It was always a good party. My friends and I just came to escape the campus and get into the musical part of it. There were times when we would go that Smitty's would be packed with people and—you know, cigarette smoke clouding up the air and the noise could get really loud. Those were mostly weekend nights. But all kinds of people came to party. . . . We generated the music ourselves. People played live music, playing old blues tunes, folk, and some popular tunes current at the time.

"And it was just a wonderful experience as far as my memory goes of having a place to go where we felt welcome. Especially my musician friends loved going to Smitty's because they could jam with different types of musicians and discover new kinds of music. The doors were always open in this place because it was in the middle of nowhere and it didn't matter if the doors were open. You wanted to be able to catch a breeze. I remember my favorite place to be was on the porch just looking out at the night sky and listening to all this music and just kind of getting into the vibe of the place.

"Smitty's was a good ways away from the campus. I would say it was thirty or forty minutes outside of Tallahassee. I have no idea what direction. It wasn't as far as the border with Georgia and it wasn't at the Gulf Coast. It was just out there. We would drive out there and sometimes we could stop and collect mushrooms on the way. Other times we would just go straight there for the music. Yeah, you could drive there but it was dirt-road driving and surrounded by woods and cow patties. Way out in the woods.

"I was sitting out there at Smitty's one time and I was—you know—I was a little high. I was just sitting there looking at this magnolia tree full of big beautiful white blossoms. And as I was watching, the blossoms just burst into flames, like a giant chandelier out in the middle of nowhere. It was truly the most wonderful thing I ever laid eyes on. I have an active imagination, but yeah, it was probably a psilocybin delusion.

"We were college students, we were working on degrees, and we would party at Smitty's and then get up to go to class the next day. But that was the culture back then. We were all reading these wonderful, heady road books, Kerouac and Ginsberg, and having all these great adventures: social adventures and hallucinogenic adventures. It was just the time. So I guess I'm a woman of her time."

Rob Slater: A Walk to the Stax Museum

Many of the musicians who contributed stories to this book have gone to Memphis to compete in the annual International Blues Challenge. Rob Slater competed twice with two different bands. For Rob, the trip to Memphis provided a bittersweet appraisal of what the contemporary scene represents.

"I think the historicity of blues is just really staggering, especially in Memphis. There it is. The river is just a monumental presence. *Huckleberry Finn* is one of my favorite books . . . and the Mississippi River and all it signifies is just this compelling presence in town, just like the grinding poverty, racial inequality, and white privilege. The irony of black music being played almost exclusively by middle-aged white guys in its ancestral home was not lost on me. The irony of it all . . . and I know I'm guilty. I am absolutely guilty. Memphis and Beale Street in particular have become this paradox because during the IBCs, Beale Street was blues Disneyland with ribs and beer. Which is not to say that there are not great players, great music, great scenes, great riffs, and all that. It's all there, but it seemed to me that it's become the bailiwick of fairly well-heeled middle-aged white folk—at least from what I saw at the IBCs. I love the fact that that the music is being kept alive, but there's a pretty heavy rock quotient to a lot of the music that happens out there. I saw it all during the Blues Challenge. I saw really, really well-done traditional acoustic stuff, and then I saw stuff that was barely recognizable as blues. It seems disingenuous to me somehow. There was a lot of atmosphere that seemed—I might be completely wrong about this, but it seemed—imitation. Like, 'I'm here. Watch me, listen to me; I'm going to play really

12.1. Rob Slater. Courtesy Doug Mokaren.

loud. I'm going to inflict my deluded interpretation of blues with way too many notes on everybody because I've got a captive audience here.' But there was everything in Memphis. There were great performances, great interpretations, and some genuine stuff. But then there were also way too many Kangol hats on backwards and way too many Stevie Ray clones. It's like, 'Here's my blues cred. I'll get a Kangol hat, like a newsboy hat, and turn it backwards, and I'm an instant blues badass.' Those players were everywhere, all over Memphis. You know, the black leather jacket or the faux sharkskin suit.... Too much of it was just the affectations and the trappings. I don't think many of these people got their start in a drink house. When I was in Memphis, I wanted to hear people testify and *get* it. But a lot of the music seemed diluted to me, which is not to say that blues shouldn't evolve, because it has, but a lot of what was going on seemed more like an amusement-park imitation than genuine musical progress; blues Disneyland with ribs and beer.

"I just have to feel that the most monolithic and entrenched *given* in our culture—in contemporary American society—is racial distinction and a de facto segregation. Things cross the lines, but it seems more of like . . . I don't know. It's really complicated. We could have this sociological, philosophical discussion of why racism is, if it is, how it is, but

12.2. A walk to the Stax Museum. Courtesy Alex Forsyth.

I think race trumps everything in America. I think there have certainly been good things that have happened, incidentally and accidentally, but all the good stuff happens with individuals. . . . I just am really pessimistic about this globally *integrated party* . . . I just don't think it's happening. As astonishingly powerful as music is, I think even music is really having a hard time pushing against the entrenched racism in this country. That's how bad the racial disparity is, the actual problem and the perception of the problem. Even music is having a really hard time pushing back. . . . I don't think music is the integrative entity that we all wish it was. . . .

"So let me tell you the story about going to the Stax Museum in Memphis.

"It was this gorgeous day. We didn't know exactly where the museum was. Beautiful day, so we started out, all of us, the whole band. That included me, John and Leigh Olsen, and Bruce Wassel, who was playing drums with us, and Alex Forsyth, the photographer, came along. We were walking south in Memphis. The plan was that we were going to wind our way down to the Stax Museum because we heard it was so phenomenal and we wanted to see it.

"We walked and walked and it became increasingly more blighted and there were increasing numbers of blocks where, obviously, buildings had

12.3. A walk to the Stax Museum. Courtesy Alex Forsyth.

been razed and weedy grass was growing up there, or there were buildings where there was just two or three walls left standing and no roof. . . . It was that old cliché: looks like a war zone. It was rough. Not rough like violent rough; like just . . . decrepit. It looked like nothing had been going on here, just railroad tracks, graffiti, and abandonment. And the few businesses you'd walk by, like a body shop or something like that, those businesses had razor wire on the tops of the fences. It looked pretty bad.

"We walked and walked. . . . Things were looking pretty rugged. We walked past an old burger stand that had been abandoned when this pickup truck pulled into the parking lot. John and Leigh were walking up ahead of us. I saw this truck stop and this guy, this *white* guy, got out of the truck. He was talking to John kind of animatedly. Alex and I were in the back, trailing them because Alex was looking around, taking photographs. We eventually caught up to them. The man from the truck was this really nice guy and he was talking to John and Leigh.

"He was telling them, 'Y'all can't walk there. You'll be killed.'

"He was serious. As it turns out, he was a guy who ran a heavy-truck dealership down on the next block and he was heading off to lunch. He saw us and he's probably seen people like us before. We were getting to the pretty dire part of Memphis. If you don't know, Memphis is one of

12.4. A walk to the Stax Museum. Courtesy Alex Forsyth.

the most violent cities per capita in the country.[5] We were just walking farther and farther south toward the worst of it. When John told him what we were doing, this guy goes, 'You can't do that. You'll be killed.' He was serious. It was another two or three miles through south Memphis before we would get to Stax.

"He told us, 'I'll tell you what I'm going to do.' He was in his pickup truck. He says, 'I'm going to go back to the dealership and I'm going to get my van. I'll be back here in a minute. You guys can get in and I'll take you there. Don't walk any farther.'

"We were thinking, holy shit, huh? But this guy is real sincere. So we sat there twiddling our thumbs for a couple of minutes before he came right back with the dealership's van. We all piled in and he drove us. He knew exactly where we were going and he knew exactly how to get there. We drove through progressively rougher and rougher neighborhoods. His buddies, the people who he was going out to lunch with, were following behind us in the pickup truck. He pulled into a lot across the street from the Stax Museum and his pals pulled up to the curb in the pickup. We were expressing our gratitude and we were going to give him some money.

"He goes, 'Oh, no.' He wouldn't take our money. He was a really, really nice guy. He said, 'When you're done with the tour, before you're finished, call a cab company. They have a list of cab companies at the desk in the museum.' He says, 'Call a cab and get a cab back to your hotel. Do *not* walk in this neighborhood. In fact,' he told us, 'do not walk away from the Stax Museum in either direction. Do not step off this block.' He was emphatic. It was kind of stunning how insistent he was. I had wandered over to the curb and I was talking to the guys in the pickup truck, thanking them for looking after us. Telling them, 'We really appreciated this. We had no idea. This is a shame. It's a really sad situation, but here we are.'

"And this one guy in the pickup truck said to me, 'Yeah, not too long ago, there was a guy shot right here. I mean, right here.' He leaned out of the window of the pickup truck and pointed down right where my feet were. He goes, 'This guy got shot right there trying to do the same thing y'all are doing.' Forewarned is forearmed.

"We went in and did the Stax tour. It was just unbelievable. Really wonderful. And we called a cab before we left. No sooner had we walked out the front door to wait for the cab, a half a block up, some guy is getting cuffed and stuffed. There he was, hands behind his back and a cop putting the zip tie on him, then the cop was pushing his head down as he got jammed into the backseat.

"So we got in our cab and the cab driver was telling us, 'It's a good thing you guys called us while it's still light because there's not a cab driver in Memphis who'll come down here after dark.'"

Sheila Grady Carlisle: Hippie Sings the Blues

Sheila Carlisle is the vocalist for Arhooly, a group that played together for more than sixteen years and recently (2014) had a reunion at the Double Door[6] in Charlotte. I spoke with Sheila by phone in December 2014.

12.5. Sheila Carlisle. Courtesy Max Drake.

"In the '70s I was living on a dairy farm, a hippie dairy farm. Renting it, I didn't own it. I had bluegrass musicians out there all the time. We ended up playing some for Tommy Faile.[7] It was a very good bluegrass band. We won third place in the World Fiddler's Convention up in Union Grove in 1973. . . . Basically, we were sitting around the farmhouse, you know, drinking moonshine and smoking hash under glass. People had been playing music and drinking. We'd build a fire and I started putting quilts over people so they could sleep there and not have to drive anywhere. About three o'clock in the morning, Max Drake just shows up at the farmhouse. He has a resonator guitar. He says, 'Come over here.' He'd been hanging out with a bunch of black blues players and he wanted to show me some stuff he'd learned. I sat and sang with him, sang some stuff, and that's how it all started, because I just loved it. I'd never really been exposed to blues before and I *loved* it. We started jamming. I eventually moved to Troutman [North Carolina] from the farmhouse and we'd have little jam get-togethers with the people and one day somebody in Hickory [North Carolina] asked us, 'Why don't you come down here and play live?' The rest is history. . . .

"Back then I was wide open. I had no fear, no sense, and no idea of danger. Yeah, I got in dangerous situations but I was a tough girl. I've been hanging out with guys most of my life and preferred hanging out with guys. I could cuss and spit with the best of them. People out there on the road respected that. I can remember jumping on the back of a motorcycle, with a motorcycle gang from somewhere in South Carolina, and I had a skirt on. It was just flapping in the wind. They ended up going into—it was almost like a fort. It was all gated and fenced but it was a dope house, a crack house with crystal meth. They were out there patrolling the gate with guns. When I got there, I was the only female in the place, but I went for the drugs, the alcohol, and the party. I did that stuff all the time. When I first got in there, one of the guys grabbed my thigh and I just punched his hand out of the way. I said, 'I'm not here for that crap.' . . . This was a serious, serious place and there I was, the only female, but I never came to any harm. I did lots of stuff like that. I truly think that not having any fear kind of took anybody that does that sort of thing—well, it didn't inspire them to—I'm just not a victim type. I would never do anything that crazy now. I have more sense now, but back then, it just never occurred to me that anything bad would happen. I never had any fear and I think that's what protected me. . . . I threw caution to the wind. . . . I wouldn't advise other people to do it, especially in this day and time, but it worked for me then. It was my personality—I'd just go up to the scariest guy outside the bar and start hanging out and talking. I was wide open, afraid of nothing or nobody. That's not intelligent, I know, but that's just the way I was and it protected me. The roughest—hookers, bikers, street people—loved me. I was one of them. . . . Once I spent the night at a hooker's place where they did business and was sitting around eating an apple in the living room the next morning. The johns started coming in and somebody pointed at me. I went, 'Oh, no, no, no. I don't work here. I'm just visiting.' I just hung out with all kinds of people. It was fascinating to me. I loved to be right in the middle of it. . . .

"When we were on the road, we only actually went to two establishments that were illegal . . . two black clubs. We went there because we were really mesmerized by the whole black experience and the music and wanting to hear the real stuff, not covers played in white clubs. We ended up going to a couple of those clubs and it wasn't any problem. I only did that twice. Both times I was a customer, just wanting to go and listen to . . . the real stuff . . . and it was exactly what we wanted, the feeling that we wanted to learn. It was like a research thing, like trying to keep it authentic and to the roots. That was mostly Max's [Drake] influence because he's a purist when it comes to blues. . . . The only thing for me was some women weren't too happy about me being there until they realized that I was truly there just to listen. . . . They didn't want no white bitches in there dancing with their guys. . . . If I'd go to the restroom or something, they would give me a hard time. I'd just tell them, 'I'm here for the music. That's all.' They respected that.

"Really, I think the fascination for the music had a lot to do with the hippie generation, and the rebelliousness—well, that's what we were all about during that age—rebelling every way we could. It was kind of, if not forbidden, kind of racy and wonderful to hang out with black people and play black music. . . .

"I don't think the scene is as loose as it used to be. It could be the area that I'm in now; I'm kind of out of the loop. I moved back home to the foothills near Morganton [North Carolina] There are great musicians in this town. They're all successful. . . . They're very good musicians but they're not concentrating on music. They're concentrating on putting their kids through college and this and that. Back then—in the '70s—you could travel and make a living and even stay semi-local and raise a family with music. The money is exactly the same now as it was in the '70s. There's been no pay raise for musicians and I don't think people support it. I can remember going up to Asheville and going to a little club. Jimmy Thackery[8] is a real good friend of mine. I sing with him when he's in town. We went to see him up there. There was nobody in there to see Jimmy. *Jimmy Thackery*! I walked up the street to get some French fries . . . and it was like all these young kids were packed in this little brewery just drinking beer, eating pizza, hanging out, and meat marketing. Nobody was interested in the real music that was three doors down. . . ."

The Bigger Story the Smaller Stories Tell

The old drink house, juke joint, chitlin circuits, and gritty local bars with down-home blues were beginning to lose their appeal for young black audiences just as young white audiences and musicians went looking for that authentic experience. It is not a coincidence that blues societies began to appear in the '80s, at a time shortly after younger white musicians and audiences were discovering the "genuine" stuff. By the turn of the millennium, blues societies and their festivals would become a necessity for fans looking for that experience. Max Drake complained that a person could not just wander into a bar and hope to hear some blues. "If I want to just go hear some blues, what are my choices? My choices are—I don't know where to go to hear any blues. Not now. It was rough back in those days [the '70s and '80s], but it was a golden time. We all knew it was near the end. When all this is over, there's nothing that's going to replace it. It's going to be done and over with, so we did it to death the best we could." Storytellers talk about "keeping the blues alive," but note that the music has to evolve right along with race relations and liquor laws.

Some storytellers seemed to believe that players who did not have that southern drink house or bar-jam experience could not claim blues authenticity. Yet others noted that some of the best players at the IBCs in Memphis come from Europe and Asia. As one player observed, "Other than some of the places on the IBC list [of venues], what do kids from the Philippines know about southern bars? They can still play the hell out of some blues."[9] For many players wanting that "genuine experience," finding the bona fide southern bar with a live-music jam these days is a rare if not near impossible mission.

Even if many of the venues have been tamed or have disappeared, there is still a familiar virility, an undercurrent of dangerous, black male authority that continues to echo in the blues, although it may take older ears to hear and recognize the sexual prowess the music suggests. It is no accident that in 2011, Howlin' Wolf's "Smoke Stack Lightning" became the background music for a series of television commercials selling medication for erectile dysfunction. In one of these, an aging but rugged white cowboy "doesn't back down from a challenge" but manages to get his truck out of the mud while the raw blues soundtrack suggests his other manly capabilities. The commercial highlights the multiple ironies of the blues narrative.

By the 2000s, musicians like Roy Roberts were complaining that black youth no longer seemed interested in their musical roots at all, calling it "slavery music." In particular, the old-time folk blues represented misery for younger listeners, but Roy lamented that even electrified R&B seemed to have lost the black audience. His explanation was that "black audiences want glamour. They want to dress up in stylish clothes, go to the nice club where they can go looking and be looked at. Not much glamour in some old shack out in the woods or some old guy playing and singing about misery. Old blues doesn't seem to have a connection to their lives now." Mike "Wezo" Wesolowski echoed this complaint, adding that young people seem ignorant of their heritage, even ignorant of the great local legacies. "In Winston-Salem, the kids—even the black kids—have no idea who the "5" Royales were, and this was a local group recording for Apollo Records; they had an important and lasting impact on all popular music."[10]

Other storytellers remarked that we have not even come close to integrating our southern party. In 2008, with the election of Barack Obama, it seemed that the promise of Sam Cooke's "A Change Is Gonna Come" had arrived and the achievement of our civil rights ideal was within our grasp. However, by 2015, a resurgence of civil rights protests following the deaths of unarmed black men at the hands of white police and a neighborhood-watch patrolman showed that those goals are still elusive.

It is tough for some to escape the snare of undue identification or categorical thinking. Not every poor black man is a violent criminal, not every poor white man is a vicious redneck, and not every policeman is a sadistic racist. It takes a moment's consideration to realize that the person in the bar behaving like a total jerk represents only himself or herself, not an entire race, gender, or nationality. A few observers remarked that the "rainbow coalition" of protestors in the fall of 2014 was a sign that people were learning to see beyond the boundaries of race to the inclusiveness of human experience.[11] However, until a majority of the population can overcome categorical thinking and preconceptions about race, we may never be able to truly integrate our southern party. As Rob Slater observed, all the "good stuff" happens between individuals; it seems we have not have learned to share our festivities—or our resources and opportunities—as a nation, and that is a bitter disappointment. Some boomer storytellers observed that as the hippies aged, many became complacent. No longer interested in rebelling against mom and dad's strict southern values, they learned to live with them. As Big Ron Hunter observed, the confirmed hippies ran off to the mountains but others "got jobs," consequently falling under the economic yoke that rarely supports youthful idealism. Chick Willis predicted that the full evaporation of bigotry might have to wait until miscegenation is so complete that we are visibly one people: "We can't rely on music, good intentions, and a good time to make us all gentle and color-blind."

Looking back over this collection of narratives, the temptation is to try to find the big story that all these little stories tell. Oral history, like any history, is the personal perception of events; the various "takeaways" from the moments of a life. A story is not the truth, but like music and art, stories can help us see the truth. Although this is not social science research and the experiences from these stories cannot be generalized to a larger population, there does seem to be a common theme among the interwoven threads of music, liquor laws, and race relations. The clearly reverberating theme that echoes with nearly every storyteller is an economic one. Although a bar can exclude live music, patrons can self-segregate, and musicians can perform in venues where no liquor is sold, the subject of economic survival is a steady, often directly mentioned, and frequently emphasized theme in every narrative. The story of the drink house or bar, legal and illegal, is a story of entrepreneurship.

The bar owner is a businessman, but so is the musician.

One of the axioms of small businesses is that they are fragile; less than half of small businesses make it past four years of operation. It is even tougher for a business that is unsure of its product. Superficially, the products of the bar and the musician are alcohol and music. But the real product their clients are chasing is something as ephemeral and formless as experience: the good times. Like any prized abstraction (such as love, freedom, or justice), the good time is as difficult to price as it is to define. Its worth and definition vary with every individual. There is no fair market value for a good time. Furthermore, it is impossible to refund time when the good mood evaporates and the gig goes bad. And gigs do go bad. Sometimes they go terribly, terribly bad and someone is hurt or killed. Although the fans and working-class musicians telling stories here seem to share the creed of nonviolence, many carry firearms or knives for self-protection. There are brutal realities (or brutal perceptions) about dancing and gigging in certain bars, whether they are legal or illegal, black or white. Despite the rhetoric of nonviolence, southern culture still seems to be gun culture, and if alcohol is involved, the party can be one insult away from a fistfight, and one fistfight away from a bullet. Though patrons will go to the bar looking for good times and a temporary escape from what Bill Moore describes as "the crying shame of life," sometimes trouble follows and fists, knives, and bullets fly. However, those dangerous possibilities might also be part of the allure. At least in the imagination and until a person is sitting in the emergency room with a bloody towel against his or her head, dangerous can seem exhilarating.

Although appearing to be about public safety, the of role liquor laws in the larger story also has a strong economic pulse; they are a significant part of the costs of doing business. In many ways, the laws drive the illegal business, but they can also shut it down.

While the bar owner understands that a bar is a retail concern, a complication for musicians is that many, perhaps even most, see themselves as artists. The axiom about art is that "if it makes money, it's a business; if it loses money, it's art." The working-class musician willing to work for tips in a drink house may have developed some wicked musical skills but was less likely to have developed solid business expertise. Max Drake said Taj Mahal once offered him a bit of advice: "He told me, 'Keep your own hands on your own business.' What he meant was, don't let somebody else handle your money." Of course, you have to make some money before anyone can handle it. A recurring economic theme from musician storytellers is the tale of the rip-off, not only from managers of venues who won't pay at the end of the night but also from partners, producers, studios, and agents, and even customers who walk past the tip jar and look to download music for free. All are potential thieves.

A further disappointment for that musician who looked backward for the genuine art behind the virility of blues music and finally found and mastered it is the dwindling public appreciation for the real thing. White veneration of the authentic black sound helped to bring about commercial victory for a few artists, but thousands more talented individuals struggled to pay the bills; they were only one heart attack, burst appendix, cancer diagnosis, car crash, or other catastrophic event away from homelessness. Economic survival often meant adapting, playing different genres, finding different bars, and maybe putting their talents and artistic happiness aside for the "real job."

Storytellers disagreed about the ending of this bigger story and whether there is an ending. Some claim it is over without a "happily ever after." For these storytellers, the narrative about discovering the drink house, the blues, and the integrated party is unmistakably over and was likely a fairy tale from the start, as much a myth as the romanticized legend in the film *Crossroads* (1986). In *Crossroads*, a young white musician discovers his elderly black mentor and travels to the South to charm juke-joint audiences and finally defeat the devil with his own blend of black magic and classical white sound. Maybe the story of the integrated southern party we want to tell is pure myth like the movie: there are no crossroads; we walk separate paths and very few make any money on the journey. Still, a few white musicians believe they found their authentic black mentors and experienced the drink house in its glory, but that golden era faded every time a bar with live music shut down.

Still others warned not to be too quick to scribble "the end" to all of it. Tim Duffy says folklorists are often eager to see the end of an era: "The genuine drink houses may be harder to find now, but they do exist; the music is still here and people still love it." Michele Seidman is encouraged to see younger players, black and white, at the IBCs in Memphis: "Music with this much passion won't die out; I don't care where you play it." Observing firsthand the enthusiasm for blues music in other countries, Roy Roberts, Chuck Cotton, and Melva Houston believe the music has a permanent home in foreign venues if not in southern bars.

Before she died, Naomi Alexander was confident of one thing: "The party will go on." She was right. People may be broke, disappointed, and protesting, but some are still drinking, some are still dancing, and a few are still singing the blues.

NOTES

Introduction

1. Stone, *End of the Beginning,* 34.

Chapter 1. Buckets of Blood to the Better Clubs

1. In 1951, the city of Greensboro voted to approve, operate, and control the sale of distilled products. However, many neighboring cities and counties maintained a prohibition on liquor sales. Even where sales were permitted, some establishments never bothered with any kind of legal permit, which put them squarely in the category of the illegal drink house. *ABC Quick Guide: An Overview of North Carolina's Alcoholic Beverage Control Laws, Rules and Information*. Raleigh: ABC Commission, 2012.

2. On the website "Big Government. Small Brains. Dumb Laws" and two radio station websites, WSOC 103.7 and Kiss 95.1 FM, listings of the "Top 11 Most Bizarre North Carolina Laws," the state is noted for making it a misdemeanor to "sing off-key" (Dumb Network). Perhaps they refer to North Carolina general statute § 14–288.4, disorderly conduct. I could find only one "off-key singing" case from 1873, against William Linkhaw of Lumberton, who sang hymns too loudly and in an "abnormal tone." After hearing the evidence regarding Linkhaw's zealous yet appalling singing, which he demonstrated for the court, the judged fined Linkhaw a penny for disturbing the peace. Linkhaw appealed the decision and it was overturned the following year. In a 1971 statute on noise regulation (§ 160A–184), cities are allowed to restrict or prohibit amplified music or any other noise that might disturb citizens. Noise ordinances have been applied in Greensboro after eleven o'clock at night, particularly in 2010, when people began to move back to the downtown area, and nightclubs along Elm Street became not only noisy but violent. The city responded with ordinances on loitering, noise, and an 11:00 p.m. curfew for teens under eighteen. However, I have never heard of anyone arrested for "off-key singing" in North Carolina, though I have been witness to more than one occasion when such an ordinance might have been applied. See "Big Government. Small Brains. Dumb Laws," http://www.dumblaws.com/laws/united-states/north-carolina, and "Top 11 Most Bizarre North Carolina Laws," 17 June 2013.

3. The chitlin circuit was a series of venues considered safe for African American performers who were not welcome at whites-only bars and clubs. Greensboro was nicknamed the "Gate City" because it was a centrally located transportation hub in the state, and this also helped black entertainers traveling the East Coast; see Lauterbach, *Chitlin Circuit.*

Interestingly, some of the earliest music festivals hosted by the Piedmont Blues Preservation Society were held at the railroad depot from 1989 to 1992.

4. Mr. and Mrs. Alexander Faucette owned the El Rocco Supper Club. Minnard H. Peek opened the Carlotta Supper Club in 1961; see Otis L. Hairston Jr., *Greensboro, North Carolina* (Black America Series), (Charleston, SC: Arcadia Publishing, 2003), 64. Green's Supper Club (1952–2012) was primarily a white establishment in the early years but became more racially diverse by the time it closed. Roy Roberts also noted that the Plantation Supper Club was another important music venue of this type, where black musicians often entertained white audiences until patrons became more racially diverse.

5. A short picture and bio of Sam Red appears in Duffy, *Music Makers,* 128–29.

6. For more stories about unwary sailors walking into the wrong bar, Ralph referred me to *American Folklore and Legend* (Pleasantville, NY: Reader's Digest, 1978), 248–51.

7. A&T University is North Carolina Agricultural and Technical State University, which opened 1890 as a land-grant university. The historically black college has a strong civil rights legacy and prepared black men for what was often the only really reliable job they could rely on even with a degree. On February 1, 1960, four freshmen A&T students, Ezell Blair Jr. (Jibreel Khazan), Franklin McCain, Joseph McNeil, and David Richmond, walked to the Greensboro Woolworth's and "sat-in" at the whites-only lunch counter. They refused to leave when denied service and stayed until the store closed. This was not the first sit-in, but was instrumental in the civil rights movement, helping to achieve the desegregation of lunch counters and other public places.

8. Betty Jean Jones was a Bennett Belle and a professor of drama at the University of North Carolina–Greensboro from 1982 to 1995, when she left to take a position at the University of Michigan. She was locally famous in Greensboro for hosting parties and for her sweet-potato pie. Dr. Jones was killed in a plane crash in 1997. The American Theatre and Drama Society accepts nominations each year for the Betty Jean Jones Award in her memory.

9. In *The Language of the Blues from Alcorub to Zuzu,* Debra Devi explains that an "easy rider" is a faithless man who sponges off a woman (103).

10. Tommy Johnson (1896–1956) was a blues vocalist and guitar player from Terry, Mississippi. Dick Weissman, in *Blues: The Basics,* describes Johnson as an alcoholic and a showman who played guitar behind his back. Tommy Johnson is not related to Robert Johnson, but both men have a similar legend attached to them about making deals with the devil in exchange for musical talent. Tommy Johnson may have encouraged and even helped to spread this story. Tommy Johnson's practice of occasionally drinking Sterno inspired his 1928 song "Canned Heat Blues" (99). For more on Tommy Johnson, see Evans, *Tommy Johnson.*

11. After 1984, the National Minimum Age Drinking Act prompted states to raise the legal age from eighteen to twenty-one or risk losing federal funding dollars for highways.

12. "My Father Said" is on the CD *Pouring Out the Blues*, Rock House Records, 2006.

13. Richard Ripani makes a similar argument about rap music in *New Blue Music.*

14. Logie Meachum is a past recipient of the Keeping the Blues Alive Award for his efforts to perform and promote blues music. Perhaps best known for his work with Bubba

"Big Bump" Klinefelter in the group Bump and Logie, Logie sings and plays acoustic guitar and washboard while "Big Bump" plays guitar and harmonica. The duo won the national single/duo qualifier for the Piedmont Blues Preservation Society Challenge, which sent them on to compete in the International Blues Challenge in Memphis in 2009. In 2008, Logie received the O. Henry Award, which recognizes an individual for extraordinary contributions to arts and culture. In 2009, the Greensboro Public Library selected him for Greensboro's Literary Laurel Award. He is featured in the feature film *Bone Creek* (2008) and the Oscar-nominated short *Two Soldiers* (2003).

15. From *Florida Folklife WPA Collections, 1937–1942,* there is an audio clip by the author and anthropologist Zora Neale Hurston (1891–1960) that provides a more detailed explanation of the rules of the card game Georgia Skin. Each player gets a card face up on the table. The dealer puts the deck on the table so he can't cheat and the players place bets that the card matching theirs won't be uncovered as the dealer turns up the cards from the deck, one by one. Once the players have their cards and the game is set to commence, the dealer will tell them, "Put the money on the wood and let the bet go good."

16. Except for James Brown, the acts Logie named are well-known gospel artists. The Blind Boys of Alabama are a gospel group that began singing in 1944 and continue to perform with changes in the group's original members. Sister Rosetta Tharpe (1915–75) was a gospel vocalist and guitar player who opened gospel to pop with her 1939 hit, "This Train." Mahalia Jackson (1911–72) was another gospel artist known for her powerful vocals. James Brown (1933–2006) is the only act better known as a high-energy soul and R&B artist from Georgia.

17. Andy Coats is a guitar player and singer who formed the band Andy Coats and the Bank Walkers in 2007 and released the CD *Owe the Devil* (2013).

18. Arhooly should not to be confused with the record company Arhoolie Records. Max said that Bruce Cook's book, *Listen to the Blues,* a book his mother gave Max when his interest in this music became apparent, suggested the name, but the band dropped the *ie* for a *y.* Max said the founder and president of the record company, Chris Strachwitz, called him, glad that Max respected the record company and used a different spelling for the band name. The name comes from a term for field hollers. Over a fifteen-year period, Arhooly members changed but consistent musicians were Max Drake (guitar), Sheila Grady Carlisle (vocals), Aristotle Georgio (harp), Chris Grant (bass), and Bob Dunlap (drums). Earlier incarnations included David Clark (drums), Conrad Bender (keyboard and harp), Bill Ward (bass), Kirk Vernon (sax), Dan Rose (guitar), and Steve Barker (guitar).

19. Roy continues to record, tour, and play a variety of music, including country music that Obie Burnett McClinton inspired (see chapter 10). Roy's studio, Rock House Records, produces his own CDs along with the CDs of many other artists. In 2002, *Living Blues* magazine featured Roy on the cover and awarded him the title Producer of the Year. I interviewed Roy on several occasions from 2006 to 2014.

20. Conversation with African American informant Moneek Allah, December 21, 2014. Interview recorded by Robin Stamps Doby Easter.

21. Conversation with African American informant, May 26, 2014.

Chapter 2. The Bar as a Music Venue

1. Places that allow underage drinking.

2. Rick Estrin is a blues harmonica player and songwriter with the band the Nightcats. He was awarded the Blues Foundation's prestigious Blues Music Award for Best Harmonica Player at the Thirty-Fourth Annual Blues Music Awards in Memphis, Tennessee, in January 2013.

3. Brett Chambers is the drummer for the band the Usual Suspects and a host for open jams. Chambers teaches in the Department of Mass Communications at North Carolina Central University (NCCU) located in Durham, North Carolina. NCCU was the first public liberal arts institution for African Americans and one of the sixteen campuses of the Consolidated University of North Carolina.

4. Jalacy "Screamin' Jay" Hawkins (1929–2000) was a blues musician and actor known for his theatrical performances and often wore ghoulish, eccentric costumes. He performed the song "I Put a Spell on You" with macabre props and hints of hoodoo. Video versions of this song available on the Internet show various interpretations ranging from a black-and-white version with a creeping hand prop from *The Merv Griffin Show* on September 21, 1966, to a color version from a concert in Tokyo in 1990 that included the coffin and full witch doctor costume.

5. Elvin Bishop is a guitarist, vocalist, and songwriter from Glendale, California. He may be best known for the song "Fooled Around and Fell in Love" (1976). Bishop claims to find survival value in music. In August 2000, *People* magazine reported that the dismembered body of Bishop's daughter, Selina Bishop, had been found in a duffel bag floating in a marina in the Sacramento River Delta. Bishop's mother had died a few weeks before his daughter was murdered. He told reporters, "The only good thing I've got is the blues"; see Patrick Rogers, Maureen Harrington, Michelle Bowers, Bob Stewart, and Gary Delsohn, "Blues for Selina," *People,* 4 August 2000, 81–84.

6. Sam John Hopkins (1912–82) was a guitarist, vocalist, and songwriter from Texas who recorded on multiple labels. He is featured in *The Blues Accordin' to Lightnin' Hopkins* (1968). He also performs in *Warming by the Devil's Fire*, one of seven parts of Martin Scorsese's PBS series *The Blues* (2003). Television appearances included *The Tonight Show with Johnny Carson* (NBC, 1962–92). See Alan Govenar's book, *Lightnin' Hopkins: His Life and Blues.*

7. P. B. Scott's Music Hall operated in Blowing Rock, North Carolina, in a geodesic dome–shaped wooden building from 1976 to 1983, and continued to hold reunion parties even after losing long-running battles with the town of Blowing Rock over noise and liquor and finally closing; see Paul T. Choate, "Seventh Annual P. B. Scott's Reunion Party," *High Country Press,* 25 April 2012. Web. 29 December 2014.

8. Napoleon Brown Goodson Culp (1929–2008) was a vocalist and songwriter. Max played with Nappy on the CD *I'm a Wild Man* (1994).

9. Blues and soul vocalist Lester Chambers was attacked in the middle of his performance at the Hayward Russell City Blues Festival on July 13, 2013. Lester had just dedicated a song to Trayvon Martin, the unarmed black teen fatally shot by neighborhood-watch volunteer George Zimmerman in 2012. Trayvon Martin's death and the jury acquittal of Zimmerman produced rallies and protests across the country and provoked a nationwide discussion

about racial profiling. Some people viewed the attack as a hate crime, but the woman who assaulted Lester, Dinalynn Inez Andrews Potter, was charged with felony assault and felony elder abuse. Lester was seventy-two years old at the time of the attack. He had dedicated his performance of a Curtis Mayfield song, "People Get Ready," to Martin and had asked the audience to "come together in the mind, in the heart, in the soul . . . let's color the world with love." Many blues artists in venues across the country dedicated music to Trayvon Martin's memory. See the Internet video on the story: Lisa Fernandez, "Woman Charged with Felonies in Soul Singer Lester Chambers Assault Suffers from PTSD," NBC Bay Area, KNTV, 16 August 2013.

10. The original bar, the White Horse Tavern, was owned by John "Ziggy" Ziglinski in the 1970s. After closing and reopening in different locations, Ziggy's continues to operate in 2015 as a large nightclub and live-music venue in Winston-Salem. Charles Womack, Brad McCauley, and the original owner, Jay Stephens, own and operate the bar.

11. Peter Madcat Ruth is a Grammy Award–winning harmonica player from Ann Arbor, Michigan. James Whiting or Sugar Blue is a harmonica player, vocalist, and songwriter from Harlem who appeared in the film *Angel Heart* (1987) along with Pinetop Perkins and Piedmont guitarist Walter Brown "Brownie" McGhee. The movie tells a story about music and voodoo. Louis Cyphre (the devil) hires detective Harry Angel to track down a singer named Johnny Favorite, who sold his soul in exchange for stardom, a familiar blues legend.

12. Howard Levy is a harmonica player from Brooklyn, New York, and founding member of Béla Fleck and the Flecktones.

Chapter 3. Blues, Booze, and "Occupying a Dive"

1. The acetate disc was dubbed from the master recording and served as a demo.

2. Rudy Ray Moore was originally an R&B singer turned comedian who was known for his explicit humor. He may be best known for his comedy role in the 1975 film directed by D'Urville Martin, *Dolemite*. Jimmy Lynch was also a singer and comedian, telling jokes as the character "Funky Tramp." He also appeared in the *Dolemite* film with Moore.

3. LaVal Records was a label out of Kalamazoo, Michigan.

4. "Stoop Down, Baby. Let Your Daddy See" was considered too lewd for radio play, with sexual innuendo that was bold for the time. Some of the verses tell the story of two frustrated women: "Two old maids they're layin' in the sand / One rolled over and said, 'I wish you was a man' / She said, 'No, no, child, I ain't no man / but keep still, baby, I'll do the best I can.'" The chorus repeats the song title, adding, "You got something down there, baby / Worryin' the hell out of me."

5. Oliver Sain (1932–2003) was a legendary saxophone player, drummer, and songwriter from Mississippi. He played and collaborated with many notable blues artists including Howlin' Wolf, Ike Turner, and Little Milton Campbell.

6. Gussow, *Seems Like Murder Here*, 196.

7. The Hi-Hat was not a "bucket of blood," but a well-respected club. Formerly known as the Embassy Club, the Hi-Hat Club in Hattiesburg is famous for hosting performers like

B. B. King, Otis Redding, Ike and Tina Turner, and others. The owner, Milton Barnes, was one of Mississippi's most successful black businessmen. The club closed in 1994.

8. Here I believe Chick was speaking in general about the hypocrisy of the law and its role in hindering the civil rights movement, not specifically about the experience of the Freedom Riders in Georgia in 1961. In that specific event, the Freedom Riders encountered violence in South Carolina and in Alabama, but the ride through Georgia was without incident. It wasn't until the riders reached Alabama that buses were attacked. Klansmen ambushed the riders in Anniston, firebombed the buses, and assaulted the riders. In many cases where the civil rights movement met with organized violence from the Ku Klux Klan, police authorities were believed to have been involved and supportive or at the very least, sympathetic. For example, the Greensboro massacre on November 3, 1979, resulted from a rally in the Morningside Homes housing project, where the Communist Party was attempting to organize black industrial workers. There was no police presence at the rally when Klansmen and members of the American Nazi Party arrived and fired shots at the demonstrators. In 2005, the Greensboro Truth and Reconciliation Commission determined that police had infiltrated the Klan and knew about their plans to attack the rally; see the documentary *Greensboro: Closer to the Truth*, directed by Adam Zucker.

Chapter 4. White Kids on the Chitlin Circuit

1. Big Jack Johnson (1940–2011) was a guitarist and vocalist who received multiple Handy Award nominations for his guitar playing and songwriting and in 2003 won the Handy Award for best acoustic album for his CD *The Barbecue Sessions.*

2. Sam Carr (1926–2008) was a blues drummer whose father, Robert Nighthawk, was also a blues guitarist and vocalist. Sam began his career playing with his dad. In the 1960s, he joined guitarist Big Jack Johnson to form the band the Jelly Roll Kings. He was featured in *Feel Like Going Home,* which is part of the Martin Scorsese series *The Blues* (2003).

3. Frank Frost (1936–99) was a harmonica player who began touring as a young man with Sam Carr and Robert Nighthawk. Sam Phillips of Sun Records recorded some of his work, including the album *Hey Boss Man* (1962). See Neil Strauss's tribute: "Frank Frost, 63, Who Played Delta Blues," *New York Times*, 14 October 1999, B13.

4. The "Boogie Man" Jerry McCain was known for his harmonica playing. McCain was born in Gadsden, Alabama, in 1930. He recorded on Trumpet Records, Columbia Records, Jewel, Ichiban Records, and Music Maker before he passed away in 2012.

5. Tyrone Davis (1938–2005) was born in Mississippi but moved to Chicago when he was fifteen. He worked as a chauffeur for blues vocalist Freddie King and then began in Chicago clubs. He became known as an R&B singer and had several hits with Dakar Records before signing with Columbia Records.

6. Chicago Bob Nelson (1944–2013) was known for his harmonica and vocal style and for working nearly every blues venue in Chicago. Muddy Waters gave him the nickname "Chicago Bob."

7. James Cotton became famous for his work on the harmonica, playing with Howlin' Wolf in the early 1950s. He also played on Muddy Waters's album *Hard Again*, which was produced by Johnny Winter in 1977.

8. Billy Wright (1932–91) was a blues vocalist from Atlanta who did a number of recordings with Savoy Records.

9. Little Richard (Richard Wayne Penniman, b. 1932) is known for his extreme high-energy performances with songs such as "Tutti Frutti" (1955), "Long Tall Sally" (1956), and "Good Golly Miss Molly" (1957). Billy Wright was the flamboyant, Atlanta-based artist who helped Little Richard get his early recording career going.

10. Sonny Terry (1911–86), or Saunders Terrell, was a blind harmonica player from Georgia. He recorded a cover of Robert Johnson's "Crossroad Blues" for the film *Crossroads* (1986) and is featured in *Godfathers and Sons*, which is part of the Martin Scorsese series *The Blues* (2003).

11. Jerry McCain was proud of his car. He recorded the single "Courtin' in a Cadillac" and released it on Excello Records in 1965 (Excello 2268).

12. The Tutwiler Hotel is a historic luxury hotel in downtown Birmingham near City Hall. The original building was demolished in 1974, but in 1986, the Ridgely apartment building (built in 1913) was converted into a hotel and named for the original Tutwiler.

13. James Harman (b. 1946) is a blues harmonica player, singer, and songwriter from Anniston, Alabama, who has played drink houses all over the South but now tours internationally. He was inducted into the Alabama Music Hall of Fame, won numerous Handy Awards, and recorded on labels such as Black Top, Blind Pig, and many others.

14. Werner, *Change Is Gonna Come*, 184–86.

15. In the song "Burn the Crack House Down," Jerry "Boogie" McCain calls for people to "Come go with me / We got a job to do / Get a plastic jug or a gasoline can / We're going down to the filling station and fill it up with 93 octane gasoline / And when we get through, the whole doggone neighborhood gonna be clean / 'Cause we're gonna burn the crack house down . . . we're gonna clean up this town." McCain also wrote another song with similar sentiments about what was happening in his neighborhood, "Ain't No Use for Drug Abuse."

16. According to the *Gadsden Times*, the only survivor of the 1995 arson that killed two men named Carl Weaver as one of the conspirators in the double homicide; see Andy Powell, "Hokes Bluff Man Sues in Coosa County Murder Case," *Gadsden Times*, 14 September 2010. The case was further complicated when the assistant DA and a lawyer were accused of attempting to extort millions of dollars from Weaver.

17. Jimmy Hall was a vocalist and harmonica player from Alabama who became the lead singer for Wet Willie. He was nominated for a Grammy Award in 1985 for his vocals on Jeff Beck's album *Flash*.

18. John Everett Sandlin Jr. was a music producer for the Capricorn record label and was well known in the Muscle Shoals music scene. Sandlin was also a musician, playing guitar, drums, and bass. He worked at FAME recording studios as a session guitarist in the 1960s.

19. The 1995 television documentary that resulted was *Jerry McCain's True Blues*.

20. Permits for liquor sales can be very specific. An owner of a business with an alcohol beverage license generally must buy alcohol from a wholesaler with a permit issued by the

state. Generally, a business may not purchase for resale from another retail licensee, even if they only hold a temporary license.

21. Sandra Hall (b. 1948) is a vocalist from Atlanta, Georgia, known for her earthy style. Hall had a background as an exotic dancer but has always been a singer. She became a mentor to Shemika Copeland and a visitor to public schools, where she teaches about blues culture.

22. Morris Holt was known as Magic Slim (1937–2013), a guitar player with four fingers on his left hand who moved from Mississippi to Chicago and began a recording career in the 1960s. Magic Slim and the Teardrops won the W. C. Handy Award in 2003 for Blues Band of the Year.

23. Napoleon Brown Goodson Culp or Nappy Brown (1929–2008) was a vocalist and songwriter from Charlotte, North Carolina. Numerous artists have covered his hit song "The Right Time" or "Night Time Is the Right Time" (1957), which was also featured in a memorable episode of *The Cosby Show* (1984–92), where the cast lip-synched to the Ray Charles version. He was a featured guest on Garrison Keillor's NPR radio variety show *A Prairie Home Companion* in 2007. Scott Barretta writes about his musical comeback in "Long Time Coming," *Sing Out* 52, no. 1 (Spring 2008): 107.

24. Eddie Kirkland (1923–2011) was a blues musician born in Jamaica but who lived in Dothan, Alabama. He was known for his guitar, harmonica, and vocals as well as writing original songs.

25. Bobby Rush (Emmit Ellis Jr.) is a vocalist and songwriter from Louisiana who began playing juke joints as a teenager. In 2000 he was nominated for a Grammy Award and has won Blues Music Awards for best acoustic artist and album. He appears in *The Road to Memphis*, one of the seven shows in Martin Scorsese's series *The Blues* (2003).

26. Carey Bell Harrington (1936–2006) was a harmonica player and vocalist from Mississippi who moved to Chicago, where he learned to play harp. In 1990, Bell collaborated with other harp players—Junior Wells, James Cotton, and Billy Branch—to release the album *Harp Attack* (Alligator Records). The year before he died, Carey Bell made a duet album, *Second Nature*, with his son, Lurrie Bell.

27. Chan's Fine Oriental Dining is a restaurant in Woonsocket, Rhode Island, which also has a blues and jazz club with a stage. The club books national and regional musical acts and also hosts a jazz jam.

28. Lovie Lee (1909–97) was a keyboard player from Tennessee who grew up in Mississippi and did some vaudeville before joining the Muddy Waters Band. He became a mentor to his cousin, Carey Bell, moving with him to Chicago in the mid-1950s.

29. Big Chief Eddie Clearwater is the stage name of Edward Harrington (b. 1935), a guitar player from Alabama who moved to Chicago in the 1950s. He is a guitarist who plays left-handed and upside down.

30. The Slippery Noodle is a popular bar and restaurant in Indiana that features live local, regional, and national blues acts on two separate stages, nationally recognized by *Blues Revue* as one of the top twenty blues venues. The location has an important history as a link in the Underground Railroad. It is associated with Slippery Noodle Sound, Indiana's blues recording label.

31. Johnny Mars (b. 1942) is a harmonica player, singer, and songwriter from South Carolina who moved to California and then London in 1978. He has toured extensively in Europe and has worked with Magic Sam, Earl Hooker, and B. B. King, among others.

32. Arthur "Guitar Boogie" Smith (1921–2014) played banjo, guitar, and fiddle but is best remembered for his live television broadcast on WBTV in Charlotte, *The Arthur Smith Show*.

33. William Thomas "Champion Jack" Dupree (1908–92) was a piano player from New Orleans. Hank Bordowitz writes about "Champion Jack" Dupree along with other blues artists in "Blues for the Blues," *American Visions* 7, no. 4 (August/September 1992): 43–46.

34. Tom Dooley refers to Thomas C. Dula (1845–68) a Confederate soldier from Wilkes County, North Carolina, who was convicted and hanged in the murder of his fiancée, Laura Foster. The folk song by Thomas C. Land, "Hang Down Your Head Tom Dooley," was a murder ballad based on Tom Dula's trial and became a popular hit when the Kingston Trio recorded a version of it in 1958.

35. Etta Baker (1913–2006) played acoustic guitar as well as banjo. Her playing style was considered to be the true Piedmont blues style with back picking, in which the thumb plays downward on the bass strings with the index finger picking backward on the higher strings.

36. Howard Colbert is a versatile guitar, banjo, and keyboard player who made his first recording with the King Bees.

37. Charlie E. Bristol is one of many lesser-known but powerful Piedmont-style guitar players, a longtime player of the black Gibson guitar known as Lucille, a name B. B. King bestowed on his black Gibson guitar. The legend goes that King rescued his guitar when the gig he was playing literally caught fire from two men fighting over a woman named Lucille and caused the deadly fire.

38. Blind Boy Fuller (Fulton Allen, 1907–41) was a vocalist and guitar player in the Piedmont tradition from Rockingham, North Carolina. He grew to popularity playing house parties in North Carolina cities like Winston-Salem and Durham and became extremely popular, recording for the American Recording Company.

39. Ora Watson is a guitar player, banjo player, and an old-time fiddle player from Watauga County in North Carolina. She is known for bluegrass and traditional mountain music at events like MerleFest.

40. Johnny Shines (1915–92) was a vocalist and guitar player from Memphis, Tennessee, who was influenced by the music of Robert Johnson. He recorded for Columbia Records, Chess Records, and J.O.B. Records. He moved to Alabama in 1969 near Tuscaloosa and continued to play in local bars and on the international blues circuit. He played with many of the original blues greats: Robert Johnson, Robert Lockwood Jr., Snooky Prior, and many others.

Chapter 5. Muscle Shoals, Dry Counties, and the Hooch Run

1. Like any good legend, there are several versions of this story, some with romantic, almost fairy-tale-like overtones, some much darker and ghostly, depending on who does the

telling. All versions agree that the singing Indian girl blessed the Shoals with extraordinary musical talent.

2. Colonel William Lindsey McDonald, the Shoals historian (1927–2009), knew this story growing up locally but it is also related in Handy's autobiography, *Father of the Blues.* Colonel McDonald was a retired army colonel and author of several books on Shoals-area history, and I interviewed him at his home on September 21, 2007. Colonel McDonald passed away on June 20, 2009.

3. The Beatles would record Alexander's song "Anna (Go to Him)" in 1963. Ike and Tina Turner played his song "Every Day I Have to Cry." The Rolling Stones and the Hollies played his song "You Better Move On."

4. James Joiner and Tom Stafford invested in a small recording studio above a drugstore on Seminary Street in Florence from which Stafford would later develop FAME recording studios. See Alabama Music Hall of Fame (alamhof.org).

5. Magnolia Pictures released the documentary *Muscle Shoals* on September 27, 2013.

6. King, "Blues Tourism in the Mississippi Delta," 456.

7. In a few cases, informants suggest that locations where the rough drink houses or "buckets of blood" once operated have become even "rougher" places catering to the drug trade.

8. George "Wild Child" Butler (1936–2005) was a guitar player, vocalist, and harmonica player from Alabama who moved to Canada in the 1980s.

9. "Deep Elem Blues" (popularized by Joe and Bob Attlesay in 1935) is a tune covered by Bob Dylan and others. The song warns listeners that there's a certain town in Texas where you might get robbed if you aren't careful.

10. Johnny Shines (1915–92) was a blues musician born in Memphis, Tennessee, but finally settled in Alabama in the late 1960s. He toured with Delta blues guitarist Robert Lockwood Jr. but when he was in Alabama, he frequently played at a coffeehouse on the University of Alabama campus in Tuscaloosa and was invited to the Handy Festival before he died in 1992.

11. George Martin is a musician, record producer, arranger, and composer from London associated with the Beatles' early years and Abbey Road Studios.

12. *Coal Miner's Daughter* is a 1980 biopic of Loretta Lynn in which Levon Helm made his screen debut in the role of Ted Webb, Loretta Lynn's father. Michael Apted directed the film, which starred Sissy Spacek as Lynn.

13. In the 1970s the minimum drinking age in Alabama was lowered to nineteen. After 1984, the minimum drinking age was raised to twenty-one; see Susan Kay Arndt, *Adolescent Alcohol Consumption and a Changing Legal Drinking Age* (Bloomington: Indiana University Press, 1988).

14. Andrew Wright was a keyboard player who cowrote "When a Man Loves a Woman" with Calvin Lewis and Percy Sledge. Percy Sledge, a vocalist from Leighton, Alabama, recorded the song in 1966 at Norala Sound Studio in Sheffield, Alabama.

15. Rod Stewart was in the area in the mid-1970s to record for the album *Atlantic Crossing* (1975).

16. George Jones (1931–2013) was a country music singer who recorded at several studios in the Shoals. Ironically, one of Jones's early hits that became a signature song in his

repertoire was the rockabilly song "White Lightning" (Mercury, 1959), which was recorded in Nashville. Rumor was that Jones was drunk while recording it. The lyrics tell a story about a family still in North Carolina that revenuers couldn't find and moonshine so powerful that it could knock out a tough city slicker. The song was a Shoals-area front-porch favorite because the story could easily swap locations from North Carolina to north Alabama.

17. Jerry Lee Lewis ("the Killer") is a pianist and vocalist from Louisiana.

18. The Tams were a vocal group from Atlanta, Georgia, who recorded their hit "What Kind of Fool (Do You Think I Am)" at FAME recording studios in 1963.

19. The Drifters were a vocal group widely known for R&B and soul music but had various incarnations. In 1979 the group was Bill Pinkney, Andrew Lawyer, Chuck Cockerham, Harriel Jackson, and Tony Cook.

Chapter 6. Juke Joints, Bootleg, and Moonshine

1. R. L. Burnside (1926–2005) was a Mississippi guitar player who began to get attention in the 1990s for his electrified blues (see Weissman, *Blues: The Basics*, 32). Burnside traveled to North Carolina several times in the 1990s, playing gigs in Greensboro and at the Double Door Inn in Charlotte, North Carolina. Burnside also spent some time in Chicago and Memphis before returning to live in north Mississippi.

2. David "Junior" Kimbrough (1930–98) was a Hill Country blues–style vocalist and guitar player. He recorded on High Water, Fat Possum, and Capricorn Records.

3. Bill Moore wrote about some of this odyssey in an article for the Greensboro *News and Record*: "A Search for the Blues: Pilgrimage Takes Devotee from Slick City Nightclubs to Countryside Juke Joint," 21 August 1991, A8.

4. Kaopectate is the brand name of a liquid medication taken orally for symptoms of diarrhea, nausea, and stomach cramps.

5. *The Blues Brothers* (1980) is a musical comedy film developed from a comedy sketch on the NBC variety series *Saturday Night Live* (1975–). The movie tells the story of two brothers from Chicago on a mission to reunite their band and play a fund-raiser to save the Catholic boarding school where they were raised. The movie features several well-known blues, gospel, and soul performers such as Cab Calloway, James Brown, Aretha Franklin, Ray Charles, and John Lee Hooker. It also features a scene in a bar where there is chicken wire around the bandstand. In this scene, a rowdy country audience does not appreciate blues music and pelts the band until they begin to sing their own version of Frankie Laine's "Rawhide" (1958). Although more appreciative of the country song, the audience now throws bottles at the band with approval rather than derision. It seems that whether the audience is annoyed or enthusiastic, debris will get tossed at the band.

6. In Ray Browne's book *Rituals and Ceremonies in Popular Culture*, Steven Del Sesto writes in his chapter "Dancing and Cockfighting at Jay's Lounge and Cockpit: The Preservation of Folk Practices in Cajun Louisiana" about this important part of Cajun subculture. The cockfight functions as a "symbolic representation of man's continual struggle for survival" and contributes to social solidarity in rural communities. Like dancing, cockfighting has "tension-management functions," venting hostility and pent-up emotions "with few or

no deleterious consequences for the individuals involved . . . no one really suffers but the cocks. Death and destruction is confined to the wire surrounding the pit" (279). According to Mel, there were occasions when fighting escaped the cockpit, entered the bar, and even spilled over into the parking lot.

7. Tabby Thomas (1929–2014) was a guitar player, pianist, and vocalist from Baton Rouge who recorded on Excello Records. His son, Chris Thomas King, is a singer, actor, and guitar player known for his performances in *Ray* (2004) and *O Brother Where Art Thou?* (2000), in which he plays a guitar-playing character based on the folklore of Robert Johnson (1911–38) and Tommy Johnson (1896–1956).

8. As of this writing, the Fairlanes include guitarist/vocalist Mark "Buddyro" Harrison, drummer/vocalist Chip "Memphis" Click, and bassist/vocalist Ken "Lil' Kenny" Graham, and have added Philadelphia native Glenn Bickel on keyboards and vocals. Previous members of the band before 1990 included Gary Collins on drums, Chris Carroll on bass, and Kevin Wilson on keyboards. Mark's band should not be confused with the vocal trio Robert Knight formed in the 1960s in Nashville, Tennessee, also called the Fairlanes.

9. Some bars and clubs will have "band houses," which are places where musicians who are booked in the bar can sleep for the night as a substitute for providing hotel rooms. Penny Zamagni complains that most of these are pretty awful. "You certainly wouldn't let your mother sleep there." However, for some clubs, having a band house was the only economically feasible way to book an out-of-town group.

10. Danny Thomas (1912–91) was the star of the television sitcom *Make Room for Daddy* (later called *The Danny Thomas Show*, 1953–65), which was about a family man and entertainer at the Copa Club.

11. *The Color Purple* came out in 1985. More than one informant mentioned scenes from this film as an accurate portrayal of a drink house. Even though the movie depicts a 1930s juke joint and most stories that informants told occurred thirty to sixty years after the setting of this film, some storytellers believed that the juke scenes were reflections of their more recent experiences.

Chapter 7. Roots

1. See Hazzard-Donald, *Mojo Workin'*, 29–33.

2. Spencer, *Blues and Evil*, 99.

3. Devi, *Language of the Blues*, 134.

4. Hazzard-Donald, *Mojo Workin'*, 65–66.

5. Malbrough, *Hoodoo Mysteries*, 132.

6. Palmer, *Deep Blues*, 95.

7. For the magic of knotting, see Hazzard-Donald, *Mojo Workin'*, 147–50. For the use of whiskey-spitting on knots, see Owens, *Voodoo Tales*, 175. The famous voodoo queen Marie Laveau was said to blow a mouthful of whiskey in dancers' faces as part of her ritual; see Ward, *Voodoo Queen*, 116.

8. Hazzard-Donald, *Mojo Workin'*, 69.

9. Gussow, *Seems Like Murder Here,* 16.

10. For a discussion of this legend, see Graves, *Crossroads,* 39–43, or Schroeder, *Robert Johnson.* For a discussion of Johnson's death and the black arts, see Guralnick, *Searching for Robert Johnson,* 49–55, and Pearson and McCulloch, *Robert Johnson Lost and Found,* 15–17. In Pearson's interviews with David "Honeyboy" Edwards (1915–2011), the story is that the man who owned the bar where Robert was playing convinced someone else to poison his whiskey: "and he didn't go to the penitentiary; he didn't go to jail"; Pearson, *Sounds So Good to Me,* 16–17.

11. Interview with Tammy Armstrong, Elizabeth City, North Carolina, September 2003. A videotaped and edited version of this story appears in the documentary *Folk Medicine* (2005). The details of what the root doctor told the husband to do to lift the lesbian's curse from his wife were never revealed.

12. Walter Davis (1911–63), "Ashes in My Whiskey."

13. Conversation with a male African American informant, Elizabeth City, North Carolina, October 11, 2003.

14. Reiki is the Japanese method of palm healing through which the healer intuitively transfers universal energy through her or his palms to the wounded body. Reiki healers tend not to touch the body, but to hold their hands, palm down, just above the physical body.

15. Conversation with an African American informant, Elizabeth City, North Carolina, October 11, 2003. An edited videotaped version of this story is told in the documentary *Wondrous Healing* (2004).

16. Hazzard-Donald, *Mojo Workin',* 98–99.

17. Ibid., 156–57.

18. Conversation with white student informant, UNCG, Greensboro, North Carolina, October 4, 1992.

19. Conversation with African American student informant, UNCG, Greensboro, North Carolina, October 5, 1992.

20. Chicago Bob Nelson (1944–2013) was a harmonica player and vocalist who played both Delta and Chicago blues styles. Penny and Rob toured with Bob for several years.

21. I had also been to Miller's Rexall to interview Richard Miller for the documentary *Folk Medicine,* which aired on South Carolina public television in 2005. The documentary also includes edited root-doctor stories from Dale Neighbors, Frank Stephenson Jr., Tammy Armstrong, Lacoyia Cobb, Darryl Napier, Jeffrey Anderson, and Richard Miller. Some of these stories are included in this chapter along with other stories not incorporated in the documentary.

22. Bend-over oil or Bendover oil is a commercial hoodoo product that promises to let the user influence others, to "bend" them to your will. There are bend-over oils and bend-over spells that are supposed to give the user power over both people and situations.

23. High John the Conqueror root is a significant ingredient in traditional hoodoo, although there is some controversy about which is the true magical root. See Greer, *New Encyclopedia of the Occult,* 226–27.

24. Reverend Billy C. Wirtz is a blues musician from South Carolina known for his comedic style. He also teaches workshops on blues and gospel music.

25. Marie Laveau (1794–1881) and her daughter, also named Marie Laveau (1827–95), both practiced and were ministers of voodoo with a large following in New Orleans throughout the nineteenth century. Their ministry was so large that the two historical women merged into one legendary figure who was said to hypnotize the white police so she could dance with snakes in Congo Square, put possession trances on people, have the power to influence court proceedings, and make the magic to acquire husbands or get rid of them, among other magical powers. See Ward, *Voodoo Queen,* 3–20. Marie Laveau's House of Voodoo on Bourbon Street in New Orleans is one of those commercial establishments that sells charms, mojo bags, voodoo dolls, spell kits, and all manner of talismans using the influence of the famous Laveau name for legitimacy. According to Hazzard-Donald, the historical Laveau women may have been midwives as well as root doctors; *Mojo Workin',* 138–39.

26. Malbrough, *Hoodoo Mysteries,* 131.

27. Conversations with Mamma Roue, intuitive root doctor, Greensboro, North Carolina, December 18, 2003.

28. There is some speculation that sweet potato is associated with High John the Conqueror root, one of the most important and powerful tools in the root worker's medicine kit. This makes the sweet potato powerful by association. Hazzard-Donald says the fabled High John has been incorrectly identified as the herb St. John's wort, but it is actually *Ipomoea jalapa,* also known as *bindweed* or *jalap root.* The sweet potato has a similar botanical name, *Ipomoea patata,* which is an indicator of the relationship between the two roots; *Mojo Workin',* 68–69. I have also heard that eating sweet potatoes is a good cure for a hangover.

29. Ibid., 66.

30. A dirty sock worn around the neck is also a known folk cure for tonsillitis; see Dorson, *Buying the Wind,* 331. However, Mama Roue's old socks were clean. My personal experience with this type of root work or folk medicine as a child in Alabama was initially with a relative who had a gift for curing warts, headaches, hangovers, and other maladies using herbal medicines or magical suggestion, or a combination of both. I did not become alert to the more deeply African-inspired hoodoo until I was in college in the early 1970s. There was an old woman living across the river in Sheffield, Alabama, who was a practicing root doctor. Several of my college friends had attempted to mimic some of her rituals. No one really believed these rituals would have any impact on events, but my white friends were especially fascinated by the idea that a ritual or charm might secure love, help them pass a college exam, help them escape the military draft, or bring them financial success.

31. In the slang from the era of this song, a *bean* is a very smart person. In more contemporary use, the word *bean* refers to a pill, usually ecstasy.

32. Pianist Woodrow Wilson "Buddy" Johnson (1915–77) recorded "Root Man Blues" with Geezil Minerve on vocals as a single 78 RPM on DECCA Personality series, #27998, in March 1951. Walter Davis also had a song with the same title, but here the lyric has a funny double entendre and no one in the song acquires a "get out of jail free card" because of a root doctor. Davis sings, "Mama, here come your root man, open up the door and let him in / It is just about time you using some of your good roots again"; Walter Davis, "Root Man" (1935).

33. "Foot track magic" or "stones in the passway" involves sprinkling goofer dust along thresholds of doors or across passageways. Robert Johnson's "Stones in My Passway" is a musical reference to foot track magic; Devi, *Language of the Blues,* 106.

34. Conversations with Constance Hayes, North Carolina, September 6, 2003. An edited videotaped version of this story appears in the documentary *Folk Medicine* (2005).

35. In Vestapol tuning, the guitar is tuned to play a chord, often D, when strummed open; several informants claim it is any tuning to an open chord.

36. Conversation with Clyde "Pop" Ferguson, Lenoir, North Carolina, June 14, 2014. Pop Ferguson is a traditional guitar player and vocalist living with his family in Lenoir, North Carolina. In 2007 the North Carolina Folk Life Institute, the Appalachian Regional Commission, the National Endowment for the Arts, and the North Carolina Arts Council recognized Pop as an important performer of traditional blues in the North Carolina foothills. In 2008, Pop was inducted into the Smithsonian Institute. Ferguson's *Big Boss Man* CD was recorded on March 25, 2009, at Star Recording, Miller Creek, North Carolina. I spoke with him at the Sixth Annual Pop Ferguson Blues Music Heritage Festival organized by his son Clyde Ferguson Jr. in downtown Lenoir, North Carolina.

37. Conversation with an African American female informant, Elizabeth City, North Carolina, October 11, 2003.

38. Cootie Stark (Blind Johnny Miller, 1927–2005) was a singer, guitarist, and songwriter known as the "King of the Piedmont Blues." The South Carolina General Assembly and the Arts Commission named Cootie Stark a recipient of the 2005 South Carolina Folk Heritage Award. Stark was a street performer until Music Maker discovered him in 1995. He recorded two CDs with Music Maker: *Sugar Man* (1999) and *Raw Sugar* (2003).

39. Oliver, *Songsters and Saints*, 58.

40. From the interview discussed in chapters 1 and 9 of this book.

41. The band plays blues music with a heavy "zyde-Cajun" influence. As of this writing, the band members for Mel Melton and the Wicked Mojos include Mel on lead vocals, harmonica and washboard, Max Drake on guitar, T. A. James on bass, and Kelly Pace on drums.

42. Devi, *Language of the Blues*, 167–70.

43. Conversation with an African American informant, Greensboro, North Carolina, October 29, 2004.

44. Palmer, *Deep Blues*, 95–97.

45. Bebergal, *Season of the Witch.* This quote is given in Greg Kot's and Jim DeRogatis's interview with Bebergal on their NPR radio program *Sound Opinions* for the Halloween episode, "Rock Music and the Occult," 24 October 2014.

46. Conversation with African American informant, Greensboro, North Carolina, September 25, 2013.

Chapter 8. Feeding the Music

1. Bill Griffin (1932–99) had a reputation in the Greensboro area as a music promoter. The year he died, the North Carolina Music Hall of Fame inducted Bill Griffin for his role in bringing important musicians to the state. The North Carolina Music Hall of Fame writes of Bill Griffin that "at some point in his career, he booked almost every marquee act on the soul, R&B and beach music circuit and was on personal terms with most of them, particularly Bill Pinkney of the Drifters and General Johnson of the Chairmen of the Board."

2. Pat is referring to Anson Funderburgh of Anson Funderburgh and the Rockets. Anson was a blues player from Texas who was a solo artist before releasing the Rockets' debut album in 1981.

3. General Norman Johnson (May 23, 1941–October 13, 2010) was known as a rhythm and blues artist most famous for his work with the group the Chairmen of the Board (Danny Woods, Harrison Kennedy, and Eddie Custis). Later, the Chairmen of the Board became Darryl Johnson, Danny Woods, and Ken Knox).

4. Pat might be referring to Charlie's Place, a black bar and supper club owned by Charlie Fitzgerald and located "on the Hill" in Myrtle Beach, South Carolina. The club operated from 1930 to 1955 and was very popular with young white audiences. The place became infamous for an incident in 1950 in which the KKK warned Charlie not to admit white kids into his bar. The KKK wanted to stop teens from mixing in public places that offered music. The Klan returned with a violent raid in which it was discovered that a Klansman killed in the raid wore a police uniform under his robes. The story is detailed in Frank Beacham's book, *Whitewash: A Southern Journey through Music, Mayhem and Murder*. In addition to Charlie's Place, Myrtle Beach was home to a number of shag dance clubs throughout the years. Later clubs included bars like the Pad, Crazy Zack's, and Fat Harold's, closed now but famous for cheap beer, good music, and shag dancing.

5. The Muddy Waters Tribute Band consisted of Pinetop Perkins (piano, vocals), Luther "Guitar Jr." Johnson (guitar, vocals), Willie "Big Eyes" Smith (drums, vocals), Calvin "Fuzz" Jones (bass, vocals), Jerry Portnoy (harmonica, vocals), and "Steady Rollin'" Bob Margolin (guitar, vocals). When Jerry Portnoy left the band to play with Eric Clapton, Carey Bell stepped in to play harmonica. During the period that Pat traveled with them, Little Feat, Dr. John, and B. B. King were also part of the tour.

6. Buddy Guy's Legends opened in 1989 and was originally located at 745 South Wabash. I visited the club with my husband Doug Mokaren in 2005 just before it closed in its original location. When we went back to Chicago in 2012, Buddy Guy's Legends had reopened down the street at 700 Wabash. The new venue was bigger but still had open jams and some of the artwork, records, and memorabilia of the original club on the walls. We saw B. B. King's daughter Shirley King at a jam there.

7. On September 17, 1994, the US Postal Service honored Muddy Waters (McKinley Morganfield, 1915–83) by putting his picture on a postage stamp as part of the Black Heritage stamp series.

8. Blues harmonica player Snooky Pryor (September 15, 1921–October 18, 2006) played at the Fourth Annual Carolina Blues Festival in 1990. Some of his hits include "Judgment Day" (1956), "Crazy 'bout My Baby" (1989), and "How'd You Learn to Shake It Like That" (1989).

9. The Nightshade Café was a bar located on Tate Street in Greensboro, on the east side of the campus of the University of North Carolina at Greensboro. It was situated in the basement under the Hong Kong House, a Chinese restaurant popular with students. Both establishments are gone now but both were destination spots during the colorful "Hippie Hill" period of Tate Street's history.

10. Phillip Walker (February 11, 1937–July 22, 2010) was a black musician from Texas known for a variety of styles but primarily traditional blues and R&B.

11. Kenny Neal (b. October 14, 1957) is one of the younger bluesmen to stay with Pat, but she remarked thinking about it that "Kenny's already pushing fifty." Kenny is a vocalist and guitar and harmonica player described as having a New Orleans flavor. Kenny played at the Ninth Annual Carolina Blues Festival on May 20, 1995.

12. The cabin where Muddy Waters lived as a boy is on the Stovall plantation or Stovall farm near Clarksdale, Mississippi.

13. Marcia Ball (b. 1949) is a blues singer and piano player from Louisiana and Texas known for her zydeco and "swamp blues" style of music. She has won multiple awards for best blues instrumentalist—keyboards and for contemporary blues artist of the year—female, and has been nominated for Grammys. She performed at the Carolina Blues Festival in 1997.

14. Jimmy Rogers (June 3, 1924–December 19, 1997) was a singer, guitarist, and harmonica player from Chicago who played with Muddy Waters in the late 1940s and early 1950s. He also played with Howlin' Wolf's band in the 1960s.

15. The Holmes Brothers performed at the Fourth Annual Carolina Blues Festival on May 19, 1990, when it was at the Depot in Greensboro.

16. Bubba "Big Bump" Klinefelter plays lead and slide guitar and harmonica and does vocals most often with the band Big Bump and the Stun Gunz, which was formed in Greensboro in 1985. He also plays in the duo Bump and Logie with Logie Meachum.

17. Earl King (1934–2003) was a singer, songwriter, guitarist, and record producer from New Orleans. King played at the Fifth Annual Carolina Blues Festival on May 18, 1991.

18. This is not a verbatim account transcribed from a recording but an account taken from notes made at an informal interview at Naomi's house in February 2012 before she went into the hospital. Laurel Matsudaira, another member of the "blues family," went with me to do a few chores for Naomi, who was getting feeble. Naomi told us several stories that day about her family and about her grandfather, who she said had been born a slave and was a "mean old man." Naomi said her grandfather once told her that she would never have survived as a slave because she was too proud, sassy, and lazy. He meant this as a criticism when he thought she was shirking her chores. Naomi didn't "talk back" to her grandfather—she said she was afraid of him—but she also told me that she considered his criticism to be a point of pride. Naomi didn't have any desire to be a good slave.

19. James Brown (1933–2006) was an important R&B artist from Georgia, and made more than one visit to Greensboro. Naomi knew he was a game changer for American music when she first met him. For more about Brown, see Kevin Powell, "Black Music's Bosses, Legends and Game Changers," *Ebony* 69, no. 8 (2014): 95–104. A 2014 musical biopic of James Brown, *Get On Up*, portrays his beginnings and rise to fame.

Chapter 9. Piedmont Personalities

1. For a portrait of James "Guitar Slim" Stephens, see Duffy, *Music Maker*, 153.

2. In the independent movie *The Retrieval* (2014), a young black boy betrays escaped slaves to "paddy rollers" and bounty hunters even as Union forces crumble in the last of the

Confederacy. The characters of Will and his Uncle Marcus refer to the brutal white bounty hunters they work for as "paddy rollers." *Paddy rollers* or *pattyrollers* is a term for white slave patrols, "patrollers" who enforced fugitive slave laws. The patrollers stopped black slaves in the antebellum South, searching for weapons and demanding to see the pass that allowed them to leave plantation grounds. The law-enforcement system intended to protect the interests of slave owners by recovering "property" continued with the rise of vigilante groups after the Civil War. Some have viewed the heavy-handed treatment of minority misdemeanors and recent deaths of black men at the hands of police as modern remnants of paddy rollers; see Turner, Giacopassi, and Vandiver, "Ignoring the Past."

3. What Logie means by the phrase *cut buddies* is friends "cut from the same cloth." In Urban Dictionary, the slang term *cut buddy* is similar to "friends with benefits," someone with whom to have sexual relations without emotional entanglement. *Cut buddy* might also refer to a partner in crime who takes a "cut" of the proceeds.

4. Stride piano is a technique of piano playing in which the left hand provides a type of rhythm by playing a single bass note in a low octave on the odd beat and "striding up" to play the accompanying chord on the even. It is a style that was popular in jazz and blues music in the Harlem music scene of the 1920s and '30s. It is particularly useful if you are a pianist playing solo without a rhythm or bass to support you.

5. Not to be confused with Johnny "Hammond" Smith (1933–97), who was a keyboard player from Kentucky known for playing the Hammond B-3 organ. John Paul Hammond or Johnny Hammond Jr. was a guitar player whose father, John Henry Hammond (1910–87), was a record producer and civil rights activist. As David Bolton told me, "His father was really important to American music because he discovered people like Stevie Ray Vaughan." John Paul Hammond or John Hammond Jr. usually plays acoustic guitars and Dobros and sings in a barrelhouse style. He was at the Nightshade for a gig when he invited Slim to play his guitar.

6. William "Billy" Ransom Hobbs Jr. (1951–2008) was a popular guitar player in the Greensboro area, jamming with a wide variety of local musicians and sitting in with different bands. He was sometimes referred to as "Hobo Hobbs" because he traveled around. In 2008 Ransom was murdered and his friend, Deborah Moy, was beaten and burned in Moy's apartment. The brutal attack happened after a night of partying and playing music. Moy survived but lost both legs and some fingers, and sustained a broken jaw, cracked ribs, and fourth-degree burns over much of her body. See Brian Clarey, "It Happened in Greensboro . . . ." Writing a year later in his book *The Anxious Hipster and Other Barflies I've Known*, Clarey laments the lack of progress in this case of "a violent beating. A sexual assault. A murder." Finally, on May 17, 2012, WGHP television reported that because of blunders in the case, police dropped charges against the man indicted with the murder and attempted murder.

7. The memorial tribute for Billy Hobbs, "Ballad for Billy," appears on the House of Dues CD *Cross That Line* (2013).

8. Short bios and photographs of these musicians can be found in Duffy, *Music Makers*. For a detailed biography with pictures of Guitar Gabriel, see pp. 62–67.

9. Walter Brown "Brownie" McGhee (1915–96) and Saunders Terrell or "Sonny Terry" (1911–86) were both Piedmont blues musicians who collaborated as a duo touring and

largely recording on the Folkways label. Sonny Terry was a harmonica player and vocalist. Brownie McGhee was a guitar player and occasionally a vocalist. In the movie *Angel Heart* (1987), Brownie McGhee plays a fictional blues singer, Toots Sweet.

10. Big Joe Williams (Joseph Lee Williams, 1903–82) was a traveling vocalist and guitar player from Mississippi who recorded on a variety of labels. He was known for playing a nine-string guitar, and is also known for the song "Baby Please Don't Go"; see Weissman, *American Popular Music: Blues,* 243.

11. *Bear's Choice* is a live album the Grateful Dead released in 1973 on Warner Bros. Records. It is a compilation of recordings made at the Fillmore East in New York in 1970. The title references Owsley Stanley, who was nicknamed "Bear" and was famous as a producer of LSD. Bear was part of the early acid-test parties and was a sound man in addition to cooking drugs when the Warlocks began performing as a band for Ken Kesey's Acid Tests. See Edwards, "Transgressive Toke," 223–43.

12. This would have been the Fourth Annual Carolina Blues Festival, May 19, 1990. Snooky Pryor (1921–2006) was a Chicago blues harmonica player who followed the Holmes Brothers in the lineup. The Holmes Brothers are a trio from Christchurch, Virginia—Sherman and Wendell Holmes and Willie "Popsy" Dixon. For more stories about the Holmes Brothers, see chapter 8.

13. Thomas "Mookie" Brill is an upright bass player who also plays electric bass. He played with artists such as Nappy Brown, Carey Bell, Louisiana Red, Pinetop Perkins, Hubert Sumlin, and Big Bill Morganfield, among others.

14. Tim Duffy explained that the actual title of the song is "You Got to Watch Yourself." He described it as a party song, "like the roots of rap. Great poetry." Tim recited a verse for me: "Pussy oh Pussy, all men crave / Deep as a dungeon, dark as a grave / Got more hair on it like a bristle on a hog / Swallow more meat than a goddamn dog." Tim summed up the song as "really just great, X-rated poetry. It's probably from the African American toast tradition of poetry and singing vulgar poetry. It was really funny but filthy."

15. Sam "the Dot Man" McMillan is known in the Piedmont area as a folk artist whose signature style is to cover things in bright paint and tiny dots. Sam is a self-taught artist who paints everything—from furniture to clothes to toys—in dots. See Keith Barber's article "Sam" in *Yes! Weekly*, 2 December 2009. My colleague at Wake Forest University, Mary Dalton, also made a documentary, *Sam McMillan: The Dot Man,* that aired on North Carolina Visions in 2003. Sam is known for saying, "If we all hold hands, then we can't make fists to fight with."

16. This description of lighters like autumn leaves on the ground puzzled me. I learned that, in addition to using them for smoking, some drug dealers would gut ordinary disposable lighters, leaving just the plastic body of the lighter, and use the empty lighter as a container for transporting crack cocaine. Each lighter was equal to a vial of crack cocaine. When I asked Abe about this, he said he didn't believe the lighters were for transporting crack; he believes there was so much smoking going on that the used-up lighters were just discarded everywhere. Ralph R. Speas, who is a substance-abuse counselor with SMART recovery (Self-Management and Recovery Training), says Abe might be mistaken about this. According to Ralph, "When lighters were first used, they were gutted and the space lined with tiny plastic

bags, plastic wrap, or tin foil to make handy carriers of emergency needs for pot and cocaine or whatever. The lighters were stolen and traded and, unfortunately, easily lost."

17. There is no explanation for the superstition of lining up different colored lighters when they were used up. However, I have heard the superstition that it is extremely unlucky to carry a white Bic lighter because Jimi Hendrix (1942–70), Janis Joplin (1943–70), Jim Morrison (1943–71), and Kurt Cobain (1967–94) all supposedly had a white Bic lighter on them when they died.

18. The musicians Chris Stamey and Will Rigby who Rob mentions here are members of the dB's. Steve Earle is a guitar player from Texas known for roots music: country, folk, and rockabilly. Mitch Easter is a musician from Winston-Salem who became a producer and songwriter, working a lot with Chris Stamey.

19. Shiela Klinefelter is a bass player with the band the Ladies Auxiliary and the After Hours Blues Band as well as Big Bump and the Stun Gunz. She has played with many different groups, including performing with Smokin' Joe Kubek and Bnois King on their overseas tour. In the Piedmont area, Shiela is known for hosting jams in a variety of bars.

20. The incident Rob refers to was a Labor Day jam Shiela Klinefelter hosted at Zion Bar and Grille, which was videotaped in 2010. Ray Burnett led the set with "I Just Want to Make Love to You." After Rob stepped out front with a complicated and risky solo, and various audience members are screaming a whistling appreciation, Ray briefly confers with other players, walks across the stage, and tosses a two-dollar bill at Rob's feet. Rob picks this up and holds it out for the Labor Day crowd to appreciate, announcing that it is a "two-dollar bill." The music continues throughout like a soundtrack to these antics, before resuming full throttle.

Chapter 10. Even Chocolate Cowboys Get the Blues

1. Obie Burnett McClinton (1940–87) was a black country music singer who also got his start as a soul singer before turning to country. Both Roy Roberts and McClinton referred to themselves as "chocolate cowboys."

2. Arthur "Guitar Boogie" Smith (1921–2014) was a music teacher who moved from South Carolina to Charlotte, North Carolina, where he had a country music television program, *The Arthur Smith Show*, which was syndicated nationally. Another North Carolina favorite, Andy Griffith (1926–2012), appeared on the show to play a guitar duo with Arthur in 1973 and discuss country ham and black-eyed peas in a popularly remembered episode of the show. Smith also built and managed a recording studio in Charlotte. Smith may be best known for a banjo instrumental, "Feudin' Banjos," which became "Dueling Banjos" in the soundtrack for the film *Deliverance* (1972). He was inducted into the North Carolina Music Hall of Fame in 2010. Arthur passed away on April 4, 2014. David Menconi, "Remembering the Late Great Arthur 'Guitar Boogie' Smith," *News and Observer*, 4 April 2014. Web. 21 April 2014.

3. WLAC is a Clear Channel radio station based in Nashville, Tennessee, that had its beginning in country music but also offered broadcasts of R&B shows at night during the 1950s through the 1970s, which were popular with African American audiences throughout the South. For more about the impact of WLAC on African American talent, see Cooper, "Radio Revolution."

4. It is doubtful that this white man understood that the term could apply to his own behavior. There is not a more emotionally charged or nuanced word in our vocabulary; see Kennedy, *Nigger: The Strange Career of a Troublesome Word.*

5. Robert Cray (b. 1953) is a Grammy Award–winning vocalist and blues guitar player who was inducted into the Blues Hall of Fame in 2010.

6. The record label was New Moon Records, which released the album in 1994.

7. Calvin "Skeeter" Brandon (1949–2008) was a blind singer and keyboard player who toured with his band Hwy 61 up and down the East Coast. He toured overseas with soul-blues singer Clarence Carter in the early 1970s and then the doo-wop group the Chi-Lites. He released several important albums, including *Hi-Test Blues* (1993) on New Moon Records and *It's Good to Go* on Rock House Records (Roy's label) in 2003. See Max Drake's stories in chapter 2.

8. The town of Pulaski commemorates the founding of the KKK with a plaque in the courthouse, which began as a social group for former Confederate soldiers before it developed into a terrorist group; see Lewis and Serbo, "Kommemorating the Ku Klux Klan."

9. A Chicago teenager, Emmett Louis Till (1941–55) was murdered while he was visiting Mississippi. The motive was that Till had flirted with a white woman. Roy remembered hearing about it because the trial caught a lot of media attention. The murderers were acquitted of their crimes and later admitted to them. For a compilation of the story taken from media accounts, see Kolin, "On the Record."

10. Joseph Arrington Jr. or "Joe Tex" was a vocalist and songwriter from Texas who performed a mixture of country, gospel, and R&B; see Alan Cackett, "More Dirty Laundry: The Soul of Black Music," *Maverick* 76 (2008): 90.

11. William Edward "Little Willie" John was an R&B vocalist from Arkansas who is remembered for the song "Fever," which was made popular in a cover by Peggy Lee, and for a lesser-known song, "No Regrets"; see Ze'ev Chafets, "No Regrets," *New York Times Magazine* 148, no. 51419 (1999): 74.

12. In his book *The One: The Life and Music of James Brown,* R. J. Smith mentions the ABA club as the musical home of saxophonist J. C. Davis, who became the bandleader for James Brown. The two were supposed to have met in this club.

13. Jackie Bell is a featured artist at 930 Blues Café in Jackson, Mississippi. The café is a two-story house decorated to emphasize a Delta heritage and has a reputation for hosting weekend parties with international blues artists.

14. Ludacris (Christopher Brian Bridges, b. 1977) is an actor, rapper, and businessman and former DJ from Atlanta, Georgia. For more on the rapper turned actor and his early career, see "Ludacris," *Entertainment Weekly,* 30 June 2006, 104–5.

Chapter 11. Traveling Blues

1. Several musicians have mentioned Jackson Station as a favorite venue. Jackson Station in Hodges, South Carolina, was repurposed from the Southern Railroad Depot known as Jackson Station Rhythm and Blues Club. One of the co-owners, Gerald Jackson, died in 2010 shortly after being bludgeoned with an ax in the parking lot of the club; see the *Index-Journal* (Greenwood, SC), 13 February 1991, 2.

2. The earlier version of Lawyers Guns & Money included Terry VunCannon (guitar), Stan Atwell (vocals and bass), Rob Slater (guitar), and Mike Thomas (vocals and drums). The current band members are Terry VunCannon (guitar), Steven Headen (vocals and bass), and Mike Thomas (drums).

3. The Tobacco Road in North Wilkesboro should not be confused with a club of the same name in downtown Miami, Florida, which advertises as Miami's oldest bar and had a reputation as a speakeasy during the prohibition era. Max Drake talks about playing Miami's Tobacco Road in chapter 2.

4. *I'm not picking* is a southern expression that roughly means that the matter under discussion is not a small thing.

5. For more about A. C. Williams and the Teen Town Singers, see Bowman, *Soulsville, USA*, 14–20.

6. Samuel David Moore and Dave Prater were a gospel-inspired duo who were involved with Stax Records from 1965 to 1968. They are multiple gold record–award-winning artists and members of the Grammy Hall of Fame.

7. There is a video of this competition on the Eric Gales Band website and on YouTube, which shows a young Eric Gales in a very interesting outfit rocking out with his brothers; see "The Eric Gales Band WINS the Battle of the Bands in Memphis 1989."

8. Blues with a Feeling is a band that included Mike "Wezo" Wesolowski on harmonica, Max Drake on guitar, Bob Dunlap on drums, and Lou Ann McCarthy on bass and vocals. "Blues with a Feeling" is also a celebrated harmonica song popularized by Little Walter in 1953.

9. The Void Brothers is a traditional black gospel group from Chatham Country that has been performing since 1979. Landy Void is the lead vocalist and Larry Void is vocalist and keyboards.

10. Southern Culture on the Skids or SCOTS is a rockabilly and blues band from Chapel Hill, North Carolina, formed in 1983. In 2014 the membership of the band includes Rick Miller on guitar, Dave Hartman on percussion, and Mary Huff on vocals and bass guitar.

11. The Ministers of Sinister was an acoustic blues group with Mike Wesolowski (harmonica), Calvin "Loudmouth" Johnson (electric bass), and Russ Wilson (drums, washboard).

12. The Aryan Nations is an extremist white supremacist group with neo-Nazi, paramilitary connections. The group claims a Christian base and has had members in common with several other white supremacist and neo-Nazi groups, including National Alliance, the Ku Klux Klan; see Ridgeway, *Blood in the Face*.

13. The Willie Boy Band was named for the movie *Tell Them Willie Boy Is Here* (1969). It featured Terry VunCannon (guitar), Mike Rowe (keyboards), Eric Smith (drums), Reese Hughes (bass), and Warren Phillips (guitar).

14. Held since 2002, FloydFest is an annual celebration of Appalachian mountain-music culture held near Floyd, Virginia. In addition to music and camping, there is storytelling, arts and crafts, and other workshops. Robin says FloydFest is "mind-blowing. It was wonderful. That's where people really stayed in the thicket. I mean roots and trees all over the place and then thousands at night would gather to watch and listen to the music." She also mentioned enjoying the comfort of real showers, which might not be available at every outdoor festival.

15. Smilefest was originally organized as a local attempt to fill the massive void Triad-area Deadheads felt after the death of Jerry Garcia (1942–95), who was the beloved front man for the Grateful Dead. The festival was envisioned as a continuation of music and artistry that formed the Deadhead Tent City, a place for those still seeking the transcendent qualities of the Deadhead experience. The first Smilefest was held in 1996 at Castle McCulloch in Jamestown, North Carolina, and later moved to a natural amphitheater in Pinnacle, North Carolina. The festival ran for thirteen years with two years of "Reunion," celebrating a "family" of musicians and fans "united through music and like-minded ideas." The music at Smilefest was a mixture of rock, blues, bluegrass, and jam band with acts like David Grisman, Derek Trucks, Yonder Mountain String Band, Vassar Clements, and Leftover Salmon. Robin and her band played the last festival in 2011. The Jomeokee Music and Arts Festival supplanted Smilefest in 2012.

16. Performing since 1958, the Embers is an R&B band well known in the beach-music circuit.

Chapter 12. Baby Boomer Blues

1. Lee Atwater was George H. W. Bush's campaign manager. Several people have remarked at the irony of this concert. Twenty-five years after Bush's inauguration, PBS aired a version of the concert in March 2014. A longer DVD version was released in April, *A Celebration of Blues and Soul: The 1989 Inaugural Concert* (2014).

2. Adelt, *Blues Music in the Sixties,* 140.

3. Adrianne Carageorge has worked as the editor on feature documentary films and political media campaigns. She has screened her work on cable channels such as HBO, and has published articles about media in scholarly journals.

4. A brochure for the North Leon County Heritage Trails lists Smitty's Joint as number eighteen on the self-guided tour of African American historical sites of North Leon County, Florida. According to the brochure, Mr. McKinley Smith Sr. purchased 186 acres there in the 1940s and opened Smitty's Nightclub on his birthday in 1955. Smitty's Farm, Smitty's Joint, or Smitty's Place had a reputation as the "rocking place to be" until it closed in the late 1990s.

5. Memphis has consistently ranked as one of the most violent cities in the United States, reaching number one for violent crime in 2006. Hanna Rosin's article, "American Murder Mystery," portrays Memphis in 2008 as "America's new South Bronx" and links some of the crime problem to housing; see *Atlantic* 302, no. 1 (July/August 2008): 40–54.

6. The Double Door Inn has been a popular bar and live-music venue in Charlotte, North Carolina, since 1973 and is currently recognized as one of the oldest blues clubs. Many of the musicians and music fans contributing stories have mentioned the Double Door as a favorite venue.

7. Tommy Faile (1928–98) was a country music singer especially known in North Carolina for the song "The Legend of the Brown Mountain Lights." He also appeared on Arthur "Guitar Boogie" Smith's country music show. "The Legend of the Brown Mountain Lights" is a well-known ghost, UFO, or odd geological phenomena story in Linville, North Carolina.

The story of Tommy Faile's lyrics suggests that the lights belong to a lantern carried by the ghost of a "faithful slave, come back from the grave," searching for his master.

8. Jimmy Thackery is a vocalist and guitar player from Washington, DC. Rich Del Grosso reviews his CD *Solid Ice* (2007) in *Sing Out* 51, no. 4 (Winter 2008): 154–55.

9. This is a reference to the band Brat Pack, which made the 2014 finals at the IBCs in Memphis.

10. The 5 Royales were inducted into the Rock and Roll Hall of Fame on April 18, 2015. The group was Lowman Pauling, Jimmy Moore, Obadiah Carter, and brothers Johnny and Eugene Tanner. See Lisa O'Donnell, "Family Members Excited over Rock and Roll Hall of Fame Induction for "5" Royales," *Winston-Salem Journal*, 20 December 2014. Web. 22 December 2014.

11. For one example of this optimism, see syndicated columnist Leonard Pitts, "Rainbow Coalition of Protestors Holds Promise," *Greensboro News and Record*, 11 December 2014, A9.

BIBLIOGRAPHY

Adams, Rebecca G., and Robert Sardiello, eds. *Deadhead Social Science: "You Ain't Gonna Learn What You Don't Want to Know."* Walnut Creek, CA: AltaMira Press, 2000.

Adelt, Ulrich. *Blues Music in the Sixties: A Story in Black and White.* New Brunswick, NJ: Rutgers University Press, 2010.

Asma, Stephen T. "The Blues Artist as Cultural Rebel." *The Humanist* 57, no. 4 (July–August 1997): 8–16.

Beacham, Frank. *Whitewash: A Southern Journey through Music, Mayhem and Murder.* New York: Frank Beacham, 2002.

Bebergal, Peter. *Season of the Witch: How Occult Saved Rock and Roll.* New York: Penguin, 2014.

Bogdanov, Vladimir, Chris Woodstra, and Stephen Thomas Erlewine, eds. *All Music Guide to the Blues: The Definitive Guide to the Blues.* Milwaukee, WI: Publishers Group West, 2003.

Bowman, Robert M. J. *Soulsville, USA: The Story of Stax Records.* New York: Schirmer Books, 1997.

Clarey, Brian. *The Anxious Hipster and Other Barflies I've Known.* Greensboro, NC: Cold Type Press, 2011.

———. "It Happened in Greensboro . . ." *Yes! Weekly*, 3 December 2008.

Cook, Bruce. *Listen to the Blues.* New York: Charles Scribner's Sons, 1973.

Cooper, Daniel. "Radio Revolution." *American Legacy Magazine: Celebrating African-American History and Culture* 6, no. 4 (2001): 14–21.

Davis, Angela Y. *Blues Legacies and Black Feminism: Gertude "Ma" Rainey, Bessie Smith, and Billie Holiday.* New York: Pantheon Books, 1998.

Del Sesto, Steven L. "Dancing and Cockfighting at Jay's Lounge and Cockpit: The Preservation of Folk Practices in Cajun Louisiana." In *Rituals and Ceremonies in Popular Culture,* edited by Ray B. Brown, 270–81. Bowling Green, OH: Bowling Green University Press, 1980.

Devi, Debra. *The Language of the Blues from Alcorub to Zuzu.* Foreword by Dr. John. New York: Billboard Books, 2006.

Dicaire, David. *More Blues Singers: Biographies of 50 Artists from the Later 20th Century.* Jefferson, NC: McFarland, 2002.

Dorson, Richard M. *Buying the Wind: Regional Folklore in the United States.* Chicago: University of Chicago Press, 1964.

Duffy, Timothy, ed. *Music Makers: Portraits and Songs from the Roots of America.* Hillsborough, NC: MM Press, 2004.

Edwards, Emily. "The Transgressive Toke: Art and Misdemeanor in Deadhead Imagery." In *From the Arthouse to the Grindhouse: Highbrow and Lowbrow Transgressions in Cinema's First Century,* edited by John Cline and Robert G. Weiner, 223–43. Lanham, MD: Scarecrow Press, 2010.

Evans, David. *Tommy Johnson*. London: Studio Vista, 1971.

Friedman, Douglas E. *Who Sang Our Songs? The Official Rhythm and Blues and Doo-Wop Songography*. West Long Branch, NJ: Harmony Songs, 2003.

Govenar, Alan B. *Lightnin' Hopkins: His Life and Blues*. Chicago: Chicago Review Press, 2010.

Graves, Tom. *Crossroads: The Life and Afterlife of Blues Legend Robert Johnson*. Spokane WA: Demers Books, 2008.

Greer, John Michael. *The New Encyclopedia of the Occult*. St. Paul, MN: Llewellyn, 2003.

Guralnick, Peter. *Searching for Robert Johnson*. New York: Penguin Putnam, 1998.

Gussow, Adam. "Racial Violence, 'Primitive' Music, and the Blues Entrepreneur: W. C. Handy's Mississippi Problem." *Southern Cultures* 8, no. 3 (2002): 56–79.

———. *Seems Like Murder Here: Southern Violence and the Blues Tradition*. Chicago: University of Chicago Press, 2002.

Hall, Hiram. "From Down South to Up South: An Examination of Geography in the Blues." *Midwest Quarterly* 42, no. 3 (Spring 2001): 306–19.

Handy, W. C. *Blues: An Anthology*. (1926). New York: Macmillan, 1972.

———. *Father of the Blues: An Autobiography*. New York: Macmillan, 1941.

———. *Negro Authors and Composers of the United States*. (1935). New York, AMS Press, 1976.

Hardert, Ronald A., and Linda B. Hardert. "Peace and Equality Themes in Popular Music." *International Journal of Humanities and Peace* 19, no. 1 (2003): 61–64.

Haskins, Jim. *Voodoo and Hoodoo: Their Tradition and Craft as Revealed by Actual Practitioners*. Lanham, MD: Scarborough House, 1990.

Hazzard-Donald, Katrina. *Mojo Workin': The Old African American Hoodoo System*. Urbana: University of Illinois Press, 2013.

Jackson, Buzzy. *A Bad Woman Feeling Good: Blues and the Women Who Sing Them*. New York: W. W. Norton, 2005.

King, Stephen A. "Blues Tourism in the Mississippi Delta: The Functions of Blues Festivals." *Popular Music and Society* 27, no. 4 (December 2004): 455–76.

Kennedy, Randall. *Nigger: The Strange Career of a Troublesome Word*. New York: Vintage Books, 2003.

Kolin, Philip C. "On the Record: The Emmett Till Murder Trial and the Southern Press." *Southern Quarterly* 50, no. 3 (2013): 28–31.

Komara, Edward, ed. *Encyclopedia of the Blues*. New York: Routledge, 2006.

Lauterbach, Preston. *The Chitlin Circuit and the Road to Rock 'n' Roll*. New York: W. W. Norton, 2011.

Lewis, Michael, and Jacqueline Serbo. "Kommemorating the Ku Klux Klan." *Sociological Quarterly* 40, no. 1 (1999): 139–59.

Lomax, Alan. *The Land Where the Blues Began*. New York: New Press, 2002.

Malbrough, Ray. *Hoodoo Mysteries: Folk Magic, Mysticism and Rituals*. St. Paul, MN: Llewellyn, 2003.

McGeachy, Margaret G. *Lonesome Words: The Vocal Poetics of the Old English Lament and the African-American Blues Song*. New York: Palgrave Macmillan, 2006.

Moore, Allan, ed. *The Cambridge Companion to Blues and Gospel Music*. Cambridge: Cambridge University Press, 2002.

Neal, Larry. "The Ethos of the Blues." *Black Scholar* 3, no. 10 (Summer 1972): 42–48.

Neal, Mark Anthony. *Songs in the Key of Black Life: A Rhythm and Blues Nation*. New York: Routledge, 2003.

Oakley, Giles. *The Devil's Music: A History of the Blues*. New York: Taplinger, 1977.

Oliver, Paul. *Broadcasting the Blues: Black Blues in the Segregation Era*. New York: Routledge, 2006.

———. *Songsters and Saints: Vocal Traditions on Race Records*. Cambridge: Cambridge University Press, 1984.

———. *Yonder Come the Blues: The Evolution of a Genre*. Cambridge: Cambridge University Press, 2001.

Owens, Mary A. *Voodoo Tales*. New York: Negro Universities Press, 1969.

Palmer, Robert. *Deep Blues*. New York: Viking Press, 1981.

Pearson, Barry Lee. *Jook Right On: Blues Stories and Blues Storytellers*. Knoxville: University of Tennessee Press, 2005.

———. *Sounds So Good to Me*. Philadelphia: University of Pennsylvania Press, 1984.

Pearson, Barry Lee, and Bill McCulloch. *Robert Johnson Lost and Found*. Urbana: University of Illinois Press, 2003.

Ridgeway, James. *Blood in the Face: The Ku Klux Klan, Aryan Nations, Nazi Skinheads and the Rise of a New White Culture*. New York: Thunder's Mouth Press, 1990.

Ripani, Richard J. *The New Blue Music: Changes in Rhythm and Blues, 1950–1999*. Jackson: University Press of Mississippi, 2006.

Roberts, John. *Trickster to Bad Man: The Black Folk Hero in Slavery and Freedom*. Philadelphia: University of Pennsylvania Press, 1989.

Schroeder, Patricia R. *Robert Johnson, Mythmaking, and Contemporary American Culture*. Urbana: University of Illinois Press, 2004.

Spencer, Jon Michael. *Blues and Evil*. Knoxville: University of Tennessee Press, 1993.

Smith, R. J. *The One: The Life and Music of James Brown*. New York: Gotham Books, 2012.

Springer, Robert, ed. *Nobody Knows Where the Blues Come From: Lyrics and History*. Jackson: University Press of Mississippi, 2006.

Stanfield, Peter. *Body and Soul: Jazz and Blues in American Film, 1927–63*. Urbana: University of Illinois Press, 2005.

Stewart, James B. "Message in the Music: Political Commentary in Black Popular Music from Rhythm and Blues to Early Hip Hop." *Journal of African American History* 90, no. 3 (Summer 2005): 196–226.

Stone, Robert. "End of the Beginning." In *Garcia*, 32–35. Boston: Little, Brown, 1991.

Taft, Michael. *The Blues Lyric Formula*. New York: Routledge, 2006.

———, ed. *Talkin' to Myself: Blues Lyrics, 1921–1942*. New York: Routledge, 2005.

Turner, K. B., David Giacopassi, and Margaret Vandiver. "Ignoring the Past: Coverage of Slavery and Slave Patrols in Criminal Justice Texts." *Journal of Criminal Justice Education* 17, no. 1 (2006): 181–95.

Ward, Martha. *Voodoo Queen: The Spirited Lives of Marie Laveau*. Jackson: University of Mississippi Press, 2004.

Weissman, Dick. *American Popular Music: Blues*. New York: Facts on File, 2006.

———. *Blues: The Basics*. New York: Routledge, 2005.

Werner, Craig. *A Change Is Gonna Come: Music, Race and the Soul of America*. Ann Arbor: University of Michigan Press, 2006.

FILMOGRAPHY

Angel Heart. Dir. Alan Parker. TriStar Pictures, 1987.

Antone's: Home of the Blues. Dir. Dan Karlok. Silver Star Entertainment, 2004.

The Blues. Prod. Martin Scorsese. PBS, 2003.

The Blues Accordin' to Lightnin' Hopkins. Dir. Les Blank. Flower Films, 1970.

The Blues Brothers. Dir. John Landis. Universal, 1980.

Blues Brothers 2000. Dir. John Landis. Universal, 1998.

Bone Creek. Dir. Emily Edwards. Carolina Collaborations, 2008.

Can't You Hear the Wind Howl? The Life and Music of Robert Johnson. Dir. Peter Meyer. WinStar Home Entertainment, 1997.

A Celebration of Blues and Soul: The 1989 Inaugural Concert. Howell Begle, prod. 2014.

The Color Purple. Dir. Stephen Spielberg. Warner Bros., 1985.

Crossroads. Dir. Walter Hill. Columbia Pictures, 1986.

Deep Blues: A Musical Pilgrimage to the Crossroads. Dir. Robert Mugge. Tara Releasing, 1991.

Deliverance. Dir. John Boorman. Warner Bros., 1972.

Dolemite. Dir. D'Urville Martin. Dimension Pictures, 1975.

Feel Like Going Home. Dir. Martin Scorsese. *The Blues*, Martin Scorsese, prod. PBS, 2003

Folk Medicine. Dir. Emily D. Edwards. South Carolina Public Television, *Southern Lens,* 2005.

Forever Blues. Dir. Franco Nero. Moviemax, 2005.

Frankie and Johnny. Dir. Frederick De Cordova. United Artists, 1965.

Get On Up. Dir. Tate Taylor. Universal Pictures, 2014.

Godfathers and Sons. Dir. Marc Levin. *The Blues*, Martin Scorsese, prod. PBS, 2003.

Greensboro: Closer to the Truth. Dir. Adam Zucker. Longnook Pictures, 2007.

Hellhounds on My Trail: The Afterlife of Robert Johnson. Dir. Robert Mugge. MugShot, 2000.

Jerry McCain's True Blues. Dir. Carolyn Hales. University of Alabama Center for Public Television, 1995.

Killer Diller. Dir. Tricia Brock. Freestyle, 2004.

Lackawanna Blues. Dir. George C. Wolfe. HBO, 2005.

Lady Sings the Blues. Dir. Sidney J. Furie. Paramount, 1972.

Leadbelly. Dir. Gordon Parks. Paramount, 1976.

Mo' Better Blues. Dir. Spike Lee. Universal Picture, 1990.

Muscle Shoals. Dir. Greg "Freddy" Camalier. Magnolia Pictures, 2013.

O Brother Where Art Thou? Dirs. Joel and Ethan Coen. Buena Vista Pictures, 2000.

Piano Blues. Dir. Clint Eastwood. *The Blues.* Martin Scorsese, prod. PBS, 2003.

Ray. Dir. Taylor Hackford. Universal, 2004.

The Retrieval. Dir. Chris Eska. Variance Films, 2014.

Rhythm 'n' Bayous: A Road Map to Louisiana Music. Dir. Robert Mugge. Cowboy, 2000.
The Road to Memphis. Dir. Richard Pearce. *The Blues.* Martin Scorsese, prod. PBS, 2003.
St. Louis Blues. Dir. Allen Reisner. Paramount, 1958.
Step It Up and Go: Blues in the Carolinas. Dir. Susan Massengale. UNC TV, 1989.
Stormy Weather. Dir. Andrew L. Stone. 20th Century Fox, 1943.
A Tribute to Stevie Ray Vaughan. Dir. Gary Menotti. Sony, 1996.
Tell Them Willie Boy Is Here. Dir. Abraham Polonsky. Universal Pictures, 1969.
Two Soldiers. Dir. Aaron Schneider. World Film Magic Distribution, 2003.
Warming by the Devil's Fire. Dir. Charles Burnett. *The Blues.* Martin Scorsese, prod. PBS, 2003.
Wild Women Don't Have the Blues. Dir. Christine Dall. California Newsreel, 1989.
Wondrous Healing. Dir. Emily D. Edwards. Penn State Media, 2004.

INDEX